BEYOND THE HORIZON

COLIN ANGUS

BEYOND THE HORIZON

HORIZON

THE GREAT RACE TO FINISH THE FIRST
HUMAN-POWERED CIRCUMNAVIGATION OF THE PLANET

DOUBLEDAY CANADA

Doubleday Canada and colophon are trademarks.

Library and Archives Canada Cataloguing in Publication

Angus, Colin
Beyond the horizon: the great race to finish the first human-powered circumnavigation of the planet / Colin Angus.

ISBN-13: 978-0-385-66123-2
ISBN-10: 0-385-66123-1

1. Angus, Colin—Travel.   2. Human powered vehicles.
3. Voyages around the world.   I. Title.

G440.A56A56 2007   910.4'1   C2006-906348-6

Jacket and text design: Kelly Hill

Printed and bound in the USA

Published in Canada by
Doubleday Canada, a division of
Random House of Canada Limited

Visit Random House of Canada Limited's website: www.randomhouse.ca

BVG   10   9   8   7   6   5   4   3   2   1

To Julie

CONTENTS

O N SEPTEMBER 6, 1522, a lone and tattered sailing ship ghosted into Seville Harbour, Spain. On board the *Victoria*, 18 ragged crew members rejoiced at the end of their long voyage. Three years earlier, the expedition had departed from this same port as an armada of five ships and 270 men. During those three years, the crew had endured starvation, bloody combat, mutinies, shipwrecks, scurvy, and other disease. The captain of the expedition, Sir Francis Magellan, died in battle. The remaining crew struggled against all odds to make it home to Spain. In doing so, they completed one of the most notable maritime achievements ever: the first journey around planet Earth.

I first learned of Magellan's remarkable voyage in grade seven. What must it be like, I wondered, to embark on a journey with so much uncertainty and danger? The men must have known when they left that they most likely would never see their families again. From my sheltered North American upbringing, such hardship seemed beyond comprehension. I could imagine, however, the magic of exploring new lands; discovering peoples, places, and natural wonders that we now take for granted; seeing strange creatures, such as elephants, or devouring tropical fruits for the first time after months on the unforgiving seas.

It's easy these days to dismiss the hardships that early explorers endured. Modern "adventurers" only have to save a few months' wages from waiting tables to purchase a round-the-world airline ticket. With a few expedition supplies—a backpack, a swimsuit, a digital camera, a pack of condoms—they are ready to explore the world. Six months later, the modern explorer returns to beaming parents and regales them with tales of traipsing up Ayers Rock, trekking through tropical rainforests and bungee-jumping into deep gorges.

Travelling around the world has become an activity now marketed as a honeymoon excursion. Still, the goal of circumnavigating the globe has fascinated explorers for centuries. Many notable twentieth-century expeditions included attempts at circling the planet using different modes of transportation. Globe-girdling odysseys now account for firsts by airplane, balloon, helicopter, orbiting spacecraft, and even by Zeppelin.

The consensus is that the greatest explorations have all been accomplished. The tallest mountains have been climbed, the most distant poles reached, the deepest ocean trenches visited, and the longest rivers navigated. Expeditions making headlines these days tend to be subtle, sometimes comical, variations on what has already been done: First Muslim Woman Ascends Everest, First African-American to Row Atlantic, First to Trek to Both Poles in Back-to-Back Seasons.

With the arrival of the new millennium, modern expeditions seemed a matter of adding personal footnotes to more famous firsts. So, in 2001, it was with great surprise that I learned, after a quick Google search, that one of the most basic quests remained incomplete: nobody had ever circumnavigated the earth solely by human power.

While riding my bicycle or going for my daily jog, I idly imagined what such a journey would be like. How would it feel to reach the spot from which you started after years of toil—rowing across vast oceans and trekking and cycling over the continents? I never seriously thought of undertaking this journey. Such wild imaginings were in the same category as how to spend the proceeds of the winning lottery ticket or which restaurant to take Angelina Jolie to when she asked me out.

The concept of such a journey was simple: travel around the world using only your own steam. The planning and execution of such a feat, on the other hand, would be complex, expensive and precarious. The expedition would involve crossing at least two oceans in some type of paddle craft. Three continents would have to be traversed by foot, bicycle, or another mode of human-powered transportation. Funding such a multi-year expedition would be staggering. Even more daunting was the back-breaking work that would be required to pull off such a feat. Essentially, whoever did it would have to run a marathon or more—every day, week after week, year after year.

No, although it was an extraordinary concept, such an expedition was beyond my limited means. Although I had completed a few smaller adventures in the past, I was in no way qualified to pull off a first of this magnitude. Someone would do it one day, I was sure. But it would be one of those special people we hear about so often in the media—a visionary with unlimited finances and superhuman abilities.

1

TAKING THE PLUNGE

A YEAR AFTER MY GOOGLE DISCOVERY, in 2002, I was feeling philosophical. Like so many people, I was struck by the paradox that the human struggle for advancement was killing the planet that sustains us. The scientific community agreed that global temperatures were rising as a direct result of human intervention. If this pattern continued, within decades climatic conditions on our planet would change at an unprecedented rate. Coastal cities would flood from the rising oceans, lush agricultural land would turn into desert, and storms would increase in both strength and number. Millions would die from displacement and starvation.

Despite this apocalyptic forecast, the solution remains simple. Humans need to reduce their emissions of so-called greenhouse gases. The one hitch: such conservation may result in a short-term dip in the global economy. Quality of life—as defined by economists—might decline, especially for those who prefer driving their SUV to fetch a carton of milk rather than walk or ride a bicycle. The immediate benefits, however, would be less air pollution, a healthier population and a rise in innovative technologies and industries that cater to a less destructive society. Most important, a reduction of emissions would ensure atmospheric equilibrium and ultimately benefit all of our children, and their children, and their children's children.

These are the facts.

Although the appropriate course of action is clear, our society has chosen a different route. Total greenhouse-gas emissions increased by 50 per cent between 1970 and 2000. This trend is not changing.

Like many socially conscious citizens, I did what I could. I used my bicycle or public transit for almost all my transportation needs. I kept the heat low in my home. I tried to minimize my reliance on the power grid. It was frustrating, however, that despite the changes and efforts made by a few, overall greenhouse emissions steadily continued to rise. What else could I do to make a difference?

I revisited my daydream about a human-powered circumnavigation of the planet from a more serious perspective. Such a journey would garner much publicity, and this media attention could be leveraged to promote zero-emissions travel. If I could make it around the entire planet using my own muscles, it might inspire others to ride their bikes to work or walk to school. Suddenly, I realized that this expedition would be more than just a once-in-anyone's-lifetime adventure. It could also be a loud and clear statement about the urgency of climate change, an action that would speak louder than mere rhetoric about the issue. I could chronicle the expedition in a book to convey the message to a wide audience.

I ran my finger over the surface of a globe. I tried to imagine the easiest route and how I might traverse the various regions. By the middle of 2002, I had decided that I would do it. I would attempt the first muscle-powered journey around our planet.

I FELT SOMEWHAT LIKE A CHILD who declares he is going to fly to the moon. Although I had stated to myself that I would do it, and had every intention of carrying through, I still struggled to believe I would be successful. As the child starts clearing toys from the launching area, I began tapping on the computer, doing Google searches to glean some rudimentary information about what I was up against.

Because of these extreme nagging doubts, my initial preparations weren't accompanied by the usual enthusiasm I feel when striving for a more simple and achievable goal such as building a small boat or planting a vegetable garden. Instead, I laboured on the project simply because I said I would. It felt as though I were begrudgingly working for the small part of my brain that felt success was a possibility.

When I think back to those early days of preparation—so weighted with doubt and self-questioning—I often wonder what was my true motivating force. Perhaps the root of my drive was simply a primeval desire to explore and to discover new lands. Regardless of whether the expedition was successful in its stated objective, it would certainly offer excitement and adventure.

Preparing for an expedition that, at the bare minimum, involves rowing across two oceans, trekking through the coldest region in the Northern Hemisphere, two years of slogging, and a $400,000 (Canadian) budget is an enormous undertaking. My planning had three parts: fundraising, logistics, and finding a suitable partner. For such a lengthy and complicated expedition, a team of two would be ideal. More than two would complicate the logistics, add expenses and—as anyone with two roommates or two siblings understands—make for trickier team dynamics. With so many variables already, I wanted to keep things as simple as possible.

My first choice for a partner was Ben Kozel, an Australian friend and conservationist with whom I'd explored both the Yenisey and Amazon rivers. A hard worker, a good problem solver, and an amiable friend, Ben had proven himself to be the ideal expedition mate. Most important, the tall, curly-haired Aussie had a deep personal integrity. I knew I could trust him 100 per cent. I knew I could trust him with my life.

I sent Ben an email and outlined the expedition. I explained there was a spot for him if he was interested. When he wrote back and said he would have to decline, I was disappointed. He'd just become engaged and had enrolled at the University of Adelaide to acquire his teacher's qualifications. Although he wasn't turning his back on the world of adventure, a two-year undertaking at this stage of his life was just too much.

Another friend of mine, Dean Fenwick, a fit Vancouverite with a background in physical education, passed on similar regrets. He had recently started a company that produced accounting software for denturists and wouldn't be able to take so much time from his work.

I was discouraged. Finding the right partner was vital to the success of the expedition. Most of the people I knew who had the right qualities—fitness, discipline, physical and mental toughness—also had family or career commitments that prevented them from undertaking an extended expedition.

Out of the blue I received an email from Tim Harvey, a casual friend. He had just returned from El Salvador, where he had been working as an intern for a branch of the Sierra Club. He was wondering if he could borrow my LCD projector so he could give a presentation to his old school. I lent Tim the projector and accepted an invitation to go kayaking. I began to wonder if perhaps he might be my missing partner.

I had first met Tim, a student of journalism, in late 2000, during a swimming-pool session held by the University of Victoria's kayaking club. I wasn't a student, but I was friends with the club president, and she had invited me to do some training. Tim was interested in an expedition I had done, a voyage down the length of the Amazon River, and asked if he could interview me for the university paper. Later, we did a couple of kayaking trips together and kept in touch.

Tim stands about five foot ten, with a lean build. In the city, he usually sports a goatee and backcombs his thick brown hair into an Elvis-like swoosh. He often travels on a long skateboard, which he pilots gracefully at breakneck speeds. What struck me most about Tim was his apparent affluence, a striking contrast with the stereotype of the starving student. He owned a flashy Jeep and an Apple laptop and shared a comfortable house in the prime real estate of Cadboro Bay. I figured his lavish lifestyle was the result of hard work or smart business decisions.

The third of four boys, the son of a lawyer and a dentist, Tim grew up in the well-to-do neighbourhood of Shaughnessy and attended St. George's private school. In high school, rising conflicts in the world of scholastics resulted in his transfer to a nearby public alternative school. Tim moved out of his family home to share a house with several friends.

Despite Tim's troubled past, he seemed to have matured. He was intelligent and articulate, and he had a passion for outdoor adventure. In some respects, I felt Tim's background could be a motivating force for him. His rebellious spirit and his desire to break away from conformity could be assets. Properly harnessed, these qualities could give him the drive and energy to succeed where others might fail. The expedition ahead of us would be gruelling and dangerous. I felt Tim had what it would take to keep marching forward when things looked the bleakest.

We went for a hike on Galiano Island, and as we trekked through forests of arbutus, oaks and cedars with a panoramic view of Active Pass and the Gulf Islands, I described my proposed expedition and gauged Tim's reaction. He was clearly enthralled by the project. Finally, I popped the question:

"So how would you like to go for a paddle and hike a little longer than what we planned for this weekend?"

Tim didn't hesitate. "If it involves going around the world by human power," he said, "count me in."

I WAS STILL A LITTLE NERVOUS about the dynamics. I knew Tim only on the surface, although I liked what I'd seen. I hoped that, as we became more involved in the expedition, our inner workings would be compatible. I had completed three lengthy expeditions with different partners and didn't want to break the spell of relatively harmonious team relationships. One of Tim's greatest strengths was his sense of humour, and I figured this might help us through some of the tougher periods that lay ahead. Anger and pain can often be diminished with a few witticisms interjected at the right moment.

Shortly after Tim agreed to join my round-the-world expedition, he moved back to Vancouver from his temporary home in Victoria so that we could work together on logistics and fundraising. We had one year to plan and raise money for the journey, a full-time project for both of us. Tim worked hard. He was artistically inclined, so he finessed the graphic design of our website and poster.

Together, we tried to create a package that would impress potential sponsors. It isn't enough to have an interesting concept. As a modern adventurer, you need to convince company representatives that you will be successful and that the positive media exposure will justify their investment. Companies expect a complete and professionally polished package.

We had several strong cards to play. Doubleday Canada had endorsed the expedition by offering to publish my account of the journey. As well, the two films I had co-produced about my past adventures had won eight awards at international film festivals and had been shown around the world on National Geographic Television. Such successes illustrated the potential for a documentary covering our new expedition. Another possible draw for sponsorship opportunities was a recent partnership with Iridium Satellite Solutions. I had used their satellite phones on my previous expeditions, and the compact units were invaluable. For this expedition, Iridium offered the use of a handset and unlimited airtime—a deal worth more than $50,000. This arrangement would allow us to do crystal-clear interviews with the media from anywhere in the world.

Tim and I faced one final problem: we didn't want to publicize our expedition for fear of alerting competitors in the race to be first around the world under human power. Two other teams were attempting to achieve this very feat.

Englishman Jason Lewis had travelled almost two thirds of the way around the planet exclusively using muscle power. He had started from Britain with his friend Stevie Smith. The two crossed the Atlantic to Miami in a specially designed pedal boat, and then rollerbladed and cycled across North America. Their relationship began to falter after several years of intensive travel, and so, when their watercraft reached Hawaii, the duo split. Stevie returned home and Jason continued westwards, recruiting various crew for the remainder of his voyage to Australia. As Tim and I prepared for our own round-the-world journey, Jason Lewis had made it as far as Darwin, Australia, after ten years of travel.

Meanwhile, a Turkish immigrant living in Seattle, Washington, had even more ambitious plans. Erden Eruç was also attempting to be the first to circumnavigate by human power, while also climbing the Seven Summits—the highest peak on each continent. So far he had clocked about 8,000 kilometres and had summited Mount McKinley in Alaska.

With Jason Lewis so far in the lead, Tim and I figured we had no chance of beating him if he learned we were on his tail and increased his tortoise-like progress to a hare's sprint to the finish. We decided to promote only the first half of the expedition, from Vancouver to Moscow, as an expedition on its own. Only after we reached Moscow would we reveal the second half of our journey—and our ultimate goal.

Choosing our route was extremely important. We wanted to travel a course that would reduce risks as much as possible while staying within the rules of an official circumnavigation. A "circumnavigation" is, literally, "going around" an object. A perfect circumnavigation of the Earth would trace a great circle of 40,075.16 kilometres, for example by precisely following a path along the equator. Geographical realities, however, make it impossible to follow this arrow-straight route, and two sets of guidelines have been developed that set realistic parameters for purely nautical circumnavigation on the one hand, and for a combined land-water route on the other.

An official nautical circumnavigation, according to the International Sailing Federation/World Sailing Speed Record Council, requires, for example, that the vessel start from and finish at the same port, cross all meridians of longitude, cross the Equator, and travel at least 21,600 nautical miles (40,000 kilometres).

A continuous land–sea circumnavigation allows for a route that is closer to a perfect circle. Tim and I learned that there is only one organization that sets guidelines for such a route around the Earth: the Fédération Aéronautique Internationale. Although the FAI's rules were made with air travel in mind, they remain the only established parameters for a circumnavigation of the kind we were planning.

The FAI states that for a powered aircraft to officially circumnavigate the planet it must cross all meridians in one direction, travel a distance of at least 36,787.559 kilometres (the length of the Tropic of Cancer), and complete the journey at the point of departure. There is no requirement that it cross the Equator or touch on two antipodal points (points that are directly opposite one another on the globe). Most existing continuous circumnavigation records that are not solely nautical have followed these rules. Guinness World Records endorses the FAI requirements by recognizing feats that have adhered their guidelines: the Guinness record for the fastest circumnavigation of the planet (excluding orbiting space craft) is held by Air France for a Concorde flight that lasted just over 31 hours, and was completed entirely within the northern hemisphere.

As Tim and I mapped out our expedition route, we felt confident that if we followed the same guidelines as the Concorde flight, no one could question the validity of our claim. The 250,000 horsepower thrust of the Concorde's engines allow it to make progress against the strongest of winds, and to stay within a few hundred metres of a perfect great circle route—in other words, there is no form of transportation more capable of tracing a perfect circumnavigation of the Earth. It seemed reasonable that these same stringent rules would be sufficient for a team relying solely on their own human power.

Taking the FAI rules as our base, Tim and I also set ourselves a few extra goals to bring our expedition as close as possible to a perfect circumnavigation. We discovered that if you trace a circle equal in distance to the diameter of the Earth through either the northern or the southern hemisphere, you will touch at least three continents, span at least two oceans, and, once you take the realities of geography into consideration, you will be forced to cover more than 40,000 kilometres.

We added these three conditions to the criteria we set for our expedition. This challenge was going to take everything we had, and we wanted to make sure we did it right.

Tim and I began to plan a route. We would start on bicycle, heading north from Vancouver to Fairbanks, Alaska, where the roads ended. We would continue by rowboat down the Yukon River and then 400 kilometres across the Bering Sea to Siberia. We would trek or ski 3,000 kilometres of subarctic Russian steppe until we hit the far eastern limit of the European road system, which, again on bicycle, we would follow westwards to Portugal. From there, we would row across the Atlantic Ocean to North American shores, and then cycle the final leg back to Vancouver. We hoped to complete the 42,000-kilometre trip— 26,040 miles—in less than two years.

Our journey would take us through northeastern Siberia, which boasts some of the world's coldest temperatures, and the harsh conditions of the Bering Sea and Atlantic Ocean. Top-quality equipment would be essential to survive such extreme environments, so Tim and I sent sponsorship proposals to gear suppliers.

The response was overwhelmingly positive. It was quickly apparent that it was much easier getting product sponsorship than outright cash, so we would use these donations in any way possible to reduce our overall expenditure. Freeze Dry Foods offered us as much dried meat and vegetables as we could use. Not only would this food be good for the rowboat and Siberia, where it would be difficult to obtain other foods, but we could also use it on our cycling leg up to Alaska to cut down on costs. We would drop off food caches en route when we drove up to Fairbanks to drop off the boat. Norco Performance Bikes would provide us with heavy-duty Bigfoot mountain bikes, Valandré supplied us with down sleeping bags rated to minus 50 Celsius, Hilleberg gave us tents designed for polar expeditions, Helly Hansen offered top-quality clothing including down outfits and immersion survival suits for the Bering Sea, and Mountain Equipment Co-op offered a range of equipment that we couldn't get elsewhere.

By December, six months from departure, things were shaping up quite nicely with the logistical preparations and in obtaining the appropriate gear. However, we were still struggling to get adequate funding for the journey. No broadcasters or any of Canada's many government-supported film-funding agencies were willing to offer support for our film. Unlike our gear sponsors, companies were unwilling to make a more substantial financial commitment because they felt the expedition's goal was unrealistic. A few organizations eventually showed interest, and their support ended up being just enough to get the expedition rolling.

One of our most generous sponsors was Wallace and Carey, a Canadian distribution company. They weren't interested in promotion, as their company already had all the business it could handle. They simply wanted to see us succeed on our expedition. I met Frank Carey, the owner, and Jackie Bellerose, a member of his executive team, on an airplane and they listened intently as I told them of our plans. They ended up offering us any goods that their company distributed, which included food, film, confectionery, and other useful products. They also raised $9,000 for our expedition, which included $5,000 from a good friend of theirs, David Morgan.

A progressive school district in the southern Okanagan, SD 51, came on board as a gold-level sponsor. They realized the value of connecting education with adventure to create interest in geography and social studies among the students. We would conduct several interviews from the field with various classrooms in the district and give presentations at the schools before and after the expedition.

We raised about $19,000 from sponsors plus a few personal donations, including $3,500 from my brother, George. Our total of $24,000 was far from the $400,000 I'd estimated would be necessary to complete our expedition. We would need money to purchase our rowboat, filming equipment, to pay for shipping costs, etc. As our departure date drew closer, I felt increasing stress about this shortfall, but could see no solution. We would simply have to travel on a tighter-than-anticipated budget.

The to-do lists were endless, and invariably the number of jobs to do increased at a much greater rate than those completed. We had to learn how to row across an ocean, determine what kind of bikes can traverse thousands of bone-jarring kilometres in temperatures below minus 50, get permission to arrive in Russia's last closed state, Chukotka, in a rowboat, and determine how we would cross this frozen expanse where no roads existed and cycling would be impossible.

Tackling each job opened up new cans of worms. For example, in order to receive our entry permit for Chukotka, we learned we would need a translator and host to accompany us. These problems were compounded by the fact that our pitiful finances often wouldn't allow us to choose the easiest options.

During my research on ocean rowing I learned that this sport has become increasingly popular in recent years, and rowing across oceans has even been dubbed "the new Everest." I was shocked to learn that the average budget for these ocean rows—which includes shipping, transportation, the boat, emergency equipment and insurance—is about $200,000. The $24,000 we had collected so far for our entire round-the-world expedition wouldn't even cover half the cost of a custom-made ocean rowboat, never mind anything else.

Both my mother and father are Scottish, which gives me a genetic advantage when it comes to exercising extreme fiscal frugality. As we prepared for our monstrous undertaking, it was apparent that we would need to perform magic in the budgeting department. There was no way we would be able to afford the high-tech, sleek, and seaworthy custom-made rowboat that was typically used in setting ocean-rowing records. I had an idea, however. The market is flooded with small, dilapidated sailboats that can be purchased relatively cheaply. Surely the right design of sailboat could be converted to an ocean rower at a very low cost.

I consulted with Vancouver naval architect Patrick Bray. He agreed that the idea was feasible, and we discussed various ways to increase the boat's seaworthiness and conversions necessary to increase its ability to be rowed.

Around Halloween I tracked down the perfect sailboat on eBay, and purchased a Laguna Windrose, an 18-foot trailer sailor, from Everett, Washington, for $2,400 (which included a good quality trailer). This boat is seaworthy enough for open waters but light enough to be pulled behind the family sedan. It has a surprisingly large cabin, with two single beds and one double. Tim and I towed it back to Vancouver and set about converting it into a rowboat. Through the winter, even on days when the docks were sparkling with frost, we mucked about with plywood and fibreglass. The whir of our borrowed hairdryer warming the fibreglass resin was a common sound around the dock where our boat was berthed. We removed the sailing hardware and mast, lowered the cockpit cowling and installed oar locks and a sliding rowing seat—donated by Pocock, along with rails. We sealed the companionway—the cabin entrance—and installed a watertight hatch in its place. Croker Oars of Australia supplied durable carbon-fibre oars. After our work was completed, the boat was as unsinkable as a corked bottle and rowed with ease. We would use this boat to cross the Pacific and, if we could clear the logistical and bureaucratic hurdles of shipping it to Portugal from Siberia, also use it for the Atlantic. In total our rowboat cost just over $3,000.

Meanwhile, my basement suite became a mini sweatshop as we processed the various foods that arrived on pallets off the back of transport trucks. Wallace and Carey had provided 8,000 chocolate bars, which we chopped up, mixed with peanuts and raisins for additional nutrition and then portioned into zip-lock bags. Our freeze-dried chicken, beef, corn, and peas were similarly divided among zip-lock bags in meal-sized portions along with a liberal dose of spices. We had enough food to fuel us for seven months; we would be carrying a large portion of it across to Siberia in the rowboat.

Some logistical problems were almost impossible to solve. How, for instance, would we transport our gear to Siberia? No shipping companies or couriers serviced Russia's Far East, yet we needed to deliver all the supplies and equipment necessary to get us across this frozen landscape. Finally, after finding no other solution, we realized we would have to carry everything across in our 18-foot rowboat.

We had decided to depart from Vancouver on June 1 in order to reach the Bering Sea before the intense storms of fall and winter. As this date neared, we went into overdrive trying to get everything organized with our meagre resources. Little time was left for physical training, and most of my exercise came from riding my bicycle when running errands. Despite the limited fitness schedule, I was much less worried about my physical condition than I was about finances and logistics. I firmly believed that the success of our expedition relied much more on the mind than on the body. Personal discipline is what would get us around the planet, not having the physique of Arnold Schwarzenegger.

Almost all our planning and preparations had gone into the first half of the journey—from Vancouver to Moscow. We simply hadn't had the time or money to prepare for the second half of the expedition, through Europe and across the Atlantic, which we would need to plan, and raise funds for, while on the road. I felt nervous leaving with so much still undone. Even our permits and visas for entering Russia had not arrived, and would have to be forwarded to us on the road. There were tense moments between Tim and I as our deadline loomed, and we often disagreed about priorities. Regardless, we couldn't delay any longer. June was the latest we could leave without compromising our chances of making it across the Bering Sea.

Six weeks before departing, Tim and I rented a car and towed our heavily loaded rowboat to Alaska, where it would await our arrival by bike. The journey took almost four days and allowed us to view the remote countryside we would be crossing on our bikes. Finally, after almost two years of planning, Tim and I were set to go. We had the gear, the bicycles, and the rowboat. What we lacked in cash we made up for with enthusiasm.

2

SETTING OFF

W E HAD DECIDED TO START our circumnavigation at the base of a totem pole fronting the Maritime Museum near Vancouver's Kitsilano Beach. The location looks across English Bay to the Vancouver cityscape nestled in front of the North Shore Mountains.

The totem pole itself had been created by First Nations carver Mungo Martin, and the 100-foot monument depicts the mythical ancestors of the Kwakwaka'wakw people. We felt it would be fitting to have our human-powered journey to Russia marked by a significant piece of West Coast Native art. Our own travels would be the reverse of the great migration across the Bering land bridge that took place 13,000 years before. We would be travelling through the homelands of North America's first explorers.

On June 1, 2003, I arrived at the totem pole at 9:30 a.m. with my fiancée, Julie Wafaei. Julie had taken two weeks off from her work with a pharmaceutical company so that she could cycle with Tim and me as far as Alaska. A drizzly morning greeted us as we arrived on heavily laden bicycles. A small group of well-wishers had come to see us off. Our planned departure time was 10 a.m., so we had half an hour to savour the final moments before our two-year journey would begin.

My Norco bicycle was loaded with more than 50 kilograms of equipment, including an enormous professional video camera in a waterproof case, two tripods, an Iridium satellite telephone, an SLR camera, a seven-kilogram lead-acid battery to power all our electronics, repair and first aid kits, camping equipment, and dozens of other items. I had had trouble controlling my overloaded bike while getting used to the new clipless pedals and had fallen off once already on the three-kilometre trip to the totem pole. Julie shamed me by handling her heavy bicycle with finesse.

By ten, Tim still had not arrived. We had agreed to meet at 9:30, so we could do interviews with CBC Radio and Global Television. Finally, at 10:20, Tim arrived on his bike, with the grin of a class clown, clutching an Egg McMuffin in one hand while steering with the other. His bicycle had just recently been elongated using an Xtracycle frame extender with racks. The extra cargo-carrying capacity allowed Tim to pack his gear—an assortment of panniers, dry bags, and loose items— onto the frame in complete disarray before he strapped them into place. Hurriedly we conducted our interviews and did a last inspection of our bikes.

My mother had come out from Vancouver Island to see us off. I knew it was a hard moment for her. Tears filled her eyes as she gave a final hug to her son. It would be two years, maybe longer, before we would see each other again.

Tim, Julie, and I mounted our bicycles, waved and started the first pedal strokes of our 40,000-kilometre journey. We pedalled along a waterfront path in the light rain.

THE FINAL PREPARATIONS HAD BEEN SO RUSHED that this was the first moment in days I'd had to relax and reflect. It was exciting to finally leave, but at the same time I felt both sad and overwhelmed. I was saying goodbye to the familiar world I had known for so long. As we slipped through the comfortable, familiar surroundings of Vancouver, it was impossible to fully accept the fact that I was, in fact, on a round-the-world expedition. An expedition that promised to be more dangerous, gruelling, and challenging than anything I had ever done before. Apart from our heavy bags, we appeared no different than all the other cyclists on the road, and I couldn't help but feel I was simply running another errand on my bike.

Underlying my post-departure trance-like state of mind was a feeling of extreme sadness. Julie and I only had 10 more days together before she had to return home. It would be two long years before we would be reunited permanently, when I returned home again. I felt I was saying goodbye to everything and turning my back on a world of love and comfort and stability in exchange for a life of perpetual uncertainty and danger.

We had cycled only five kilometres when Tim's bike blew out a tire. It took us an hour to find a replacement in a nearby bike shop and install the new rubber (we didn't want to dig into our spares while bike shops were still around). Then, as we cycled through a major intersection, I heard a crash. The next thing I knew, my bike was dragged from underneath me. Unable to unclip my shoes from the pedals, I was thrown onto the street while cars swerved to avoid my head.

My homemade attachment system, by which I'd secured the pannier racks to the frame of my bike, had failed. The rear rack had crashed down backwards with all my heavy equipment. The bottoms of the racks were still fastened to the bicycle, which meant I was still connected to the mangled rack and accompanying load, now being dragged behind me. I lost control and tumbled onto the road.

I looked in dismay at the twisted racks, broken mount, and my bloodied hands and knees. Julie and Tim helped me to carry the mess out of the traffic. Nothing was broken beyond repair, apart from the piece I had made to connect the rack to the frame. With a chunk of broken concrete, we hammered the rack back into shape. I found a hardware store and bought a piece of angle iron with pre-drilled holes. With a borrowed hammer, I pounded the iron into a shape that would wrap around my seat post and secure the racks. Voila: we'd overcome our first hurdle. But we were still only in the middle of Vancouver.

Thanks to our breakdowns, we made dismal progress. By 8 p.m., we had only reached Maple Ridge, a suburb of Vancouver, a mere 60 kilometres from our starting point. Then my rear tire went flat, forcing us to stop for more repairs. While we patched the inner tube, a fellow strolled up and invited us to stay in his townhouse for the night. We immediately accepted. Dwight was also a long-distance cyclist and asked where we planned on going.

I felt almost embarrassed as Tim detailed our plan of travelling to Moscow entirely by human power. We sounded like— and were—complete novices with our shiny new overloaded bikes and unblemished gear, not the hardened, well-worn travellers that should be undertaking such an adventure.

I felt exhausted, and we had travelled only about one seven-hundredth of the total distance. I realized then that the only way to look at the challenge was one day at a time. Today, we were knocking off the easy part—cycling through our home city. Over the next two years, we would row across oceans, cycle frozen rivers, endure some of the world's most extreme temperatures and cover an unfathomable distance. Running my finger around the surface of the globe and daydreaming had been the easy part. Now, the reality was humbling—and scaring—me.

OUR TRAVELS IMPROVED as our small team cycled along the decent roads of the B.C. Interior. We seemed to have gotten most of the mechanical problems out of the way on the first day. Apart from frequent flat tires, our bicycles operated smoothly. On our third day, we clocked 96 kilometres—not too far from the daily 120 kilometres we hoped to average.

We completed day three at the 1,242-metre summit of the Coquihalla Pass. We pulled into a food stand in a checkpoint where trucks' brakes were tested before the steep descent.

"I hope you guys aren't planning on camping around here," the cook warned. "There's a black bear and a grizzly that live just down the road. And old Blackie's got cubs right now. She's a cantankerous old sow who won't take shit from no one."

With that he handed us three buns overflowing with cold corned beef from a can. I bit into the disappointing mess and wondered how many other gullible visitors had interpreted "beef on a bun" to mean a hot Salisbury steak smothered in gravy.

"It's getting dark," Julie said. "Let's just camp here and keep our food away from the tents. There are lots of truckers around here, so I'm sure we'll be fine."

Tim nodded in agreement while I tried to transform my slaughterhouse sweepings into a T-bone steak through intense imagination. A chill wind whistled over the pass and through the trees. Our day had been the most gruelling yet as we slogged up the steep grade of the Coquihalla Highway through waves of shimmering heat. My body, still soft from months in front of the computer, ached as I forced it to continue up the relentless hills. So when Julie suggested camping in the middle of a bear hangout, I couldn't think of a better idea.

We set up our two tents and placed our food bags on top of a two-metre-tall metal box of unknown purpose. Before collapsing into a state of unconsciousness I did my best to appear manly in front of Julie. I pulled out my 10-centimetre Gerber knife and winked at her as I tossed it in a sidewall pocket.

"Any bear will have to deal with me first, baby," I promised. Then I immediately forgot where I placed the knife and fell asleep.

The following morning, Tim cooked porridge while a semi-trailer with flames painted along its sides entered the check-point. The pot-bellied driver sauntered towards our campsite, thumbs tucked into his tight jeans.

"You guys staying here for long?" he inquired.

Julie told him we'd be on our way after breakfast.

The driver looked nervous. "There's a big griz about a hun-dred metres down the road," he said, "and it's coming this way."

He sauntered back to his truck and was off. A second rig entered the stop, and its driver, too, warned us of the bear. Hurriedly we packed our bikes and cycled down the road. The grizzly was nowhere to be seen, although we did see the black bear and her two cubs just off the side of the road.

OUR BODIES GOT USED TO THE CONSTANT TOIL, and I began to enjoy the surrounding mountain vistas from the slow pace of a bike sad-dle. I was also pleased by how the team was gelling. Low-stress pedalling past ever-changing natural backdrops seemed to heal some of the tensions between Tim and me that had developed in the later planning stages.

From the Coquihalla Highway, we continued north through the picturesque Cariboo region up Highway 97, past the village of Stoner and on to Prince George. It had taken us nine days to reach the city of Prince George, 900 kilometres from Vancouver, and it was our first major milestone. I was slowly learning that the only way to keep from being overwhelmed by the scope of our trip was to focus on much smaller goals within the journey. Arriving in Prince George buoyed all our spirits, and here we

turned westwards towards the town of Smithers, about 320 kilometres distant. A vacant lakeside cabin, owned by Tim's grandfather, awaited us there, and we stopped for a day's rest and
admired the alpine scenery. Tim elected to stay for another few
days instead of joining a short side trip that we had planned down
into Hyder, Alaska. He promised to catch up to us at Meziadin
Junction on the Cassiar Highway. Julie and I left Tim in the late
morning and began the remaining 330-kilometre leg to Alaska.

It was mid-June now, and at these high latitudes, twilight
stretched like taffy across the long evenings. The sun set
around 10, so Julie and I were still pedalling as midnight
neared. We had hoped to reach the junction of the Cassiar
Highway before retiring for the night, but neither of us felt like
continuing through the pending darkness.

"There's a bear!" Julie suddenly exclaimed.

I looked where she was pointing and saw a large shadow
shambling towards us. The bear didn't even look up as we
rattled past. I remembered that, when Tim and I had passed
through this region to deliver our rowboat to Fairbanks six
weeks earlier, we had counted 21 bears within two hours.

"Maybe we should cycle a little farther," I volunteered.

We continued until 12:30. By then, all traces of twilight
had faded. The forests on either side of the highway seemed
creepier than ever. Every shadow, real or imagined, took the
shape of a bear.

"How about here?" said Julie. She pointed down the
embankment to a spot that was even blacker than the adjacent
area, perhaps suggesting a clearing.

"Uh, yeah, looks great," I said. "I'll hike down and check
it out."

Julie stayed with the bikes while I stumbled down the
grassy slope. I tried to remind myself that bears had as bad
night vision as humans. Suddenly, a crashing noise erupted

several metres to my right and a large creature charged through thick bushes. I couldn't tell if it was heading towards me or away, nor did I care to find out. I bolted back up the slope and climbed onto my bike.

"What was that?" Julie asked.

"Don't know," I gasped. "Let's get going!"

We hurried on and I tried to stop thinking about the gory bear stories we'd heard from the locals we had met along the road. The grisliest attack had occurred only a few kilometres ahead, at Meziadin Junction. A woman driving along the Cassiar Highway had stopped for the evening and slept in the back seat of her car. In the middle of the night, she heard a soft tapping or scratching at her window. She thought she saw a shadow at her door and immediately thought of bears. She knew the area was full of the big creatures and had even seen a few earlier that day. She pulled her sleeping bag over her head and tried to block out the gentle thudding on her door. Perhaps it was her imagination, she told herself.

In the morning, she found a mutilated cyclist sprawled in a lifeless heap next to her car. The cyclist had been attacked by a bear and tried desperately to summon help. The young athlete had seen the woman asleep in the back of the car and tried to get her attention as his life slipped away in a puddle around his feet.

We continued for another couple of kilometres, when a looming sign warned of construction up ahead. At this time of night, the workers would be asleep, so I had an idea.

"Hey, the perfect campsite is coming up," I told Julie.

Shortly after, a ghostly collection of heavy machinery appeared, and I spotted what I was looking for.

"We can set the tent up in the back of that dump truck," I explained. "It's almost three metres from the ground to the back of the bucket. A bear fortress."

Julie looked incredulous but also pleased at the prospect of finally settling down for the night. We climbed into the massive steel bucket and set up the freestanding tent.

"Have you heard of the Dump Truck Club?" Julie asked me mischievously as she pulled shut the tent's door.

AT SIX IN THE MORNING, the alarm chime of my watch joined an orchestra of diesel engines thundering to life. Julie and I leapt out of our sleeping bags, half expecting our tent's mobile foundation to thunder into action. I pictured a large Caterpillar front-end loader dumping tonnes of rock and gravel over our tent. Fortunately, we had chosen a machine that was temporarily out of commission.

In record time, we packed the tent and loaded our bikes. In daylight, we were able to take in the size of the construction project. Traffic had been closed from both directions for one hour and dozens of dump trucks, front-end loaders, bulldozers, and other heavy machinery rumbled around the site like dinosaurs. We stood awkwardly in the middle of this scene, unsure how to proceed.

A kindly foreman pulled up in his Chevy and told us to stay put while he got help. He was not at all curious about why two cyclists had appeared in the middle of his job site. A pilot truck with a yellow flashing light arrived and led us through the chaos while the massive machines paused to let us through. Two kilometres later, we left the dust and yellow machines behind and soon arrived at the Cassiar Highway Junction. Here, we would turn onto one of the most remote highways in Canada.

The Cassiar Highway runs between the Coast Mountain range and the Skeena Mountains. The southern end borders the northwest rainforest, which gradually transforms into spruce and jack pine forests to the north. The region boasts mountains, glaciers, rivers, and abundant wildlife, including black and grizzly bears, wolves, mountain sheep and goats, moose, and beavers.

Julie's cycling journey would end in Hyder, Alaska, a 65-kilometre side trip from the Cassiar Highway. Three days after leaving Smithers, and 16 days from our Vancouver departure, Julie and I rolled into Hyder and Stewart on our bicycles with great sadness. The villages of Stewart and Hyder sit side by side at the head of Portland Canal Inlet, with the U.S.–Canada border running between the two. The remote communities look like a Hollywood movie set, and in fact the film industry has used this setting a few times for the combination of Wild West architecture and mountain-meets-ocean scenery.

We had a chance to access the Internet at the local library, and I was disappointed when I read the latest expedition update posted by Tim on our website. It had a decidedly whiny tone to it, implying that Julie and I had simply abandoned him in Smithers to go off on our own excursion. Regardless of what his feelings were, I felt annoyed that Tim had chosen the website, which was viewed by thousands, as a place to vent his frustration. The expedition was still in its very early stages, and his actions weren't conducive to strengthening team dynamics. Up until this point, I thought relations between Tim and I had been improving. Life on the road had removed many of the stresses we faced during preparations, and the light banter and jokes exchanged between us seemed promising.

Julie and I rented a hotel room in Stewart for our final night together. Julie planned to fly out to see me in Moscow, but that was worlds away now in time and distance. A small part of my brain wondered if I was saying goodbye to her forever. What if we didn't make it across the Bering Sea alive? What if we succumbed to the frozen wastelands of Siberia? I squeezed Julie tight while she cried softly.

At that point, I was tempted to quit the expedition and go home with Julie to Vancouver. My journey around the world suddenly paled before the strength of our love. Instead, I just lay quietly on the bed with a thick heart.

"I'll phone you every day," I promised. "It'll be just like I'm there, and before you know it I really will be there—cycling back into Vancouver and into your arms."

Julie stroked my head. "Don't worry, honey," she told me as she watched doubt flash across my face. "I know you'll make it. That's why I'm marrying you—because you do what you say you'll do."

When I began planning this expedition, I was single and never even entertained the thought that I would meet my life partner before I left. As Julie and I lay in bed, I thought back to when we first met, almost two years earlier.

On September 11, 2002, at Vancouver's Ridge Theatre, I had just shown my Amazon film. Near the stage, I signed copies of my book *Amazon Extreme*. I couldn't help but notice an exotic-looking girl waiting in line with her book. I wondered if she was Brazilian, perhaps interested in reading about my experiences in her homeland. The girl and I chatted for about 30 seconds while I signed her book. The presentation was part of a tour I was doing in western Canada. Although I presented to more than 2,000 people, the curly-haired girl at the Ridge Theatre stood out in my mind. I even mentioned her to Ben Kozel, my good friend and expedition partner, and hoped she might email me.

She never did.

Seven months after the presentation, I was waiting in Vancouver to catch a bus to the Sun Run, a 10-kilometre race. The buses were full, and a man flagged down a taxi and asked if anyone else wanted a ride. I packed into the taxi with a few other runners, and we headed towards the race. Through the course of conversation, I discovered that I was sitting next to the girl who had been in my thoughts for so many months. (Neither of us had recognized each other by sight.) We didn't have much time to talk, but she let me know she was going trekking in Nepal. I told her I'd love to see her pictures when she got back, and gave her my email address.

Six weeks later, Julie emailed me. Our relationship began to blossom during treks together in the B.C. mountains and an extended canoeing trip on the west coast. It turned out Julie wasn't Brazilian, but a mix of German and Syrian. Originally from Ontario, she moved out to B.C. to complete her master's in molecular biology at the University of Victoria. When we met, she was working in business development for a pharmaceutical company.

As we grew closer, I began to trouble over my planned expedition, which would separate us for two years, if not more. Who knew what might happen during such a long period of absence. Julie could take time off work and cycle with me for the first two weeks of the expedition, and we both hoped that she might join the expedition for various stages. Still, our short-term future felt uncertain. We did know, however, that after the expedition, we would get married. Two weeks before our departure, I had proposed to Julie and she accepted.

Finally, the dreaded moment arrived. We took the bus out of Stewart and I got out back at Meziadin Junction, where Tim was waiting. Julie would continue by bus to Terrace, from where she would fly home. Julie waved goodbye through a tinted window, and I stood watching as the bus roared away. And then she was gone.

NORTHERN BRITISH COLUMBIA AND THE YUKON were wilting under a record-breaking heat wave. Soon, Tim and I were cycling in temperatures close to 40 Celsius. The long dry spell had also ignited thousands of forest fires. Flames were consuming large tracts of land ahead of us in Alaska and the Yukon.

I had been troubling over the implications of Tim's update, and as we cycled along the hot gravel highway past snow-capped peaks, I decided to broach the subject.

"What update?" Tim said, looking genuinely surprised.

"The update you posted while in Smithers," I said, "I really think we should remove it, because it just isn't a suitable spot to be airing that kind of information."

Tim looked confused while I described the content of the web posting.

"My idiot brother must have posted that," he said with a pained expression. "It has nothing to do with me."

I believed him. Publishing such an update would be nothing short of shooting yourself in the foot with respect to the health of team dynamics and the overall success of the expedition. Tim was intelligent enough to consider the ramifications of these actions. The update was Tim's writing style, and I guessed that his brother Pete, who hosted the website on his server, had simply posted one of the private email updates that Tim regularly sent to his family. Tim immediately called his brother on the Iridium phone and asked him to remove the update. Although the web issue was resolved, I still worried about what was obviously smouldering beneath the surface.

On June 25, after cycling almost 1,900 kilometres from Vancouver, we reached a rather imposing hurdle on the Alaska Highway. At Swift River—just a log building with a gas pump—a huge line of traffic stretched back from a roadblock enforced by the fire marshal. Thick clouds of smoke billowed in from the west. We were soon informed that a fire was raging right next to the highway.

Four hours later the conditions improved marginally, and they began allowing traffic to move forward. Tim and I mounted our bicycles and began following the cars until the fire marshal jumped in front of us.

"Where do you think you're going?" he said.

"To Whitehorse," I replied.

"Not while on my watch you don't. It's vehicles only right now—too dangerous for bikes," he said. "You can probably put your bikes on one of those trucks over there and hitch a ride through."

"We can't because our journey is entirely human powered," Tim explained. "When do you think the roads will be safe for bikes?"

"Dunno." The fire marshal shrugged and walked away.

It might be days before the authorities reopened the roads to us, and the clock was ticking. We needed to cross the Bering Sea before summer was done, and this unexpected delay wasn't helping. It was rather ironic that these overcautious officials were endangering our lives more than they could ever guess. The hours ticked by, and nothing changed: vehicles were being allowed through but not us.

"Okay, let's make a boat," I finally said.

"What?" Tim was dumbstruck.

"Our map shows that Swift River runs parallel to the road. There are all kinds of lumber and materials here. We can build a boat or raft, load our bikes onto it and paddle down the river. It'll be a hell of a lot more dangerous, but we don't really have a lot of options. These fires will be burning for weeks."

I told the fire marshal of our new plan. Maybe it would drive home how desperately we needed to get moving. He talked to other officials and finally returned.

"Okay, you guys can ride your bikes through," he said. "Don't stop. And go as fast as possible."

We hopped on our bikes and rode through thick, billowing smoke for about ten kilometres. At times the visibility dropped to about 40 metres. We hacked and coughed as we cycled past bright flames that licked and danced at the side of the road. After about 45 minutes, the smoke began to clear and we were on the other side of the fire.

Tim laughed. "Give me that any day over a storm on the Bering Sea."

TWENTY-SEVEN DAYS AFTER LEAVING VANCOUVER, we rolled into Whitehorse, the capital of Yukon Territory. The forest fires had been growing in size and number, and it seemed that the entire territory was ablaze. A thick haze hung over the land.

We learned that the Top of the World Highway into Alaska was closed because of fires, which meant we had no means of reaching Fairbanks. The main Alaska Highway remained unaffected, but it was closed to Tim and me for an entirely different reason.

Six weeks earlier, when we were towing the rowboat up to Fairbanks, Tim and I had been stopped at the U.S. border.

"What're you doing with that boat?" the customs officer asked.

"We're dropping it off in Fairbanks so we can use it later on our expedition," I replied.

"You mean nobody is staying with it?" she asked.

"No, we're leaving it with a storage company."

"What's it worth?" she asked.

"Twenty-four hundred dollars," I replied.

"I'm afraid I can't let you into the country," she said, with a hint of a smile. "You can only leave goods unattended that are valued under two thousand dollars."

I should have just told her we were going fishing for the week-end, but it was too late now. I tried to backpedal. "Twenty-four hundred is the value of the boat *and* trailer," I said. "The boat is sixteen hundred and the trailer is eight hundred. I even have the documentation to prove it. We'll drop the boat off and bring the trailer out of the country."

"I'm afraid not," she drawled. "Anything over fifteen hundred must be attended."

"You just said two thousand a minute ago," I said, trying not to scream with frustration.

"No, I didn't," she insisted. "If you're not pleased with this, you can speak to my boss."

She summoned a stout man over to our vehicle. We explained our expedition and how the boat was only valued at $1,600.

He shook his head. "Sorry, I have to stand behind my employees," he said. "It's sort of a grey area, but once the decision is made we have to stick by it. We can't go making no exceptions."

"But what are the actual rules?" I asked. "Can you show me on a piece of paper?"

Another head shake.

"I've made a decision, guys," Tim said suddenly. "This expedition has been a lifelong dream for me, but I've decided to forfeit. Instead I'll stay here in Alaska with the boat."

The fat man brightened. "That sounds like a swell idea," he said. "Now I can let you into our country."

As Tim and I climbed back into the car, the officer turned and pointed to Tim. "If I see you riding up here on your bicycle in six weeks' time, both of you will be out on your asses so quick you won't know what happened."

At the time, we didn't worry. We would take the Top of the World Highway instead and pass through a different border crossing. Now, as forest fires raged across the Yukon and Alaska, only one option remained to sneak into America: the Yukon River.

3

PADDLING TO THE BERING SEA

A FRIEND OF MINE, Derek Law, lived in Whitehorse, and Tim and I quickly set up base camp in his suburban home while committing ourselves to the latest challenge. We would need to find a cheap boat to paddle 1,500 kilometres down the river to the Dalton Highway above Fairbanks, where our rowboat was stored.

I called several of the local outfitters who cater to the tourist industry and soon found a rental company that was willing to sell an Old Town canoe for $200. The boat had been thrashed and had a hole in it the size of a grapefruit. I sealed the deal and dashed over to Canadian Tire to buy paddles, life-jackets, fibreglass, and polyester resin. Then I patched the green canoe and we were ready to go.

Thirty-six hours after reaching Whitehorse, Tim and I loaded our bicycles, panniers, and groceries into the newly patched canoe and set off down the smoky Yukon River.

At 3,148 kilometres, the mighty Yukon is North America's third longest river. The section from Whitehorse to Dawson City has become a world-class paddling destination thanks to its northern scenery and Gold Rush ruins. During the Klondike era, the Yukon was the primary highway into the region, and shallow-draft paddle ships plied its waters. Our patched canoe glided easily through the roiling waters, past thick forests, camped Germans, and foraging moose.

Our delays to this point had been greater than anticipated, and Tim and I were already behind schedule. Although the distance along the river was only slightly longer than by road, the canoe was significantly slower than our bicycles. We decided to take turns and paddle round the clock, in the land of the midnight sun, to regain lost time. By staying on the go, we logged 150 kilometres a day, even faster than on our bicycles.

The banks of the river seemed untouched by modern development. The deforestation required to fuel the paddle boats had long since been filled in by a thick new growth of pine and spruce. Occasional ruins of log structures could be seen amongst the trees, a reminder of the boom days of the past.

My friend Derek had mentioned that there was a bakery along the banks of the Yukon River. After we'd been eating our own monotonous cuisine for a few days, the rumoured bakery became something of an El Dorado. We scanned the forested shoreline for the elusive house of treats.

"Yeah, I think I'll have a cinnamon bun and a big hot coffee," Tim mused as his paddle dipped through the silty water.

"I'll have a coffee with four big chocolate cookies," I said. "Where the hell did he say that bakery was anyway?"

"I don't remember," Tim admitted. "It doesn't really make any sense. I can't imagine someone having a bakery out in the middle of nowhere. They'd probably get two canoeists a day if they were lucky. Maybe Derek was pulling our paddles."

The days slipped by and we passed slowly through a tobacco-tinted world. Smoke from the forest fires seemed to leach all colour from the land and sky and replace it with shades of copper and grey. The only bright colours were the flames from the fires themselves, which could often be seen burning on the hillsides or on the riverbanks. We lost all hope that the bakery existed and resigned ourselves to the fact that the only treat we would be having was our sticky mess of melted Mars bars.

After four days and nights of paddling, we spotted a small white sign at the tip of an island. As we drew closer, we read "Stay right for Kirkman Creek" painted with an unsteady hand. Our guidebook indicated that Kirkman Creek was a ghost settlement of a few decaying buildings. Shortly afterwards, we saw a tattered Canadian flag flapping in the breeze just above two aluminum boats pulled up on the bank.

"Do you think this could be the bakery?" Tim asked hopefully.

We hauled the canoe ashore and hiked up the bank towards a dilapidated log cabin. The grey cracked logs leaned and twisted at all angles, and the roof was a patchwork of corrugated sheets in various stages of corrosion. The peace was shattered by the furious barking of four mangy mongrels as they dashed down to greet—or perhaps eat—us. Alerted by her canine army, a matronly woman in her fifties came down, shepherding two girls in their early teens ahead of her.

"Am I glad to see you boys," she said breathlessly. "Do either of you know how to shoot a gun?"

"I learned how in outdoor education," I admitted, "but I'm a little rusty . . ."

"There's a bear . . . was a bear . . . a big, big one," she gasped and pointed in the direction of a gully about 60 metres from the cabin. "My dogs treed it this morning and, well, I shot it. It dropped from the tree, but I don't know if it's dead. It's down in the gully now and I keep hearing noises. I'm scared it might come up and attack us—there's nothing more dangerous than a wounded bear."

"So how do we fit into the picture?" Tim asked.

"I was wondering . . . It's just me and the girls here . . . Perhaps you might be able to go down into the gully and, well, you know, put it out of its misery if it's still alive. And perhaps you can haul it up, so I can feed it to the dogs."

I looked at Tim and shrugged, and we began walking towards the ravine. The ground angled away sharply and it was impossible to see through the tangle of underbrush and trees. I imagined a big bloody bear waiting below, wishing to wreak its revenge on the monkey creatures that had caused it so much misery. The woman and her girls had gone back into the cabin and were peering through mullioned windows.

As we reached the gully floor, we peered around, eyes adjusting to the gloom. And then I saw it, a large, dark shadow 10 metres ahead of us. It was perfectly motionless. The black camouflage of the bear's coat contrasted starkly with a mass of red and pink intestines spilling out of a big hole in its side. Flies buzzed around the creature. It was clearly dead. We looped a rope around the neck of the small bear and dragged the creature up the slope towards the cabin.

The woman came waddling over to us and the carcass. She glanced at the sweat dripping from my nose and announced, "Lunch is on the house."

She ushered us into a small wooden gazebo surrounded by mosquito netting. Soon, her daughters emerged from the shack carrying trays of fine food. Sandwiches made from homemade bread and fresh salmon and beef vegetable soup were followed by lemon meringue pie and big cups of strong coffee.

"And so the bakery exists after all," I said. "God bless Derek."

THE FOLLOWING DAY WE REACHED KLONDIKE CITY, near the American border. This site is where almost all canoeists take their leave of the river, since the scenery becomes increasingly mundane farther down in the Yukon flats. Thick smoke concealed one side of the river from the other. As we approached the Alaskan border, a dog began barking. We figured we must be near the community that housed the river border crossing.

"Maybe we should just slip on by," Tim said. "They'll never see us in this smoke."

"Yeah, maybe we should. Maybe your picture's been distributed to all the border crossings in Alaska. Imagine that: 'Expedition Ends Because of Asshole Border Guards.'"

We slipped into the U.S.A. without stopping and continued our steady pace towards the Bering Sea. The Gwich'in people inhabit this section of the river. Frequently, we passed fish camps on the small islands where the Native people would catch the spawning salmon with nets and fish wheels. The river made a quick arc above the Arctic Circle, and for two hours we were in the Arctic before the river curved south below the line again.

Ten days after we had set off from Yukon's capital, a huge bridge loomed through the smoke. It was the Dalton Highway Bridge, 1,500 kilometres from Whitehorse. Despite finicky U.S. customs agents and ferocious forest fires, we had made it. Here we would pick up our rowboat, which we'd just christened the *Bering Charger,* and continue our journey on to Russia.

From here, we would have to travel more than 5,000 kilometres—down the Yukon River, across the Bering Sea, and through northeastern Siberia—before we reached roads again. In our rowboat, we would carry everything we needed to complete this journey, one that would propel us deep into the heart of the notorious Siberian winter. Our gear included three bicycles; six sets of studded bicycle tires; three sets of skis; winter Baffin boots (rated to minus 100 Celsius); Helly Hansen clothing for all conditions; Helly Hansen immersion survival suits; multiple mitts, balaclavas, socks, and ski goggles; two Mountain Safety Research (MSR) stoves; 180 litres of stove fuel; freeze-dried provisions for five months; tools and repair equipment; and much more.

We finally launched our heavily loaded boat at the exact point in the river where we had stepped out of the canoe. Now I felt especially excited. Until today, we had been travelling well-worn paths, following in the tracks of thousands of motorized travellers or touring canoeists. From this point we would be attempting something that had never been done before: a human-powered crossing of the Beringian Gap, the roadless swath of wilderness separating the American and Russian road systems.

Our 18-foot vessel had everything we needed to cross this expanse. We had spent more than a year preparing for this moment.

Smoke still suffocated the land, and after launching the boat in the river, we still couldn't see across to the other bank. Our ship was a novelty on the Yukon, so Native fisherman paused to watch as our heavy vessel glided quickly over the river's surface.

Although our heavily burdened rowboat probably weighed forty times more than our canoe, it moved faster because of the efficiency of its sliding-seat rowing system. The set-up was gentler on our bodies, too, while the featherweight carbon-fibre Croker Oars were a pleasure to handle.

We continued with our round-the-clock paddling regimen, but the full comfort of a larger vessel made life seem much easier now. The person on the off-shift had freedom to move about on the boat without risking a capsize. He could relax on the forward deck, or climb inside and sleep on a soft foam bed. Our larger craft would also allow us to travel in all weather. The river was larger now, brawny and wild. In strong headwinds, the waves would reach four feet in size. In the canoe, we'd had to wait out such conditions on shore to keep from swamping. Now, our boat would charge through the waves without the slightest hesitation. We towed our canoe behind the rowboat to have a second boat to film from.

The river meandered in giant oxbows. To the north was the Brooks Range; to the south, the White Mountains. The river was nearly two kilometres across, so we felt like we were rowing on a giant moving lake.

In late July we reached the Yukon Delta. In this wetlands expanse, roughly the size of Oregon State, the river splits into a labyrinth of channels. Most of the delta is protected as part of a national wildlife refuge. It is also home to almost 20,000 indigenous Yupik people, who lead a semi-subsistence way of life. The border between land and sea is blurred here, with channels opening up wider in the marshes until suddenly a traveller realizes there are no more marshes. The water is still fresh, however, because of the immense volume of fresh water the river pumps into the ocean. There is no swell either, since the shallows extend 15 kilometres from shore and subdue any larger waves.

We navigated through the maze of channels and reached the Bering Sea on July 31, two months and 5,300 kilometres from our clumsy first day in Vancouver. We pulled up to the last solid piece of land, an embankment with a scattering of trees and a fishing cabin, which stayed just barely clear of the water at high tide. Here, we would wait for the best weather window in which to make our dangerous self-propelled dash across the Bering Sea.

4

BY ROWBOAT TO ASIA

U NLIKE OTHER PARTS OF THE OCEAN, the Bering Sea has no prevailing winds. Instead, the wind blows from all points of the compass equally, with great variability in strength. It is one of the most dangerous bodies of water on the planet due to its cold water (4 degrees Celsius in summer), frequent storms, lack of sheltered ports, and shallow depths that can produce steep, powerful waves.

As the cormorant flies, it is 400 kilometres from the mouth of the Yukon River to Provideniya, the Siberian port of entry where we hoped to make landfall. Roughly midway across this stretch of ocean is St. Lawrence Island. We hoped to cross at least as far as the island during a favourable spell of weather. There, we could hunker down against unfavourable winds and wait for another spell of calm weather for the last half of the crossing.

On August 3 we got the forecast we had been waiting for. Julie had been relaying the marine forecast for the Bering Sea via the satellite telephone. It finally looked like we would have calm conditions and light easterly winds just long enough to reach St. Lawrence Island. In four days, the weather was expected to degrade again, but we hoped to have made it as far as the island by then.

We departed from our muddy campsite early in the morning. The water around the boat remained the colour of milky coffee, and a taste test confirmed it was still fresh. There was no telltale swell of the ocean, but we knew we were no longer on a river. At low tide, huge expanses of mud were exposed, save for a few river-carved channels.

In a short time, only six kilometres from shore, all traces of land had disappeared from the horizon. An ocean-chilled breeze blew lightly across the water beneath dark grey skies. The boat would occasionally—and disconcertingly—graze the shallow bars we crossed. It was an eerie feeling, the sensation of being in the middle of the ocean yet frequently hitting the bottom with the oars. For the longest time, depths dipped no greater than a metre, and we kept our fingers crossed that we would get away from these muddy shallows before the tide dropped and left us stranded on a sandbar.

The shallows fanning out from the Yukon River Delta pose one of the greatest marine hazards in the region. In rough weather, waves break on the shoals 15 kilometres from land and cause many vessels to founder. A Native from one of the small villages near the delta had detailed the tragic stories of stricken mariners who tried to walk and swim to shore from their wrecked vessels. Although the water averaged only a metre or so in depth, the sailors would succumb to hypothermia long before they reached the safety of land.

"We're eight nautical miles out," I said, glancing at the GPS. "Can you check the depth?"

Tim plunged a canoe paddle into the water. "Beyond dipping depth," he announced.

This was good news. The tide now was dropping quickly, so we needed to reach deeper waters. It looked as though we would make it safely through the shallows. At 10 nautical miles out, the swell of the ocean began to rock our boat. I scooped the water to my mouth and detected the tang of salt. We could now relax a little and lengthen our rowing shifts to one hour. I called Julie to let her know we were finally on the ocean and to get the latest weather forecast.

"It looks like the upcoming weather system has intensified," Julie said. "They're now forecasting 30-knot winds and 12-foot seas."

I could hear a tremor in her voice. I knew that if positions were reversed, I would be terrified—my most precious thing heading onto the Bering Sea in an untried, unconventional rowboat with a storm approaching. What if my theories about the boat's seaworthiness were wrong?

"Shouldn't be a problem," I tried to reassure her—and myself. "We'll be safe and sound at St. Lawrence Island when the storm hits."

Julie didn't sound convinced. "Be careful, honey, and always remember I love you."

I turned the phone off and stared across the sea. The water was turning clear and absorbed all light from the dimming evening sky. Small bubbles trailed the boat as Tim did his best to keep a steady speed. The rhythmic whirring of the sliding seat made a comforting sound. Like the steady tick of a grandfather clock, it seemed to represent order amidst a whirl of uncertainties. The wind was still light, but the grey anvil heads and distant squalls looked anything but settled.

BY 11 A.M., THE NORTHERLY WINDS HAD INCREASED, so we decided to veer more to the south, thereby increasing our speed. Although this tack would take us away from our rhumb line to St. Lawrence Island, it would position us nicely for when the disturbance did hit and the winds started blasting from the south: the inevitable northwards drift would bring us back in line with the island.

By midnight, the water no longer carried suspended silts from the river. I was fatigued after our marathon run through the shallows and didn't look forward to our long night of toil. On the river, during our shifts behind the oars, we had been able to take coffee breaks or the occasional rest while the current kept the boat moving. Here on the sea, with only our muscles to propel the boat, we couldn't afford to stop.

"Colin, great news!" Tim yelled through the darkness.

I lifted my head from a pile of damp, sweaty clothes. More than anything I wanted to pull my sleeping bag over my head and drift back to unconsciousness.

"Yeah?" I asked. "What's that?"

"It's your turn on the oars," Tim said. "That means I get to curl up in bed. The bad news is that it's starting to rain and the winds have moved to the north-northwest. We're only able to go due south now."

I groaned and slipped on my raingear. The torture of rowing was bearable when we made good progress, but now it looked like we would spend an exhausting night heading in the wrong direction.

At 5 a.m., an ominous red sun punctuated our five-hour period of darkness. Our nightly progress had been disappointing. We only ended up paralleling the Alaskan coast southwards instead of heading west towards Russia. There was no chance now that we could reach St. Lawrence Island before the storm. Perhaps a retreat back to the U.S. shore would be more prudent. With the northwest winds, we could get to a village called Scammon Bay, on the south end of the Yukon Delta, in four hours. We changed course and slowly closed the gap to our refuge.

"Hey, Colin," yelled Tim, who was back for his turn in the cockpit. "The winds have switched to the south and we're really slowing down."

"Crap!" I shouted back. "The forecast didn't predict the switch until this evening."

"She's picking up and we're making no progress," Tim said. "And by the way, it's your turn to row."

I grabbed the oars. For half an hour, I battled into the wind and waves before I had to admit defeat. There would be no snug harbour or hot meal, even though our intended port was only six kilometres away. We would have to face the storm. I turned the boat around and once again aimed for St. Lawrence Island.

Even though it was noon, the sky darkened like a movie theatre before the main feature, and the black waters of the Bering contrasted the growing number of whitecaps that scarred its surface. Our vessel handled the six-foot waves well, but I still felt apprehensive, knowing this test was only the beginning.

"Tim, your mother's on the phone!" I yelled into the cabin.

"Wha . . . ?" Tim slurred. His eyes looked swollen and red.

"Yeah, she says it's time for you to get on the oars!" I said and awaited my relief.

THE NEXT MORNING, WE WERE STARING INTO A FULL-FLEDGED GALE. The seas towered to 12 feet, and the occasional monster wave would break with a maelstrom of white water. These collapsing waves posed great dangers for the *Bering Charger*, and threatened to roll the boat on its side, or worse.

In the deep sea, most mariners would scoff at 12-foot waves. However, the shallow Bering Sea makes these waves treacherous. Large waves simply cannot form in shallow waters, so instead smaller and more powerful swells are produced.

More disappointing was a change in the winds to the southwest instead of the forecasted southeast. The quarter horsepower produced by our rowing efforts only allowed us to angle 45 degrees off these strong winds. The GPS verified that if the winds didn't shift, we might miss St. Lawrence Island entirely and get blown northwards.

We entered marathon mode once again and spelled each other off in intense half-hour rowing shifts as we struggled to point our craft towards the vital shelter of St. Lawrence Island. The waves tossed and rocked our boat and disrupted our efforts to synchronize the 12-foot oars and sliding seat. As it wormed back and forth, my back felt like spaghetti thrown against a brick wall.

By evening, we were both completely spent, and my mood had deteriorated with the weather. The winds had held steady, and St. Lawrence Island would soon slip past our port side. Wind speed was increasing, and now 15-foot waves were launching assaults against our boat. The weather was far too rough to cook in, while our straining bodies couldn't get enough fuel from a diet of only crackers, jam, and canned tuna.

Larger waves would break right over the stern and fill the cockpit like an icy jacuzzi. The rower would then have to wait for the self-draining cockpit to empty before resuming his efforts on the sliding seat. The onset of darkness made a nerve-racking situation even more dangerous, as the waves were now concealed in a veil of darkness. Thick cloud cover ensured zero-light conditions, and we steered the boat by keeping the wind and rain against our right cheeks and checking our heading with the compass.

At 3 a.m. my shift ended. I was almost delirious with exhaustion.

"Tim!" I yelled. I was in no mood for any more comedy wake-up calls.

The time it took for Tim to don his raingear, neoprene booties, and gloves seemed an eternity. He then emptied his bladder into the pee bottle and handed it to me to dump over the side. (During his shift it would be impossible for him to relieve himself while struggling with the oars.) Finally, he crawled through the hatch and shut it quickly to keep breaking waves from spilling into the boat. He grabbed the second tether line and proceeded to tie a bowline around his waist to secure himself to the boat.

This was the moment I had been fantasizing about for my full shift, when I could finally escape from the freezing cold, the horizontal rain, and the waves and retreat to the damp, smelly but warm bunk below and pass out. I slipped my fingers under the hatch and pulled. It didn't budge.

"The hatch won't open!" I yelled as I violently jiggled the plastic door.

"That's impossible," Tim said.

A breaking wave nailed the boat, turned it sideways and then bulldozed the vessel for 10 metres. The boat flipped on its side, and Tim spilled off the rowing seat and onto the cockpit cowling. I felt like I'd slipped into a nightmare. Our food, warm clothing, blankets, communication gear, survival suits, and tools—everything that mattered—was inside the belly of the boat. Like the ghostly hand of some trickster, gravity had somehow closed the hasp of the inside latch. There was no way to open it from the outside.

Remnants of the last wave delivered a steady dribble of ice-cold water into my boots. Tim was scrambling to regain control of the boat by hauling on the portside oar. Without any tools, the only way into the boat was to break the hatch. But if we did end up breaking the hatch it would compromise the seaworthiness of the vessel and put us in danger of swamping. A capsize would be fatal as water filled the cabin.

On the other hand, with no food, water, dry clothing, or charts, Tim and I would eventually die of exposure if we stayed on the outside of the boat. It was a classic Catch-22.

I slipped my fingers under the plastic hatch and pulled with all my might. The hasp snapped and the lid flew open. I entered the boat with a feeling of resignation. It would now be possible to sleep for 17 minutes until Tim's shift was over. However, this nap would likely rank as the least restful sleep of my life. The boat had lost its waterproof integrity, and I felt it was only a matter of time before a breaking wave would roll the vessel and plunge it to the bottom of the Bering Sea.

❖

MORNING DAWNED WITH 15-FOOT WAVES AND 40-KNOT WINDS. Unfortunately the wind direction hadn't changed, and our trajectory would slide us 20 kilometres past the eastern point of St. Lawrence Island. We had no hope of reaching any shelter. The next landfall would be 200 storm-tossed kilometres to the north.

"We're not going to make it," I said to Tim as we changed positions at the oars at 10 a.m. "It looks like our only hope is to aim for Nome, Alaska. If all is well, we'll be there in three days."

"And be farther from Siberia than when we started," Tim noted glumly as he took hold of the oars.

The torture continued for another two days. I couldn't believe it when the fierce winds finally did change direction. A hundred kilometres from Nome, they began to blow from the southeast, the direction we had so badly needed when trying to make it to St. Lawrence Island. Now these belated winds threatened to shipwreck us if we couldn't hold our line for Nome.

Despite our extreme efforts, after Tim did another chart plot, it again became apparent that we were losing our battle. "Twenty-two hours and our boat will be surfing Hawaii-sized waves onto the rocks of Alaska," he announced.

We could drop our anchor, but it wouldn't be strong enough to hold our boat in the breaking waves. It was time to make some calls on our satellite phone. Perhaps a larger ship could be dispatched from Nome to provide some assistance. I called Julie and she gave us a list of phone numbers that included the U.S. Coast Guard, the Nome harbour master, and the police.

The coast guard informed us that they didn't have any stations that far north and suggested we call the Nome harbour master. Joy, the harbour master, was sympathetic to our predicament. However, she told us there was no way any boats could leave the harbour.

"This is the biggest storm of the summer," she explained. "The entrance to the harbour is shallow and the waves are breaking right over it. Not even the biggest crab boats can get out in this."

Then Joy had an idea. "There is a Russian research vessel—*Professor Khromov*—in the region," she remembered. "They're anchored offshore, waiting out the storm, so a supply ship can meet them from Nome. Perhaps they could lift their anchor, move to your position, toss you a line, and re-anchor. You could then hold your position until the storm abates. I'll contact them and see if they'll assist. Give me a call back in half an hour."

We waited, knowing our lives depended on the decision of a Russian captain. I'd spent enough years on the sea to know that surviving a shipwreck was a roll of the dice. Lucky sailors would emerge unscathed; others would be pummelled onto the rocks by the waves, or be squashed between their boat and terra firma. *Professor Khromov* was our only chance of avoiding a high-seas game of Russian roulette.

Tim poked his head through the damaged hatch, phone in hand, while I tugged on the oars.

"She says they'll do it," he said. "In a few hours they're going to raise anchor and steam this way."

Relief washed through my body. This was our fifth day on the Bering Sea, and I had never felt so exhausted or lonely in my life. The sullen ocean seemed to be plotting against us, and I knew there was a good chance we might die. The thought of a big ship emerging from the sheets of rain and tossing an umbilical cord to our own tiny craft buoyed my battered spirits.

I had spent the last few days thinking about my future life with Julie. I imagined the plot of land we would have on B.C.'s Gulf Islands, complete with cedar and arbutus trees and a vegetable garden. We would wake up early in the morning and read to each other, sipping freshly roasted coffee, while the sun rose above the ocean. These pleasant fantasies, when juxtaposed against stark reality, were more torturous than anything else. Why was I out on this dismal ocean when I could be with my love leading a life of bliss? If I could have pushed a magic button and gone home, I would have done it without another thought.

Now that our salvation looked more likely, my thoughts grew heavy with the prospect of continuing the expedition. I felt I didn't have the strength to carry on. And yet I couldn't bear to tell the world I was quitting.

Professor Khromov finally crashed through the waves towards our boat. The 60-metre-long ship grew in size until it was a few hundred metres away. An American pilot aboard the Russian ship relayed the orders of the captain through the VHF radio.

We were to hold our position while the *Professor Khromov* approached from downwind. It would pass within 50 metres of our boat, the closest possible on these unpredictable seas. At the closest point, a crew member would throw a monkey's fist—a weighted knot affixed to a length of thin cord—to our boat. That cord would be tied to a larger rope, which we could pull to our vessel.

The skilled captain and crew members executed the manoeuvre flawlessly, and soon we were connected to the *Professor Khromov*. Towing our boat would be a dangerous manoeuvre, so the Russian ship instead dropped anchor. Together, we would wait for the weather to calm. We spent the night bouncing off the stern of the *Khromov*. For the first time in days, Tim and I were able to get several hours of uninterrupted shut-eye.

Through the night, the winds began to subside. By early afternoon the next day, the four-day storm had abated. We untied from our saviours and rowed the final 24 kilometres to Nome.

NOME IS ANOTHER PRODUCT OF THE GOLD RUSH, and that pioneering spirit survives to this day. False-fronted buildings line the short main street, and bars are numerous and popular. Despite the rough facade, the town is tidy and one of the most vibrant and visually pleasing communities we had encountered in Alaska. Businesses on the south side of the main street all border the ocean, and the Bering Sea pounds against the rocks just metres away from their doors.

We tied our boat next to a crab ship, whose crew immediately invited us on board for beers. A short time later, a local by the name of Kevin asked us to his place for a meal of fresh moose and vegetables from his greenhouse. In Nome, we were able to repair our boat, with Kevin's help, and soon the *Bering Charger* was seaworthy again.

One week after arriving, we slipped out of the harbour in calm conditions and steered once more towards Siberia. We made it halfway across before getting hit by another strong blow. This time the winds came from the north, blowing us all the way down to St. Lawrence Island, 200 kilometres to the south. Here, we anchored and waited for conditions to favour us again. We traced the length of the island, and then made a break for Siberia, fighting strong northerlies. Throughout the voyage, we were reporting our progress via the satellite phone to the authorities in Siberia, one of the requirements they had earlier stipulated.

Finally, on September 4, exactly one month after we'd left the Yukon Delta, the craggy outline of Siberia came into view. Our snaking route had led us almost 1,000 kilometres to get 400 kilometres across the sea. But we had just completed the first ever row across the Bering Sea.

5

INTO SIBERIA

UNLIKE THE FLATLANDS WE HAD LEFT BEHIND IN ALASKA, Siberia emerged from the sea like a backdrop for *Lord of the Rings*. Craggy mountains reared out of the ocean, adorned with glaciers and wave-carved cliffs. Millions of seabirds chattered back and forth from the ocean to their mountainside roosts. We struggled against a strong current as we made our way the final distance into an inlet that led to the city of Provideniya. Once we were in the shallower waters, we dropped the anchor and could finally rest.

The next morning, we rowed up the narrow fjord. I found it hard to believe that a port town lay hidden around the corner. The land looked wild and untouched by human hands. Small glaciers crawled down to the water's edge. Stunted bushes that grew no higher than my knees indicated the harsh climate that ruled this land. The temperature today at least was a pleasant 12 degrees Celsius.

Provideniya, at a latitude of 64.5 degrees north, is Russia's most northeasterly port of entry. The population of 1,900 has declined from the 10,000 who lived here in Soviet times. The town was founded to service ships plying the Northeast Passage and still has extensive port facilities, including a major repair yard. Since the break-up of the Soviet Union, shipping through the passage has all but ceased, and Provideniya is now a dying town.

We approached this remote outpost with apprehension. The state of Chukotka is the last closed part of Russia, meaning free travel is forbidden without authorization. We had waded through the bureaucratic quagmire for a year to receive permission to arrive in a rowboat and to trek through this state. In recent years, two other groups of explorers had arrived in Provideniya by their own means, only to be deported.

Mike Horn was one of these adventurers. His plan had been to trace the Arctic Circle around the world by trekking and sailing. He sailed across from Alaska in a small sailboat along with his brother and a friend. Upon reaching Provideniya, the team learned that their Russian visas alone weren't enough to get them into Chukotka. Authorities arrested Horn and ordered the other sailors back out to sea. Horn was soon deported.

With patience and persistence, it is possible to receive permission to travel through Chukotka. To acquire this magic permit, called a *rasporyazheniye,* we had to outline the precise route that we would follow. Then we needed advance permission from the border guards and from the mayors or head administrators of every single community we would pass through. We had to hire a local, who was registered with the government, to be our guarantor and companion for the duration of our visit. Any communications devices, including satellite telephones and GPS units, would need to be granted special permissions from officials in Moscow before we could bring them into the state. Every step in the permission process involved another fee. After a year of hoop jumping and palm greasing, we were granted our all-important *rasporyazheniye.*

Still, nothing was guaranteed until our passports were stamped. If the fickle officials sent us back out to sea, we might never make it back to North America. The northerly winds were becoming more consistent, and they would likely push us down into the outward-flanging waters of the Pacific Ocean.

As we turned a corner of the fjord, Provideniya came into view. Almost the entire town was composed of Soviet-style four- to six-storey concrete apartment blocks. Two thirds of the buildings were clearly vacant, with rows of broken windows and dark interiors. The whole town had been smeared grey by the bellowing smokestacks of a huge coal-fired heating plant. Below the town sat the port, with large rusted loading cranes and three 20-metre mounds of coal.

A partially submerged barge jutted out from the eastern end of the port. A dozen uniformed men and women stood on this makeshift dock. The group included customs, immigration, and the army.

We had had to inform the Russian authorities of our progress via Slava, our local liaison, so they were expecting us. Our welcoming party didn't look too welcoming, though. As our boat drew closer, the group watched, silent and unsmiling. Finally a man in camouflage issued an order in English: "Tie the boat here."

We wrapped our lines according to his directions. The camo-wearing military man was the only one who spoke English, and he translated for all the other officials. We fielded dozens of questions and then received a multitude of forms to fill out. The forms included such questions as "How many crew members perished at sea?" (nearly two) and "What is the nature of your cargo?" (mountain bikes and enough freeze-dried food to feed the Russian Army). Apart from the unlucky Mike Horn, we were the only navigators of a small boat that they had ever processed.

By the time night began to fall, we felt optimistic about our chances of getting into the country. There had been no talk of deportation yet, and negotiations seemed to be proceeding smoothly.

Finally, the officials began leaving one by one. "You are not allowed to go ashore yet," the soldier told us. "You can sleep in the harbour tug tonight, and tomorrow you will possibly be allowed off." We were led across the barge to a tidy-looking ship. Inside, two comfortable bedrooms awaited Tim and me. I brushed my teeth, climbed into the soft bunk and enjoyed my first night just metres from Siberia.

The following day, we were freed, although we didn't know that there was still over a week's worth of customs and immigrations formalities ahead—trooping between offices, filling out forms, paying small fees. Officials had confiscated our satellite telephone and our GPS because the permits had yet to arrive from Moscow.

At our tugboat, we met up with Slava, the local whom we'd paid to take care of the bureaucracy, and Yulya, our Russian translator. Slava was a rotund teddy bear of a man, well dressed in a cardigan and a tweed flat cap. He had the Asiatic features of the indigenous Chukchi people. Yulya stood by his side with a boyish face, short brown hair, and a broad smile. She had flown in from Irkutsk, a Siberian city 5,000 kilometres distant. A Russian friend whom I'd met during a previous expedition in Siberia had recommended her services. Yulya was in her young twenties, and had been immediately enthusiastic about joining our team. I had communicated with her only by email, because she had spoken almost no English and required a friend to translate. For the past two months, she had been studying intensively and now knew the basics. Slava spoke no English at all.

On paper, and as far as the authorities were concerned, Slava would accompany our human-powered expedition. In reality, he would help with the logistics, but only Tim, Yulya, and I would actually do the travelling.

Yulya's limited English was balanced by her can-do attitude, and she seemed a robust girl, with the broad frame and stout build of a babushka-to-be. I felt she would possess the necessary fortitude for the difficult journey ahead. Yulya admitted to "hating school," and yet she had a keen interest in the natural world. Her love of animals had inspired her to become a vegetarian, and the only thing more important than her four-legged friends was God. Yulya was a devoutly practising Christian.

After we all got acquainted, Slava organized a truck to ferry our equipment to a vacant apartment, which we would transform into an ad-hoc expedition headquarters. Here we would prepare for the next leg of our expedition—an 850-kilometre trek to Anadyr, the capital of Chukotka.

Our plan had been to row our boat along the coastline to Anadyr. However, the approaching winter storms made an overland trek the safer option. It was an enormous distance to travel by foot through roadless wilderness, but I felt it was better than the alternative. The Bering Sea had flexed its muscles too many times. Neither Tim nor I wished to risk those cold and capricious waters again.

We would ship our bicycles, skis, and other gear to Anadyr on a supply ship and keep only the essential equipment and freeze-dried foods we needed for the hike. Since we had never planned on hiking, we hadn't brought backpacks. Unfortunately, there was no outdoor shop in this remote Siberian town, and anything shipped from North America would take two months to arrive. Necessity mothering our inventions, we solved our dilemma by building three durable backpacks using lumber from discarded pallets, Russian strapping, dental floss, and foam from our lifejackets and boat cushions. We would store our equipment in durable dry bags and strap these onto our pack frames with bungee cords. We would store our rowboat in Provideniya and later attempt to have it shipped to Portugal.

The city of Provideniya offered to sponsor our expedition by providing a tank to drop off our freeze-dried provisions at several locations en route. It would otherwise be impossible for us to carry enough food on our backs. The all-terrain vehicle would follow an established route used occasionally to service remote coastal villages. The delivery run would also carry much-needed supplies to one of the distant communities.

Since our new route deviated from our initial plans, Slava needed to negotiate with officials to get our new itinerary authorized. While he tended to the endless bureaucracy, Tim, Yulya, and I worked in our one-bedroom apartment preparing for the upcoming trek.

Within two days of our arrival in Provideniya, Tim and Yulya had become lovers. Yulya had the flush of mad passion and proclaimed that her union with Tim was the work of God. "When I early look photograph Tim on website, I know he will be my husband," she explained one evening over a meal of borscht. "I pray to God, and I know it is supposed to be."

Tim glanced up from his heaping bowl and said, "We've only been together for a few days, Yulya. We need to spend more time together before we can make a big decision like this. We need to see if we're compatible."

"Kom-pat-tee-bull?" Yulya said with a perplexed frown. "But don't you see, Tim, we love each other. We meant for each other."

Tim nodded slowly. Tim was proud of his Casanova ways, and I worried that the relationship might not go in the direction Yulya was hoping. We would be spending months together in close quarters, and I hoped this new ingredient in the stew wouldn't wreak havoc in team dynamics.

Yulya's English was improving quickly, and she worked hard to prove her worth as both an expedition member and now a future wife. She would get up each morning at six and work almost non-stop until midnight. Her chores tended to be domestic—cooking, cleaning, and doing laundry—so I decided to talk to her about this division of labour.

"Yulya, you don't need to do all the cooking and cleaning just because you are a woman. We can all take turns cooking, doing dishes, et cetera. And that way you would have more time to do things like building backpacks or packing gear. I know where you come from men and women do different jobs, but where Tim and I are from, we are all the same and can choose to do what we like best."

Yulya looked alarmed. "Oh, no. I am very happy doing this," she insisted. "A woman need show her man what she can do."

I shrugged and continued with my own chores.

Finally, two weeks after entering Siberia, we received the official green light to travel. Our satellite telephone was released from its bureaucratic limbo, but not the GPS. Russian authorities had decided, according to Slava, that our GPS was too much of a threat to national security.

Even without our electronic navigational aid, we were ready to hike through one of the most remote and unforgiving lands on the planet. I shivered as cold winds whipped down from the mountains and through Provideniya. It was now early fall. Soon the temperatures would plummet. It was time to take the first steps on our 19,000-kilometre human-powered traverse of Eurasia.

Slava would travel in the municipal tank, along with a driver and helper, to drop off our supplies. He promised to meet us in two days. They would then travel ahead and make drops at two tiny outposts on the coast, each about ten days apart by foot. Together, we pored over our proposed route on a soiled Russian military topographical map, lent to us by a local reporter, so they wouldn't miss us. For the first stretch, we carried enough food to last five days in case Slava and crew ran into problems and were delayed.

On September 21, Tim, Yulya, and I shouldered our 30- to 40-kilogram improvised backpacks and headed into the unknown. It had been impossible to get detailed information about the area we would be travelling through because, quite simply, no Westerners had ever hiked this route. Locals may have, but their accounts have never been published. Instead we studied the map and tried to transform the squiggles and dots into mountains, rivers, and swamps. How steep would the passes be? Would we be able to ford the semi-frozen rivers? Did we have enough food? Many questions remained unanswered as we plodded slowly away from Provideniya.

It felt somewhat surreal slowly marching away from a decaying Siberian port into a vast wilderness. As Provideniya disappeared behind us and we hiked over a low pass, an icy wind raked the land, accompanied by a few snowflakes. We marched in silence through the lonely landscape, and a feeling of agoraphobia gripped me as I looked across a land empty of trees, buildings, or anything else that could interfere with the smooth rolling contours of the land.

I thought of the millions that had perished from cold and hunger in this harsh land, and wondered if we would make it through unscathed. It seemed the roar of the wind in my ears was the voice of Siberia whispering secrets of cold, agony, and death. If we were sensible we would heed her warnings and return to the comforts of civilization, but instead we were driven by our foolhardy ambitions, and we continued into the unknown.

What made this leg even more disconcerting was the fact that we were not self-sufficient. We didn't have enough food to make it to the next coastal community, and our well-being relied on our having a successful rendezvous with Slava and the tank. What if we missed each other or the antiquated machine broke down? I tried to ignore these fears, and focused instead on making good speed and progress while things were still going smoothly.

The first 300 kilometres would connect the heads of sinuous fjords. These narrow inlets were similar to the one we had arrived in, and their black waters were flanked by the charcoal grey slopes of treeless mountains. We followed the meandering routes of valleys that offered the path of least resistance. The ground we tramped over alternated between boggy tundra, gravel moraine, and loose, dry snow. With no trees, animals were easy to spot. Barely an hour would pass without one of us seeing a fox, Arctic hare, grizzly, or other tundra dweller. At night, the haunting chorus of wolves permeated our tents' thin walls, along with the chill of approaching winter.

Two days came and went, and there was no sign of Slava. By day three we all began to worry, and tension was high. We could stretch our existing food for another two days, but what if Slava still hadn't arrived with more food? We had already begun rationing and were feeling hungry, and the prospect of running out of food entirely was terrifying. I cursed myself for not insisting that we carry enough food to have lasted ten days, enough to make it to the first village. Slava had been certain, however, that they would not have any problems, and it would be foolish to load ourselves unnecessarily. Now I felt foolish as we kept hiking through an endless wilderness on the last of our food supplies.

We had to make a decision. Would we turn back towards Provideniya before it was too late, or continue on? Together we decided to continue plodding forward through the muskeg and moraine. If Slava didn't show up, we would eat the bilberries and lingonberries growing wild and struggle on to the next village.

Days three, four, and five passed, and we continued deeper into the wilderness. Still our relief crew hadn't arrived. Had we somehow missed each other? Perhaps in this maze of valleys we had taken a wrong turn. Our food was now completely gone, and with growling stomachs we took periodic breaks to pick the tart berries that peppered the tundra around us on ground-hugging bushes. We were still four days from our destination, a tiny coastal village. With no food in our backpacks now, I wondered if we would make it. The landscape around us seemed bleaker than ever. Our bright outfits were incongruous with our surroundings, and I couldn't shake the eerie feeling that the land was getting ready to absorb us. It seemed as though we stood too tall and bright in a land that favoured low profiles and shades of brown.

"I think I see building," Yulya said.

It was near the end of day five, after a long day trekking and berry picking. I squinted in the direction Yulya was pointing and made out an irregularity that was either a large boulder or a cabin. As we neared the object, we were relieved to see it actually was a small cabin, and we prayed someone would be home.

When we finally reached the tiny clapboard structure, it was apparent that it was abandoned. No smoke came out of the stovepipe, and the door was swinging open and closed in the chill wind. A broken sled, made from driftwood and bone, lay sun bleached and half submerged in the earth outside.

The entire structure was about the size of an average North American bedroom, and we slipped through the clattering door, eyes adjusting to the gloom. The glass in the lone window had been shattered, and someone had replaced it with a thick sheet of cardboard. The only light entering the building came from the open door.

Two deep wooden shelves, presumably used as beds, were set against the far wall. A woodstove, made from an oil drum with a door cut into it, was set near the cabin entrance. Near the stove was a primitive table constructed from slats of wood and two stools. Two large burlap sacks lay on the dirty floor.

Yulya and I watched intently as Tim opened them. We were all hoping for food.

The first sack contained coal—fuel for the stove in a land where wood is almost non-existent. Tim opened the second bag slowly. It contained dry bread.

"All right! We'll be living like kings," he said gleefully. "We'll get this stove going and have a feast tonight."

In the remaining evening light we picked berries, filling our cooking pots to the brim. Although we were miles from anywhere, the small cabin offered a reprieve from the fear that had been haunting us for the past few days.

We built a roaring fire in the woodstove, warming the cabin as the temperatures slipped below zero outside, and had a hearty dinner of bread stewed in water with berries. The bread seemed to be years old, and was impregnated with coal dust, giving it a horrible flavour. Nonetheless, the sour stew filled our stomachs, and we stretched out comfortably on our bunks. Enough bread remained to fuel us to the upcoming village. I fell asleep, cozy and content, and for the first time in days didn't have dreams of starvation and death.

On the seventh day of our hike, at three in the morning, our tents were lit up by the headlights of a machine that sounded like a UFO descending on our campsite. The tank had finally made it. Inside were three drunken occupants. Slava staggered out first and explained that they had been delayed because they'd found some excellent hunting and fishing en route. The men proudly displayed cords of fish and several Arctic hares they had shot. The men camped the night, left us with enough food to sustain us until the next supply point and roared away down the valley.

We continued on our trek. Eventually, the jagged folds of the mountains gave way to an easier-to-traverse coastal plain, a vast Arctic desert of gravel devoid of any flora apart from small patches of lichen. Here, most of the visible animals fed from the beaches we were marching beside. Thousands of walruses cavorted and fished, while grey whales would swim within metres of the shore searching for food.

Two days after bidding goodbye to Slava we reached a small dilapidated fishing village of about 100 souls nestled in a small bay. The village administration handed us our freeze-dried foods and we continued westwards.

Not all our wildlife encounters were benign. After three weeks of hiking, the Chukotka peninsula had broadened to the point that the larger watersheds formed substantial rivers. We found it increasingly difficult to ford these swift waters. Usually we would strip off our pants, remove our socks from our rubber boots and then crunch through the thin ice at the edges as we teetered with our heavy backpacks to the other side of the river—all while the air temperatures hovered around minus 15 Celsius.

We came across one flow so large that wading was not an option—at least not from the bank we were standing on. I set off alone upstream to seek shallower waters. Suddenly, a wolf dashed out of a ravine just ahead and startled me. I continued forward and watched the shy canine as it paused at a safe distance to scrutinize me. I entered the small ravine and skidded to a halt. I was 30 metres from a grizzly bear standing over a kill. This was a textbook way to becoming another mauling statistic.

The bear was already agitated. It had just fended off an irritating wolf. Now a new intruder was keeping it from its dinner. Instead of bolting as all seven grizzly bears we'd sighted had done, this huge brute dashed up the hillside towards me while swiping the air with a paw. He paused on a rise 15 metres from where I stood rigid with fear, and sniffed the air. Thankfully, I was downwind. I slowly stepped backwards until

I disappeared from the bear's line of sight. Then I made haste back down the river.

We never saw Slava and his merry band again, as they returned home via a different route, but we were relieved to find they'd dropped off the remaining food caches as planned. However, we were disheartened, if not exactly surprised, to learn that Slava and the boys had arrived in one village so liquored up that they'd flattened a fishing boat and driven through the side of a concrete home by accident. Luckily, nobody was hurt, and the villagers dismissed the incident with good nature.

TEMPERATURES DROPPED, and crossing the half-frozen rivers became increasingly treacherous. On some, we could walk across on the newly formed ice, which would creak and bend under our weight. If we broke through, though, we risked getting swept underwater and caught beneath a ceiling of ice. We had to wade across other rivers up to our waists, breaking the ice with our hands as we inched forward.

One river was too deep to wade across, so we searched for the thickest ice. Ice chunks had collected in one area of slower-moving water, creating a semicircle of thicker ice across the river, like a floating beaver dam. Tim and Yulya crossed the ice jam on hands and knees to distribute their weight.

I went last. Halfway across, my hands plunged through the ice into the water. The ice between my hands remained intact, and my chest was pressed against the surface. I shifted my weight to my knees and tried to lift my hands out of the water, and suddenly they broke through the ice, too. I was pinned by the immense weight of my backpack, with all four limbs dangling in the fast-flowing water.

If the remaining ice cracked, I'd be plunged into the ice-filled river. The current would suck me under the ice, and it was unlikely I would be able to break through to escape. I momentarily froze, panicked that any movements would cause the ice beneath my torso to give way. My limbs were numb as agonizingly cold water swirled around them, hinting at what a full submersion would be like. Tim and Yulya stood helplessly on the far shore watching in dismay.

Miraculously, the floe remained intact under my torso, and I rolled over to free myself. Gingerly, I crawled back to where I started, and onto the safety of shore. I walked several hundred metres along the river, until I encountered shallower fast-moving water that wasn't frozen. Here I waded across, the water reaching mid-thigh, and arrived victoriously on the far shore.

By mid-October, about five weeks after departing on our hike, winter snows began to blanket the land. They were accompanied by shrieking winds. Both left us perpetually exhausted. Sheets of ice formed across my beard and Tim's. We longed for our extreme-winter clothing, which we had shipped ahead to Anadyr. We reached a high range of mountains that blocked our path, and we had to ascend the highest pass we'd yet encountered. Blowing snow collected deeply in the col. A hard crust had formed over the snow's surface, which made trekking across it easier. Occasionally, though, the crust was weak, and we would sink up to our chests in the fluffy snow.

During this gruelling hike, my energy levels had severely diminished and I hadn't been sleeping well. I attributed my poor health to exhaustion, so I was relieved when we were finally nearing Egvekinot, a relatively large port town. As we stumbled to the summit of the pass, a collection of concrete apartment blocks, port cranes, and belching coal smoke rose into view. In my weakened state, it looked like heaven. It had taken us more than six weeks of steady hiking to reach this town.

We had covered 650 kilometres by foot, and Anadyr lay another 200 kilometres distant. It was now November, and we were already about a month behind schedule. The temperatures were plummeting to minus 35 Celsius at night and only warming up to a balmy minus 25 by mid-afternoon. We found it hard to believe, but the weather would only get colder. We simply had to fetch our warmer clothing, skis, and other winter gear if we were to continue. We would have to find a faster way to Anadyr, bring back the necessary supplies, and then close the gap by foot again.

Yulya and Tim bounded down the slopes towards the comfort and warmth of civilization. I followed at a much slower pace. I felt absolutely terrible, beyond mere exhaustion now.

When we arrived in the town, an official informed us that the last icebreaker of the year was departing for Anadyr that evening. The captain of the ship granted us free passage and cast his lines as soon as we had stepped aboard. As the great Soviet-built ship carved through sheets of ice, my health continued to degrade. I had a mild fever, zero energy, and a strange feeling twisting my lower abdomen. The captain had given us an apartment-like cabin. While Yulya and Tim rested in the bedroom, I slouched on the couch, my mind foggy and my body spent. What was happening to me?

6

FLAT ON MY BACK IN ANADYR

W E ARRIVED IN ANADYR THE NEXT EVENING and shuttled by Lada taxi to a Russian-style hotel—a collection of flats in an old Soviet apartment block. I began to wonder whether my affliction was related to my slow flow of urine. I have a congenital condition called a urethral stricture that made peeing a slow process. Recently, the flow had seemed even slower than usual. With my condition, I knew it was possible to get a bladder infection.

The proprietor of the hotel led us up a pitch-dark concrete staircase to the sixth floor. He opened a door and directed us into an apartment that had a total of about six beds scattered throughout. We would be the only occupants.

Yulya and Tim chose to sleep in the adjacent room, which left me alone in the large bedroom. Five single beds lined the room's perimeter, and I collapsed onto the one nearest the door and fell into a fitful sleep. I awoke an hour later, chilled to the bone and needing to urinate. The flow was still painfully slow, but now it also burned. My teeth chattered as I emptied a small portion of my bladder drop by searing drop. It felt like passing lava through a syringe.

Back in bed, I curled up in a fetal position and tried to warm up, to no avail. I added quilts from the neighbouring beds, wrapped a fleece jacket around my head, and at last, as my bladder started to feel full again, I drifted off to sleep.

Half an hour later, I woke up. It felt like someone had dumped a bucket of warm water over me. I had drenched the bed with sweat, my mind was confused, and lights strobed behind my eyes.

In the morning, I had a long bath and hoped the water would cleanse me of my obscure ailment. The lack of clear symptoms left me a little uneasy. I had no cold, flu, or stomach problems. What was causing my extreme fever and lethargy?

I decided I had better go to the hospital. Yulya led me down the icy streets to a modern four-storey building. A nurse handed us plastic bags at the door to put over our shoes, and we flip-flopped down the hall. Another nurse directed me into a clinical room and placed a thermometer in my armpit.

"These thermometers are new," Yulya said, translating for the nurse. "Before they didn't use armpit."

If I'd been feeling better, I might have chuckled at the thought of a meaty-armed nurse lubing up a communist-built thermometer while her patient trembled in fear. Instead I quietly waited for the instrument to register my temperature. The nurse looked at the gauge and tut-tutted.

"You have a very high temperature," Yulya informed me. "The nurse ask why."

I didn't know why. I told her that I peed very slowly and maybe the two were connected. The nurse looked confused and summoned two of her colleagues, followed by a young female doctor. She said something abruptly in Russian.

"Drop your pants," Yulya translated.

I let my pants fall to the floor while the five women looked on. The doctor pressed both sides of my thighs.

"Does that hurt?" Yulya relayed.

"No," I said.

The doctor clasped my testicles and gave them a gentle squeeze.

"Does that hurt?" said Yulya.

"No."

The doctor then pressed the area just above my penis.

"How's that?"

"Nothing other than my bladder feeling full."

The doctor grabbed my penis, looked at it matter-of-factly, then released it.

"Why can't you pee?" Yulya translated.

I launched into a monologue explaining that I had a congenital condition called a urethral stricture caused by a narrowing of the urethra. The gradually degrading condition necessitates periodic surgery to enlarge the constricted passage. The problem not only creates low flow but also means incomplete drainage of the bladder, which can lead to infection.

Yulya shook her head, still puzzled, along with the rest of my audience. I felt self-conscious as my unclothed penis jiggled with every word. "Can I put my pants back on?"

"No," Yulya said. "We are waiting for the head surgeon. He might know this problem better."

A man of about 50 with thick glasses entered. He carried an air of authority and wore a loose blue uniform that distinguished him from the nurses.

"What is the problem?" he asked. His eyes went straight to my privates.

I began to wonder if maybe I should have practised some pubic preening before coming to the hospital. A bikini wax, perhaps. I never suspected my manhood would be the subject of such scrutiny. The female doctor attempted to explain the situation, but it was clear she didn't have a clue.

I could barely understand a word she said to the surgeon, so my fevered brain filled in the blanks: "He's got a problem with his penis, although we're not sure what. We believe the only option is to cut it off."

The surgeon gestured for me to pull up my pants and follow him down the hall. Yulya and I flip-flopped after him until we reached the operating theatre. "Lie down," he ordered in English, and pointed at a bed illuminated by three overhead lights. "And drop your pants." Two assistants joined him, and suddenly a long flexible scope was fed down my urethra by the surgeon. The surgeon had a spectacled eye glued to the viewing end and he provided colour commentary to his helpers.

While I squirmed uncomfortably, Yulya translated: "He sees blockage. He is trying to push through it."

I could tell. A searing pain radiated from my nether regions. The 5-millimetre scope was too thick to fit through the stricture, but the doctor kept shoving—and I kept squirming and biting my tongue to stifle any screams.

"It looks like it won't fit," Yulya finally said. "Now he will stick hose in you to make you pee."

The catheter also proved to be too big, so after another squirm-inducing session, it was withdrawn. The surgeon frowned. "Very deefeecult. Very small."

One of his assistants found a smaller hose and, after a good shove, the plastic tube slipped through my stricture and into my bladder. Within minutes, my bladder was drained. The doctor taped the hose to the end of my penis and attached the other end to a bag. "Come with me," he said.

I walked awkwardly down the hall and we rode an elevator to the basement. My blood and urine tests had been processed. According to the results, I had a kidney infection. Then a technician ran an ultrasound wand over my kidneys while the doctor stared at the screen and shook his head. "Not one, but two keedneys," he declared. "Very eel. Your keedneys very eel. Meenimum three weeks in hospital."

I felt deflated. We were already behind schedule. Now I was destined to rot in a hospital for nearly a month with wonky kidneys. A nurse led me into a clean but crowded ward. The 10 by 15 room contained six beds, all but one occupied by patients with obvious ailments: an old man with an empty, bloody eye socket; a Chukchi man with a grapefruit-sized goitre on his neck; and a teenager with a freshly stitched incision across his abdomen. I hobbled to the empty bed, glanced at the frozen harbour view through the window, and settled wearily under the blankets. A nurse fixed an IV drip to my arm and then gave me a half-dozen shots of who knows what in my rear end.

Lunch was announced with a cackling call and patients in all shape and form walked, limped, and literally crawled to the end of the corridor where the food was being doled out. I stood in line, pushing my IV drip holder with one hand and holding my urine bag with the other. A babushka doled out a bowl of fish gruel (chunks of bony fish, some type of grain, and a lot of water), two chunks of dry bread, and a cup of tea to each set of hands thrust towards her. Patients were to look after their own bowl, cup, and spoon, which were to be washed in the bathroom sink after we'd finished our meal. My fever sapped my appetite, so I wasn't too concerned about my meagre rations. I slowly downed the food and then fell into a fitful sleep in my new home.

"TEMPERATURE TOO HIGH!"

I awoke and looked at a blue-gowned doctor who was looking pleased to at last find a use for his two semesters of English in med school.

"Thirty-nine degrees," he explained. "We give you drug to bring temperature down. Yes?"

A few minutes later a young nurse, with a glint of evil in her eye, strode to my bedside holding a gargantuan syringe. The other nurses usually had me roll over so they could jab me in the fattier tissue of my buttocks. This nurse simply loomed over me, gave me a look of disdain, and then plunged the needle into my upper thigh. Burning fluid squirted into the muscle.

I awoke again at 2 a.m. with a full bladder. The bag hanging beside my bed was empty. I assumed either the catheter was blocked or the end of the tube had slipped out. I padded down the dark halls to find someone to remedy the situation. I found the night nurse asleep in a cot at the end of the hall.

"Da?" the matronly woman said groggily as I shook her awake.

"Problem," I said and pointed to the empty drainage bag. I tried the charades for "distended bladder."

The nurse followed me back to my room, tied my pee bag to the bed frame and left. I assumed she had gone to find a doctor or get some instruments. Half an hour passed, though, and she hadn't returned. I began to wonder if the nurse mistook my gestures and just thought I was an imbecile who couldn't tie a granny knot.

I untied the bag and walked back down the hall. Sure enough, the stout nurse was fast asleep. This time I looked up the verb "to drain" in my Russian/English dictionary.

"Da?" The nurse looked downright annoyed about her second wake-up call. She glanced at the empty pee bag in my hand as if to say, "I'm not going to tie that thing on for a second time, you moron."

"Nyet drain, nyet drain," I said slowly. Again I made distended gestures towards my bladder, which now felt like an overfilled water balloon. Again we marched back to my bed and again the nurse tied my bag to the bed frame. This time she returned with a big syringe in hand.

"What's that for?" I cried in alarm, but my words fell on uncomprehending ears.

The nurse had flicked the lights on. All the other patients looked on in amusement. I wanted to scream that the blockage of the catheter was something physical and no drug would solve the problem. "Nyet, nyet," was all I could muster.

"Da, da," the nurse replied. A meaty arm delivered a mystery drug into my ass.

The nurse turned off the lights and departed while I lay sweating. What was in that needle? A sedative? A muscle relaxant? A top-secret Russian drug designed to keep patients from pestering nurses?

Several minutes passed and I felt no discernible effects from the drug. My bladder was nearing the bursting point, and I was becoming desperate. I went into the bathroom and sat on the toilet. I then disconnected the catheter hose from the bag and sucked on the tube to clear any blockages. Nothing. If it wasn't blocked, then the end of the tube must have slipped out of my bladder sphincter. I pushed the hose upwards until I felt pressure, and then pushed a little harder. I felt discomfort deep within me when finally something gave and warm yellow fluid gushed from the catheter. Within minutes, my bladder was empty and I felt a whole lot better. I'd survived, just barely, my first day in a Siberian hospital.

AT 6:30 A.M., ANOTHER FLICK OF THE LIGHTS awoke all the patients. The same night nurse sauntered in and looked at the full bag of piss hanging off my bed. "Mmm, hmmm," she muttered in a pleased tone. She seemed certain that her special injection had performed its magic.

"Nyet, nyet!" I shouted. There was no way I'd let her take credit for my painful handiwork.

She looked at me the way an adult regards a simple child having a tantrum.

Now I had a second problem. Normally catheters are anchored in the bladder by a small balloon, which is inflated at the end of the hose after it's inserted. Unfortunately, due to the limited passage through my stricture, the doctor had been unable to insert a full-sized catheter, along with its accompanying hardware. Instead a miniature tube had been inserted, which was simply held in place by a mass of tape at the end of my penis.

The tape had lost its adhesiveness, and the tube now slid in and out with my every movement. This was the very reason for my problem the night before. As I joined the rest of the patients for the trek to the food trough, I had to have one hand down my pants holding the tube in place while my other reached out to receive a dollop of semolina.

After breakfast, the young nurse with evil in her eyes entered the ward to give me four injections in the upper thigh. I had looked up the word for adhesive tape in my dictionary.

"Can I have some tape please?" I said.

She looked puzzled and perturbed at the same time and began walking out the door, obviously with no intention of bringing any tape. I threw back my covers and pointed at my penis and the mangled mess of tape that no longer served its purpose. I grabbed the tube and slid it two inches in and two inches out to demonstrate we had a problem. All eyes in the room were on my groin.

"The doctor will be here this afternoon. He can help."

I wanted to leap out of bed and put this evil nurse in a stranglehold. "All I need is some fucking tape! I can tape it on myself. Why do we have to wait six hours for a god-damned doctor, you stupid nurse!"

It's probably a good thing she didn't understand me, otherwise I may have received an injection a little less benign than my previous midnight cocktail. The nurse left the room, and I stood there, hand on cock, scared to make any sudden move lest my catheter be yanked out.

An hour later a more kindly looking nurse entered the room to give me my daily IV antibiotic. She inserted a cannula in a bulging vein on my arm, taped it in place and then started the flow. The moment she left, I pulled the long adhesive strips off the cannula and used them to affix the catheter to my schlong. Hallelujah!

Half an hour later the cannula, having no tape, popped out of my arm, and blood and IV liquids began dribbling onto the sheets. A passing nurse reinserted the cannula and taped it back up. My problems were solved.

Later in the afternoon, the head surgeon checked on me. "Normalne?" he asked.

I wanted to tell him what a nightmare the past 24 hours had been—that at three in the morning I'd been sucking on my catheter to prevent my bladder from rupturing and that his nurses had been giving me mystery injections in the wee hours. Instead, after a quick review of my 60-word Russian vocabulary, I replied, "Normalne."

"Haracho," he said. "Come with me. We X-ray your stricture."

I again felt worried. I'd always been under the impression that X-rays to the testicles are a surefire way of lopping a branch off the family tree. I pointed at my testicles and asked, "Problem?"

The doctor must have noted my look of alarm. He put a reassuring hand on my shoulder and said, "Nyet problem—lead."

I felt somewhat reassured. A good thick sheet of lead ought to prevent me from siring three-headed kids. A technician ushered me onto a flat bed and placed the exposure plate under my buttocks. The doctor then squirted a fluid from a syringe-like plunger into my urethra, inflating my penis like a water balloon. The fluid would appear in the X-ray and outline my otherwise invisible urethra. The technician placed a sheet over my testicles. Click. A few minutes later the doctor arrived with the exposed film.

"Here is the stricture," he said with satisfaction. He pointed to a spot where the urethra tapered into nothingness.

It took me a moment to absorb what he was saying. My eyes had been drawn instead to the image of my testicles, clear as day on the image. Again, images of slobbering two-headed children filled my head.

The doctor frowned as he studied the X-ray. "Stent?" he asked. "You have stent?"

I had learned about urethral stents while googling my medical condition. A stent is a mesh-like tube inserted permanently into the urethra to keep recurring strictures from closing. In theory, they sound great. In practice, they're prone to infections, discomfort, and greater complications. I was certain I didn't have a stent. Although my stricture had been operated on five years earlier in Canada, I couldn't fathom the doctors putting a stent in my urethra without letting me know. Besides, it's the kind of thing a guy would notice.

"Nyet," I replied.

The doctor tapped on the X-ray image, pointing to a coil-like tube in my urethra. It certainly appeared to be an unidentified foreign object. "It is a stent," he insisted.

I was flabbergasted. I couldn't believe the Canadian doctors had inserted this mechanical device without my knowledge or consent. Everything I had read about stents had indicated they wouldn't work well with my problem. Now the stent would create further complications with the upcoming surgery I would need. The technician scrutinized the image, too. She glanced at my fleece pants and back at the image. Her eyes suddenly lit up. She then grabbed for my pants—and squeezed the toggle for the drawstring to verify, as she'd suspected, that a spring was hidden inside. Eureka!

I was relieved that I didn't have a stent. I wasn't relieved that I would be having an operation in this hospital, with the language barrier and erratic treatment, especially with such a delicate part of my body at stake.

The days slipped by in a haze. I had no books to read, no TV to watch, and no one to talk to, apart from Tim and Yulya on their periodic visits. My health improved with a barrage of unknown drugs. Each day I received 11 injections, four pills, and a four-hour IV drip. Communication was virtually non-existent and, despite my constant efforts, I never learned what kinds of drugs they were giving me. After 11 days, my needle-pocked ass felt as if it had been attacked by a swarm of killer bees. But my fever and lethargy had vanished.

Yulya relayed the doctors' prognosis: "They are pleased with your quick recovery and say that the operation can begin soon. The problem, though, is they have decided they do not want to do it themselves. They have never dealt with such problem before and feel it is too risky. You will have to go to either Moscow or Vancouver where they have specialists for such problem."

I was secretly relieved. I had been dreading the prospect of going under the knife in Anadyr, even though, for the sake of the expedition, it would be the most cost-efficient and speedy option. Now the doctors had made the choice for me. I would fly home to Canada for the operation. Ironically, the cheapest and easiest way to get home would be to fly four fifths of the way around the planet, via Moscow.

THE AGING SOVIET-BUILT TUPOLEV TU-154 AIRCRAFT gradually gained altitude above an endless expanse of snow. Twilight was setting in quickly, and I had only a few minutes to regard the land below before it disappeared into another long Siberian night. The mountains rolled gently, with no shadowed cliffs to offer respite from the velvety whiteness smothering the land. Even the vegetation, evolved in a world that doesn't take kindly to all things sprawling, was concealed beneath half a metre of snow, protected from the perpetually shrieking winds and minus-40 temperatures above.

The cruelness of the world below was so extreme that I almost felt uncomfortable flying above it in an overheated jetliner. It would take nine hours to fly non-stop from the northeast corner of Siberia to Moscow. Within 30 minutes of leaving Anadyr Airport we were passing near the coldest spot on the planet outside of Antarctica, a village called Oimyakon. Here the mean temperature in January is minus 50 Celsius, 32 degrees colder than Winnipeg, a Canadian city considered by many to have an extremely cold environment.

Almost more disconcerting than the cold was the isolation. I scrutinized the land below for hours from my vantage in the thundering aircraft and didn't see so much as a twinkle indicating the existence of human habitation. Siberia is larger than all of Canada, and its area is fifty times greater than that of Britain.

Were we fools thinking we could cross this 14,000-kilometre expanse using nothing other than our muscles for propulsion? Northeastern Siberia didn't even have roads, and we would have to traverse a distance four times greater than that of a trek to the North Pole, just to reach the first rutted roads. From there it would be another 10,000 kilometres of cycling on dirt and asphalt roads through ice, slush, mud, and dust before reaching the nation's capital.

But these problems were reserved for a later date. My immediate concerns were making sure the pending surgery went according to plan and that my health was renewed to a state where I could continue the expedition.

My unexpected trip back to Canada was a whirlwind of activity. After 19 hours of flying by helicopter and two jet planes, and seven days of waiting in airports, I was back in Vancouver in Julie's arms. The kind folks at Wallace and Carey (one of our sponsors) provided a comfortable apartment for us, since Julie's shared accommodation had no room for an additional person.

The operation on my stricture was done shortly after my arrival, and all went smoothly. It would take almost two months for me to fully recover, and I would spend this period in Canada.

Julie had found our separation extremely difficult, and an emotional strain with the perpetual worrying. She had decided that, rather than sitting at home and stressing, she would embark on her own adventure. Julie had been helping Tim and me immensely with home-based logistics and research, and recently she had been spending much time looking into the logistics of our proposed Atlantic row. She was convinced that this was something that she too could do, and so she planned to attempt her own rowing voyage across the Atlantic Ocean in the same season that Tim and I would be conducting our crossing.

Julie's expedition was a shorter distance—from the Canary Islands to the Caribbean—but she would still need to find a partner to do the trip with her. While I was in Vancouver, Julie was beginning her preparations—building a website and developing a sponsorship proposal. Although it seemed a large undertaking, I had no doubts that Julie was taking this project seriously, and it wasn't just a passing whim. She possessed steadfast determination, and could break any task into a logical succession of easy-to-follow steps. At the same time, I began to get a taste of what she had been going through. Although she was a capable, intelligent woman, I couldn't help but worry about the dangers she would be facing.

Meanwhile, I took advantage of my time back home to try replenishing our own dwindling expedition funds. We had exhausted our meagre finances, and I had been using the last of my own money to keep the expedition running. If no more sources of cash were found, the expedition would soon come to an abrupt halt. Three thousand kilometres of remote wilderness lay ahead of us before we reached the first roads of Siberia. And we'd be travelling in temperatures much colder than those experienced in a trek to the North Pole—minus 40 to 50 on average, with frequent gale-force winds and complete whiteout conditions. Weeks would pass between communities, and there was no guarantee we could obtain food at some of the more remote outposts.

None of our team had any experience trekking in cold temperatures, and our recent slog was an eye opener. Living perpetually in the cold is nothing like stepping out of a warm home or car for a few hours, comfortably insulated in thick clothing, and then returning home. Instead, your clothes become damp as condensation builds over the weeks and there is no way to dry off. Small chores such as tinkering with a broken stove or fixing a bike become almost impossible while wearing necessary but restrictive mitts. Our recent trek from Provideniya seemed to have stretched for an eternity, and yet it was less than one quarter of the roadless distance ahead of us.

I was nervous about what we were getting into. Crossing Antarctica from one side to the other via the South Pole is considered at the limits of human endurance, and yet we planned on trekking the same distance, in similar weather conditions, and through even more rugged terrain. Such an endeavour usually involves years of planning, yet for us it was just one small part of our overall adventure, and we could not devote unlimited resources, time, and energy to get across.

After considering the logistical hurdles of doing the journey self-supported, we finally decided that the realistic way to get through eastern Siberia was to use a support all-terrain vehicle. A large six-wheel-drive truck or tank would be able to cross the frozen land and carry our supplies. We would be able to move unencumbered, and be able to switch easily from our bicycles to skis depending on the conditions. We would also be able to make it across the tundra, lakes, and rivers before spring melt, when the land would become an impenetrable quagmire.

Tim and Yulya had been looking into the cost of such support, and it would be close to $10,000—money we simply didn't have. However, Bema Gold, a Canadian mining company that was setting up operations in the Russian state of Chukotka, received my sponsorship proposal with enthusiasm. Two days before my return to Russia, Bema Gold offered to cover the costs of our support.

Meanwhile, back in Russia, Tim and Yulya were in a stalemate with the authorities about receiving new travel permits for our revised route. Locals had informed us that a better winter route lay along the course of the Kolyma River, north of Anadyr. In late winter, when the river is frozen, its surface is ploughed, and transport vehicles use it as a highway to reach remote villages. This frozen river would also allow us to make excellent progress on our bicycles with their studded tires.

When I returned to Siberia in mid-January, two months after I had left, Tim and Yulya had still not been able to get permission for us to travel. We decided to contact the Canadian embassy in Russia, and the Canadian ambassador, Christopher Westdall, sent a strongly worded letter on our behalf to the local authorities, urging them to allow our expedition to proceed.

The day after this letter was received, our permissions were granted.

A senior in the Department of Transportation had offered to provide a government vehicle, a Russian Ural six-wheel-drive truck, to be our support, in exchange for a large sum of cash to be paid outside of the office. This vehicle was driving south over the frozen tundra from the northern town of Pevek to deliver supplies, and it could carry our gear on its return journey. We were pleased that our mode of support would only minimally increase CO_2 emissions, since the truck would be running this route anyway. The support vehicle would meet us 88 kilometres north of Egvekinot, the town where we had finished our trek. From Egvekinot, a municipal truck would carry our gear to the rendezvous point.

As it turned out, my journey back to Canada barely delayed the expedition. The lakes and rivers aren't solid enough for ATVs to cross until late January or early February. If we had started earlier, we would have had to do so without support. But, even if we had proceeded without assistance, we would still have had the same delays in receiving permission.

The sea was now frozen and no more ships were servicing the coastal communities. To get back to Egvekinot from Anadyr where our trek would resume, we hired a tank that was capable of travelling over the deep snow and carrying our mounds of equipment and food.

Finally, almost three months after we had completed our trek to Egvekinot, we were once again ready to resume our expedition.

7

LOST IN CHUKOTKA

B Y NOON ON FEBRUARY 7, we had loaded our gear into the Ural truck and were ready to leave on our bikes. Two and a half months had passed since we had last been here, after the hiking leg from Providenya. Now, as I stood at the same spot, it seemed as though no time had passed. The icebreaker, the hospital, Vancouver, and all the bureaucracy seemed to be a dream. We were once again entering our reality: ice, rock, and snow. The wind shrieked down from the mountains and fired needles of snow into our faces.

According to the latest meteorological report, the temperature was minus 35 Celsius, with average wind speeds of 65 kilometres per hour. Ten kilometres inland, the thermometer would drop to minus 45, and the wind chill would make it feel like minus 100. Over the next couple of days, an approaching blizzard was expected to intensify these already intense conditions.

We looked each other over for patches of bare flesh. Any exposed skin would quickly resemble five-year-old freezer-burned steak. The dangers of sweating made it surprisingly difficult to dress for extended cardiovascular activities in extreme cold. Our clothing had to be as breathable as possible and always keep our core temperature on the cool side to prevent perspiration. On this day, I wore long underwear made from a merino wool–polypropylene blend that would wick moisture away from my skin. Over this I had on fleece pants and a fleece jacket. The third and outer layer was a set of Interface pants and jacket. These tightly woven garments would block most of the wind yet are many times more breathable than Gore-Tex-type fabrics. In the extreme cold it is not advisable to use water-resistant clothing because of limited breathability. Since all liquid is frozen, external moisture is not a concern.

Our feet were protected by Baffin boots, Canadian-made and rated to minus 100 degrees. The boots have two components: a leather and rubber outer shell, and inch-thick boot liners made from layers of hi-tech materials—aluminum reflective lining, foam insulation, and other synthetic insulating and wicking layers, along with good old-fashioned wool. Within our boots, we wore vapour-barrier socks—essentially plastic bags over the feet—to keep moisture from our skin from building up inside the boot liners. Inside the vapour barrier, we wore thick wool socks, and beneath them, a pair of thin polypropylene socks. With five layers between our tootsies and the snow, our feet should always stay warm over the coming months, even when the wind chill dropped below minus 100.

We kept our heads warm with a thin polypropylene balaclava followed by a second, thicker one made from windproof fleece. Ski goggles covered the vulnerable skin around our eyes. Keeping our hands warm and dexterous would be vital. In an emergency, functioning fingers could make the difference between life or death. We'd keep our hands happy with polypropylene inner gloves, thick, puffy Prima-loft (low-density synthetic insulation) mitts, followed by outer shells, used more to protect the inner mitts than for insulation.

We had done our homework about cold-weather clothing. Now it was time for our final exam.

A SCATTERING OF BRICK HOUSES STOOD BEHIND US, the last vestige of civilization we would see for some time. Ahead, a track of compressed snow led down a wide valley before it disappeared into a veil of blowing snow. The absence of houses, trees, or any other objects to give the land perspective enlarged the feeling of emptiness. We mounted our bikes, settled on our reindeer-skin-covered seats and began pedalling into the heart of Siberia. Finally, our expedition was back on track.

We were heading into the worst weather on the planet. Temperatures in this part of Siberia are colder than in any other country, and the winds are more violent and sustained than in any other polar region. Our path of travel would take us directly into the icy northern blasts, which peaked at a progress-stalling 80 kilometres per hour. We'd drop gears until all of us were pedalling in lowest speed, legs spinning wildly while the bikes inched forward at 3 kilometres an hour. When the wind gusted or swirled unexpectedly from the side, all three of us would fall over simultaneously.

Despite our windproof fabrics, knives of cold air cut through the tiny gaps in our zippers, up the base of our jackets, or slipped into our sleeves and stabbed at our flesh. Our goggles steamed up, froze, and rendered an already white and shapeless world into a new dimension, one in which up and down and around all looked the same—white. A world where perspective was given not by space and time but by cold. I pedalled hard, trying to raise my core temperature, trying to make those icy leaks in our winter armour more bearable. The thundering roar of the wind filled my ears and conspired with the icy knives to fill my brain with nothing but the sensation of cold. Roaring cold.

Behind us rumbled our security blanket: the Ural truck. Designed to cope with all but the worst conditions, Urals are the mechanical workhorses of Siberia. They roll on six knobby wheels attached to the drive train, allowing them to drive over the frozen tundra where no roads exist. The windows are double glazed to keep out the cold, and the engines are big, reliable diesels. Even the fuel has been modified with chemical additives to prevent jelling in the cold. Our Ural had been fitted with a bucket in the back so it could be used as the town dump truck.

Generally, Urals travel along the winter roads in convoys for safety. Stories abound detailing lone trucks that broke down in remote locations. Invariably, the driver and his helper would perish within hours. In this environment, simple mistakes or malfunctions could quickly amplify into tragedies. The engine of a Ural is well and truly its heart, sustaining not only the vehicle but also its occupants. Once a wilderness journey has begun, the engine is never turned off, because the cold will silence it forever, given the chance. Even at night, as the drivers sleep, the engines will idle reassuringly.

Our driver was a mustachioed man in his late thirties who worked for the council of Egvekinot. He didn't say much, but seemed content to be given the tedious job of following three painfully slow cyclists for two days. He expressed concern over the degrading weather, but felt the Ural would be up to it. He had some doubt, however, when he eyed our bicycles. Our two-wheeled transportation looked as out of place in this desolate land as beach balls on the moon.

We gained elevation as our bikes crawled towards a pass 18 kilometres inland. The track surface at least was good: ice formed from compressed snow that our studded tires bit eagerly into. Occasionally, drifting snow would block the path and we would have to push our bikes through the dry fluff.

At two in the afternoon Yulya made a monumental decision and traded the agony of cycling for a comfortable seat in the truck. She had travelled more than 600 kilometres by human power. Now, when faced with the true wrath of Siberian winter, she decided that the conditions were just too unbearable.

Tim and I continued alone. Yulya's absence from our side made the world seem an emptier place. We had been a team of three for so long and now, even though she was a few hundred metres back behind a double pane of glass, it was as though she had been removed entirely from our little world.

Parts of my face were going numb, and I wondered if frostbite were setting in. My whole lower belly had lost sensation where the wind had been gushing up the bottom of my jacket. Still, my core temperature remained warm, and the passing hours seemed to dull the agony of being alive in Siberia.

At 6 p.m., bathed in the headlights of the truck, we arrived at a stone building capacious enough to house two tractor-like vehicles used to maintain the winter tracks. The three men who operated these machines stayed here through the winter, in living quarters tucked into one end of the cavernous building. They welcomed us with typical Russian hospitality. Soon we were all sitting around a roughly hewn wooden table and sipping cups of tea. The walls were adorned with photos of women cut out from magazines and shopping bags.

Both Tim and I discovered frostbite on our bodies. My lower belly was turning purple, as though I'd taken a Mike Tyson body blow; patches on my neck were red and swollen. Tim's chin had a large red lump on it where the wind had squeezed past his balaclava. Still, our frostbite looked mild, and I felt proud to have made it through our first day intact. We'd travelled 19 hard kilometres, and it was time for bed.

THE NEXT DAY, Tim found the soft snow more of a challenge. Every ten minutes or so, I circled back so I didn't get too far ahead. Again I was wearing a thin layer of clothing, to avoid sweating too much, so stopping to wait for Tim was out of the question. I couldn't even slow down without a chill setting in.

Our Ural truck trailed 30 metres behind whoever was in the rear, so I had to keep pace with Tim. I had packed two bicycle panniers with survival essentials, in case we ever got separated or lost in a storm. This gear included a down jacket and pants, a small tarp, an 18-hour candle, a lighter, two bags of trail mix, a headlamp, and the satellite phone. Although the panniers didn't weigh much, the wind tore at them and slowed our progress. We had decided to remove these safety bags because our support vehicle was always close by.

As afternoon approached, visibility improved a bit and my speed picked up. I caught myself daydreaming and realized I'd gotten well ahead of Tim and the Ural. I circled back for more than two kilometres before the cloud of snow parted to reveal my lagging companions. I couldn't help but feel frustrated. Tim would take breaks in the Ural every 20 minutes, while I rode in circles outside. The truck wasn't roomy enough for all four of us, and I didn't want to take a turn in the vehicle while Tim rode, as it would slow our progress even more. By day's end, with all my circling, I would cycle more than twice the actual distance we had travelled.

We quickly lunched, in the lee of the truck, before the cold reached into our very marrow. Sheets of ice had formed around our mouths and our balaclavas had frozen to our beards, which made eating tricky. Once we'd freed our mouths, we shovelled the frozen sandwiches down our throats before frostbite set in. Our driver told us we had only 30 kilometres to go to the next roadhouse, which would be the last shelter for the next 300 kilometres. The weather had cleared slightly, and I considered continuing ahead alone. Tim would be safe with the support vehicle. And if I had any problems, the reliable Ural would catch up with our cache of food, clothes, and tools.

I told Tim and Yulya of my plans. Within minutes, I was alone, pedalling furiously through snow slithering like lost ghouls across the road. The ruts of ice I followed had been blown clean, which made the going relatively easy. I felt good. An hour earlier, we had passed a steel monument that marked our crossing of the Arctic Circle. I was riding a bicycle through the middle of Siberia in the middle of winter. I was just a speck in an incomprehensible vastness and had trouble believing that I shared the planet with six billion other people. I have never felt so alone.

My elation was soon replaced by nagging doubt. The air was intensely cold, and my clothing was only suitable for heavy cardiovascular activity. If my fast-burning metabolism slowed to a resting rate, I would likely die of exposure in a few short hours. What if I had misunderstood and the roadhouse wasn't really just ahead at Kilometre 86? What if the Ural got stuck in the snow and my bike broke down? I imagined various scenarios that all ended badly—for me. Perhaps I'd let my impatience cloud my better judgment.

Markers on the side of the track ticked off the kilometres from Egvekinot. At Kilometre 70, just 16 kilometres from my goal, drifting snow completely obliterated the track. To orient myself, I had to follow metal stakes spaced about 50 metres apart, erected for whiteouts such as this.

The weather continued to worsen, but just when I was ready to turn back and rejoin the others, the ice ruts reappeared and the surface improved enough for riding again. I passed Kilometre 73 at 3:30 p.m. I imagined I could knock off the final 13 kilometres before total darkness set in at five. The dimming daylight and my steamed goggles made it diffi-cult to differentiate between the hard-packed snow and the soft adjacent surface. Every ten minutes, I had to remove the goggles and scrape away the ice crystals with my inner gloves. The frigid air against the exposed flesh around my eyes created an instant ice-cream headache and froze my eyelids shut. I had to delicately prise my own eyes open before I replaced the mask.

Deeper snow slowed my progress. By 4:45, I could no longer make out the tracks I was supposed to follow. At five, I was pushing the bike through nearly pitch black. A kilometre marker loomed in this darkness. I walked over to it, wiped off the snow, and used the light from my watch to illuminate the numbers: Kilometre 86!

This is where the roadhouse should be, where tea and warmth would greet me. Instead it was dark. And bloody cold. The wind battered my fatigued body. Blowing snow worked its way into the cracks in my clothing. Where the hell was the roadhouse? In the blizzardy night, I felt blindfolded. No distant glow in the darkness offered evidence of a cozy abode anywhere.

Suddenly I felt very, *very* scared.

USING THE DENSITY OF THE SNOW AS A GUIDE, I tried to stay on the ruts, but I soon realized I had lost them altogether and was crunching randomly across the frozen tundra. Pushing my bicycle through the deep snow only hindered my progress, so I dropped it. My bike was of no use to me any more. I was getting cold, and as I staggered around, lost in the blizzard, my only desire was to stay alive by whatever means necessary.

I oriented myself with the prevailing wind and made zig-zagging sweeps to find the track again. No luck. The tracks were likely buried in loose snow. Our direction all day had been straight into the wind, so I decided to march directly into the gale and prayed this tactic would lead me to safety. My eyes had become fused shut within my goggles. For ten minutes, I didn't bother separating them. Finally I lifted my goggles, peeled open my lids with trembling fingers and scanned the darkness for any kind of glow. Nothing.

My teeth chattered uncontrollably, like a skeleton in a haunted house. I was nearing the point of hypothermia. Normally, after a hard day of exertion, my metabolism would slow and I would feel chilled even in a warm building. It was strange to think that I could be dead in a few hours. I felt guilty as I imagined the anguish Julie would go through. I knew my death would taint my mother's remaining years of retirement.

I felt desperate, like a chess player who has just lost his queen in what had been an evenly matched game. He plays on, but in his heart he knows the odds are against him. But this clearly wasn't a game. In failure, I would forfeit everything I had.

I began digging in the snow beneath my feet. My short-term survival depended on getting out of the wind as quickly as possible. The only way to do this was to build a snow cave. I knew the theory of snow caves. I'd seen them built on TV and read about them in books. Now I hoped to save my life with this survival trick.

Four inches down, the snow grew hard and crusty. My gloves scratched futilely against the ice. I pulled out my Gerber pocket knife and scratched through the crust. My efforts seemed so slow, I was tempted to give up and keep staggering through the wind. But I told myself to keep digging. Eventually I created a four-foot-diameter hole, about three feet deep, bottoming out in the vegetation of the tundra. I then undercut the windward wall until I had excavated a shallow cave three feet long and two feet high. It wasn't long enough to lie prone in, but by crossing my legs and leaning forward over my knees,

I could contort into a position that conformed to my cave's claustrophobic dimensions. I wriggled into my new home.

Silence.

It was unreal. All day, the wind had been a constant roar. Now it was completely gone. The only sounds were my breathing and the shuffling of my body as I shifted in my icy tomb. I was out of the blizzard.

The minutes ticked by. I was still terrified and very cold. I never expected anyone to find me in this lonely part of the tundra. I weighed my options. If I tried to keep travelling through the night, I was as good as dead. Even as I dug the cave, I could feel my strength seeping away. I'd known that if I didn't escape the wind within an hour, I would collapse and quickly die of exposure.

My only chance was to weather the long night and hope I could find the roadhouse in the light of day. I looked at my watch. It was just past 6 p.m. I had 13 hours to go.

My body spasmed, and I would yell to vent my agony and to produce a few extra joules of heat. I knew that my semi-crazed screams wouldn't penetrate more than a few feet into the stormy blackness beyond my cave. After half an hour, my shivering stopped. I was well versed in the physiological progression of death by hypothermia and felt fairly confident this wasn't the drowsy, almost comfortable post-shivering stage people experience before they fall asleep and then die. How did I know? I didn't feel drowsy, and I did feel as excruciatingly uncomfortable and as cold as ever. The shivering had been replaced by a panting that increased in intensity until I was gasping as though I were in a foot race. I had to pull my balaclava open slightly to keep from suffocating.

BEFORE WE LEFT ON THE EXPEDITION, Julie had presented me with a portable hard drive. Into this pocket device, she had downloaded thousands of songs as well as several audio books. While cycling along the highways or paddling down the Yukon River, I found it remarkable that I could listen to a book through a tiny set of headphones.

One of the titles Julie had included was *Last Breath* by Peter Stark. In the book, the author details the physiological and psychological stages that people go through in various forms of death. The stories were about happy, adventurous young people who invariably died horrifically by falling off cliffs, or drowning in whitewater, or asphyxiating in the thin air of some obscure mountain in Nepal. I found the book depressing, morbid, and all-round bad expedition reading material. At the same time, given our dearth of entertainment, I kept going back and listening to the cautionary tales, one by one. Now, as I lay in a snow cave in Siberia, hypothermic and scared, one of these stories returned to saturate my consciousness.

It described a young man driving to meet friends at a mountain cabin. It was a miserable winter's night and his jeep slid and got stuck in a ditch. Only a few kilometres away from the cabin, the man decided to strap on his skis and travel the rest of the way by the most direct route, away from the road.

After a series of mishaps—first he broke a binding and then he lost a glove—the party-seeking young man lay dying as his precious body heat evaporated into the night. In his last moments of mobility, the man ripped off articles of clothing and lay half naked in the snow. Apparently, this hypothermic striptease is a common occurrence—a bizarre crossing of the wires as our complex nervous circuitry shuts down. Ironically, the final stage of death by cold feels like a sweltering day at the beach.

This thought haunted me. Would I rip off all my clothing in a state of delirium? Would Tim and Yulya find me snuggled up in this cave, naked as the day I was born? I swore to myself that, no matter what happened, I'd avoid such an ignominious end. Nor would I fall asleep when the soft wind-driven snow looked as comfortable as a down duvet on a four-poster bed.

My panting continued. It wasn't due to a lack of oxygen, as plenty of air ventilated into my cave. I wondered if some primal physiological response had been triggered and my metabolism had been sped up to unbelievable levels to cope with the otherworldly cold.

In my cross-legged position, one of my legs was falling asleep. This sign worried me, as I had no idea how much the reduced blood flow would increase my vulnerability to frost-bite. I had visions of my leg never waking again. I would be left banging a cold, lifeless lump of flesh against the snow. I climbed out of the cave and into the driving snow to shake life into my numbed legs. The wind almost bowled me over. I hopped up and down, trying to muster more internal warmth. It was useless. The wind drew heat from my body as fast I could stoke what inner fire remained.

I dove back into the cave. It was 8 p.m., and I still wasn't dead. It was now 12 hours since I had left the security of our previous night's shelter.

Locals back in Egvekinot and Anadyr had revelled in rattling off stories of the countless souls who had succumbed to Chukotka's extreme climate: people who stepped out for a pee and were found two hours later frozen solid. And these people usually dressed in warm, padded clothes and thick fur hats. This morning, our driver had described a friend who had stopped his tank in a whiteout to relieve his bladder. He wandered about 10 metres from the vehicle to do the deed and wasn't seen again until spring melt released his blanched corpse. What were his final thoughts, I wondered.

My panting had intensified and my throat felt raw from

drawing cold air in too quickly. I wondered if my esophagus was becoming frostbitten.

The next time I checked my watch it was 10 p.m. I'd been in the snow cave for four hours. I felt alert but miserable. This was a good sign. Only nine more hours to go. I climbed into the night for another crazed jig. After pogo-ing a few times, I suddenly realized I had no idea where my hole in the ground was. Panic tore through me. It had to be within a metre or so of where I stood. But without the use of my eyes, I could lose it forever once I started stumbling around. Instead I kicked a small hole in the snow and lay down with my right foot firmly lodged in this indentation. I then rotated my body in a four-metre radius, groping with my arms. At last, I found my cavern and scuttled back inside.

My body had found a sort of equilibrium in this meat-locker environment. I felt frozen and tortured beyond comprehension and simply remained in this state, hour after horrendous hour. I might have welcomed the drowsy phase, but it never came for me. I celebrated the arrival of midnight with a few more sub-sub-sub-zero dance moves, embraced by wind so cold I imagined its icy force to be the embodiment of every one of the millions of gulag prisoners who had perished in this wretched land. I imagined my graceless flapping and unfettered groans as a dance of defiance in the face of death.

"Fuck you, Siberia!" I screamed.

And then I slithered back into my hole.

BY 1:30 A.M. I WAS BEGINNING TO FEEL OPTIMISTIC. I had survived in the cave for seven and a half hours. It would be light in another five and a half. I could do it. A simple, all-encompassing thought focused my will: Stay alive for five and a half hours. I will live.

I climbed into the winds to shake my atrophying legs again. Jump, jump, shake, shake, jump, stumble. I pulled off my goggles and squinted into the wind. I had given up all hope of seeing anything, and removing my goggles was now just part of my routine.

My frosted eyes opened wider. At a slight angle from the direction of the wind, I could make out an anomaly in the blackness. Was it a glow? I stared and became more certain my retinas weren't playing tricks on me.

Could it just be moonlight permeating through the blizzard? I wasn't sure. It was so faint that it would vanish when the wind intensified. I began to wonder if the whole thing had been a cold-induced hallucination. I was quickly losing heat as I contemplated this mysterious light.

I had to make a decision. I could march towards the glow and hope that it would be my salvation. If it wasn't my longed-for outpost, I would, without the slightest doubt, die. Alternatively, I could stay in my cave and try to make it to morning. Even if I did, there was no guarantee I would find the shelter in the blizzard.

I decided to start walking. Half an inch of ice had collected inside my ski goggles, so I had to leave them off. I knew frostbite would ravage my face as I walked through the cyclonic winds, but I wasn't willing to do anything that would impede my view of the light even for a moment. It was my one beacon out of this storm. Frequently, the glow would disappear altogether, and I carried on by keeping the wind at a 45-degree angle against my right cheek. My eyes would stick together every couple of minutes, and I would have to tear them apart and pluck ice balls out of my eyelashes.

My legs were rubbery but I kept crunching forward. The glow was getting brighter. In my right hand I clutched my knife, not for fear of wolves but because I couldn't close it with my numb, bundled-up hands.

I ascended a low rise and saw three distinct points of light. My life had been spared! A feeling of jubilation filled me, and my stride went from a stagger to a bound. Fifteen minutes later, I stood in front of a wooden door. As I was about to barge in, I caught a glimpse of the gleaming knife in my right hand. I must look like some evil cross between the abominable snowman and Jack the Ripper. I decided I'd better leave my open blade on a window ledge. Then I readied myself to leave behind this wintry fury and enter a world of warmth.

I opened the heavy wooden door and staggered into a dimly lit room. Six men were sitting around a wooden table, and one of them I recognized as our driver. Their look of shock quickly transformed to beaming smiles, and the driver rushed forward and embraced me in a bear hug.

He led me upstairs to a room where Tim and Yulya were sleeping and woke them up. Relief washed over their faces as they caught sight of their lost comrade.

"We thought you were dead," Yulya said with wide eyes. "They send out search party from Egvekinot. Three tanks out looking for you, and finally they give up. Nobody think you can live this long in the blizzard. We think you dead."

I saw myself in a small mirror hanging on the wall, and indeed, I looked like an apparition from the dead. My blue lips were a stark contrast to the rest of my blanched skin. Snow and ice still adorned my shoulders and beard.

"Holy shit," Tim said. "That was too close for comfort. We had a hot bath ready for you hours ago, in preparation for when the search party dragged you in hypothermic, but it's long gone cold. Let's get that thing refilled."

As I looked around and saw the anxiety and stress that my disappearance had caused, I felt awful. At the same time, the warmth and light, and my new lease on life, created a feeling of complete elation. I had been granted the greatest gift of all: life.

A few minutes later I was stretching out in a hot tub of water, away from the shrieking winds, driving snow, and minus-45 temperatures.

8

ON THE ROAD OF BONES

WHILE I RECOVERED IN THE ROADHOUSE, I worried about the journey ahead. We still had more than 35,000 kilometres to go, and our progress so far had not been easily earned. What if we'd ended up being dashed on the rocks during the storm crossing the Bering Sea? What if my kidney infection had commenced a little earlier when we were days from civilization? And what if I never saw that glow of the roadhouse in the blizzard? The source of illumination was a dilapidated light hanging off a pole. I shuddered to think that if that light had gone out, my life would have been extinguished along with it.

Were we foolish to keep going? We still had the rest of Eurasia to cross, a journey that promised more cold temperatures, busy narrow roads, and possible bandits. This would be followed by our attempt to be the first to row from mainland Europe to mainland North America.

It seemed we were playing one game of Russian roulette after another. It was easy to say that we would exercise the ultimate in caution and prudence, but there was no getting around the fact that we would be encountering many more unavoidable dangers. No amount of prudence can stop a semi-truck from squashing you on the highway or protect a rowboat in a hurricane.

Despite having second thoughts, I decided I would carry on. When I had made the choice to undertake this expedition several years earlier, I promised myself I would give it every-thing I had. At this stage my health was still excellent, and there was no reason physically why I couldn't continue. I knew if I went home defeated, I would trouble over my decision for the rest of my life.

Tim, Yulya, and I began preparing for our journey onwards while we waited for our new support vehicle. Our driver would return to Egvekinot and we would await a supply truck return-ing to Pevek to the north that would act as our support. I took advantage of our break by calling Julie on the satellite tele-phone, but refrained from telling her about my close brush with death. It would only make things more difficult for her. She informed me cheerily that she had found a rowing partner to join her for her Atlantic crossing. She and her new partner, Cathy Choinicki, were working hard with preparations and their website was up. A friend of Cathy's who headed market-ing and promotions for the Vancouver Canucks hockey team had offered to help produce an inspirational video featuring their quest.

From the roadhouse at Kilometre 87 (actually Kilometre 88), our travels went relatively smoothly. Our new support Ural truck, with a heated cabin in the back, met us here, and we continued on bikes and skis, following our support vehicle over the frozen tundra. Each night we would stop and enjoy our lit-tle oasis from the wind and snow within the truck's cabin.

Eventually we reached the Kolyma River, which flows into the Arctic Ocean, and we were able to pedal easily up this river, our studded tires keeping a firm grip on the ice. Cycling on the ploughed river was almost easier than road cycling because it was perfectly flat.

Near the mouth of the river the surrounding terrain was level and mundane, but as we made our way towards the headwaters, our river wended through deep gorges below jagged mountain peaks. In some areas the river flowed too quickly to freeze over, and the track followed precarious routes beside the river.

Finally, in mid-March, we reached the town of Ust Nera, on the Road of Bones deep within northeast Siberia. We had officially completed the first human-powered crossing of the Beringian Gap. The rutted dirt Road of Bones was connected to a highway system that would take us all the way to Moscow, 10,000 kilometres distant.

IN UST NERA, we reorganized ourselves in a Communist-era hotel of mostly hostel-style shared rooms. I paid the matronly babushka for a private room for Yulya and Tim and a cheaper dormitory one for me. From this point on, we would have no support vehicle, and we would have to carry every item of gear on our bicycles. It was time to sort through a mound of equipment and make some hard decisions. The equipment that wasn't coming with us would either have to be sent home by post or left behind in Ust Nera to be given away.

Postal costs were a major consideration, as we had long ago depleted our expedition funds. My savings were down to $3,500, and this money would need to get us all the way to Moscow. Yulya and I went to the post office to check into rates and procedures, and I was shocked by both. Rates to Canada were much more expensive than when I had previously sent equipment from Canada to Russia. Also, every item would need to be examined by the postal staff before it could be packed. Gear going to Canada had to be placed within 6- by 12- by 12-inch boxes provided by the post office. If it didn't fit, it couldn't go. Gear going ahead to Irkutsk had to be sewn within a special white burlap cloth we had to buy. The sewing had to be immaculate, the clerk informed us.

She went on to show us the "post office stitch" that had to be used.

I could feel the worn gears of Russian bureaucracy grinding again, and knew this was going to take a while. I had been hoping for a one-day turnaround in Ust Nera before being back on the road heading to Portugal. Instead, posting our gear was turning into a 64-man-hour ordeal and was threatening to take longer. After two days in Ust Nera, we were still sewing up packets, and long queues at the post office were a popular hang-out spot for us. I had spent almost $800 on postage and still there was more gear to be sent on.

I was getting impatient and annoyed. I had sacrificed sending a lot of my own belongings home for the sake of expediency and saving precious dollars. It seemed, however, that every item I put in the "giveaway pile," Yulya would pick up to include in another parcel to Irkutsk. At first I let it go, since such quality gear would be of extreme value to her when she returned home. Eventually, as time and money slipped away, I began to feel the expedition was being jeopardized. I couldn't keep spending the last of the cash posting unneeded gear when we barely had enough to feed ourselves for the next few months.

"We will need another day to sew up the rest of this gear," Yulya said.

It was the end of our second day in Ust Nera, and for the past 48 hours we'd been doing nothing but catering to the inefficient Russian postal system.

"Yulya, we don't need the rest, and we don't have the time or money to send it," I said.

Yulya was indignant. "This expedition is taking months to do. What is one more day?"

"We need to be on the Atlantic well before stormy season and we are currently behind schedule," I replied. "We need to deal with our chores each day as efficiently and quickly as possible and the cumulative effect will be much greater speed."

My logic didn't jive with her philosophy, and she simply shrugged and continued slowly with the "post office stitch." I went down the hall to do a final sort of the gear we would need for the journey ahead of us.

We left late the next day. We had either packed our essential gear into our panniers or sent it ahead to Irkutsk. The winter weather doesn't fluctuate much in this region, as a huge, immovable high-pressure system builds over the republic of Yakutia each winter, ensuring months of windless, cloudless, and extremely cold days. Currently, nighttime lows dropped to between minus 35 and minus 45 Celsius, while the daytime highs reached a balmy minus 25.

Our plan was to camp when necessary and, whenever possible, overnight in villages and road camps. One problem: most of the tiny villages on our map were rumoured to be abandoned. A trucker who knew this remote gulag highway warned us that, for the next 400 kilometres, there were no villages in which to buy food. There was only a gold mine, closed to the public and heavily guarded, and a few road-building camps.

The road, which passes through some of Siberia's most picturesque wilderness, is a marvel of engineering and a symbol of what can be accomplished with virtually limitless labour. Unfortunately, it is also a symbol of one of the most despicable crimes in Soviet history. It is said that one gulag prisoner died for almost every metre of the road built. The dead were buried in the roadbed, hence the name Road of Bones. Beneath our wheels lay the remains of the intellectuals and political opponents that Stalin so despised.

Along this lonely, beautiful road of cold and death, we would pedal to Yakutsk, the capital of Yakutia. Our biggest danger would come from the cold and isolation. We would pass within 200 kilometres of Oymyakon, a village that boasts the world's coldest temperatures outside Antarctica. Here the January temperature averages minus 50 and regularly dips into the minus-60s. In summer, the mercury soars and occasionally reaches plus 40, which also gives the area the greatest temperature range on the planet.

We cycled along the hard-packed snow out of Ust Nera while locals watched in disbelief. By mid-afternoon, we had reached the summit of an enormous pass, one of the two highest cols we would encounter over the next 1,000 kilometres to Yakutsk. Giant peaks stretched off in both directions under a cloudless sky, and the road snaked into the distance. The only trees growing in this region were larches. Being the only coniferous tree that sheds its needles in the winter, the trees were lifeless and brown.

We took it easy for the first few days, so that Yulya could build up her stamina—after riding in the truck for so many weeks, she was out of shape. We coasted down the long, gradual decent from the path and set up camp after 60 kilometres.

CAMPING AND LIVING IN THE EXTREME COLD requires enduring a permanent state of extreme discomfort. Everything needs to be done while wearing bulky insulated gloves. Thick sheets of ice coat your beard at night.

We spent two hours melting snow for our dinner, tea, and drinking water for the next day, which we poured into thermoses. For dinner and making drinking water the stove burned half a litre of fuel, four times as much as it would need in summer conditions. While we waited, we hopped around to maintain our core temperatures in the minus-34 cold. After wolfing down our freeze-dried rations we retired to our pair of tents and crawled into the sleeping bags.

Moisture build-up can pose a dangerous problem when using sleeping bags in the cold. Somewhere between your body and the exterior of the bag lies the freezing point. Here, the vapour released as you perspire will condense. After a few days, the sleeping bag will become soggy (or crispy in sub-zero temperatures), and the vital insulation of its down and feather fill will be rendered next to useless.

The only solution is to use a vapour barrier—an impermeable plastic membrane that prevents the moisture from entering the fabric. Essentially, you climb naked into a giant condom and then slide into the sleeping bag. The moisture condenses inside the vapour barrier rather than spoiling your sleeping bag. But it guarantees you a cold and damp exit in the morning.

A thick sleeping mat between the bag and the tent floor provided essential insulation from the cold grip of the Siberian ground. Tim and Yulya used their Therm-a-Rest pads along with reindeer skins. I just used the skin. The thick, hollow fur of the reindeer resists compression and provides unbelievable insulation from the snow below.

Reading or writing before going to sleep was next to impossible. Once cocooned within the vapour barrier and sleeping bag, we needed to pull the draw cord tight, with just our mouths and noses protruding, keeping our hands and arms restrained within the bag.

This was the most comfortable moment of the day—lying warm and cozy in our high-tech sleeping bags without needing to rely on cardiovascular activity to keep warm. Despite the warmth, each breath of frosty air still felt uncomfortable, like inhaling shards of glass.

Morning was the toughest time. It required the utmost discipline to get going. My watch alarm would chime at seven and welcome me into a dark world and the coldest temperatures of the day. After climbing naked and dripping wet from the vapour barrier, I would dress quickly before I lost too much of my core warmth. Once I'd donned the thick down jacket, Baffin boots, head gear, and puffy mitts, I would make a dash to Tim and Yulya's tent and wake them up. Since the first night, Tim and Yulya had not used their vapour barriers, fearing it would interfere with their intimacy inside their zipped-together sleeping bags. Now their bags were saturated with moisture. I would then light the stove in their tent's vestibule and cook a breakfast of oatmeal and coffee.

After breakfast, I would begin to pack up, while Tim and Yulya took care of their own equipment. Invariably I would be finished 30 to 45 minutes before them and would have to jog on the spot or do sprints along the road to stay warm. By the time we mounted our bicycles, I felt like I'd already done a hard day's work.

Despite its ominous name, travel along the Road of Bones proved relatively easy. The wheels of countless transport trucks had compressed the winter snow and the rutted dirt surface below into a hard, smooth layer of white ice. Our studded Nokian tires gripped the surface, and the ride didn't feel much different from cycling on asphalt. Negotiating the steep hills with our heavily laden bicycles gave us the most concern.

We cycled slowly through the day and took frequent breaks so Yulya could catch her breath. After eating no breakfast, she nibbled on her trail mix, one peanut at a time, and barely made a dent in the large bag.

"Yulya, you must eat more," I gently urged her. "Your body is like a car. If it doesn't get any gas, it doesn't go. Simple as that."

"I too tired to eat," she said. "My heart hurts, too."

"Your heart?"

"Yes. When I was little I have many illness of heart."

"Uh . . . did you get your heart checked before the expedition?" I asked.

"Yes, doctor say my heart is good," Yulya replied. "But he did say I shouldn't go on expedition."

"Why did he say that?"

Yulya looked down at her handlebars. "I don't remember!" she finally blurted.

I cycled ahead and thought about what Yulya had just said. Why hadn't she told us of her heart problems before the expedition? And exactly what condition did she have that her doctor would recommend she not undertake such a physical endeavour? I wasn't too concerned with Yulya's slow progress. She had been a long time without exercising much, and I felt it would take a few days for her to get back into the routine of heavy slogging.

AFTER CYCLING 40 KILOMETRES, we reached a gold mine on a hillside. A female security guard, in thickly insulated camouflage, stood beside the road that led into the operation. A clean-cut man strolled towards us along the main road as we hovered by the entrance. He introduced himself as the mine's doctor. The mine was closed to the public, he told us, but he would talk to the administration and see if we might be able to stay for the night.

Fifteen minutes later, he returned and told us with a smile that we could have our own guest house for as long as we wanted. We were also welcome to eat with the mine's staff in the cafeteria. The following morning we would get a guided tour.

The mine site was the size of a small village, its wooden buildings heated by a central boiler plant that belched coal smoke into the azure skies. At the far end, a throaty rumble voiced the presence of the ore-processing plant. The mountain's flanks were riddled with tunnels that traced veins of gold deep into the earth's crust.

We were led into a two-bedroom wooden house with triple-glazed windows, and traded the minus-35 temperature outside for a pleasant plus 21 degrees inside. "Don't eat dinner," the doctor told us. "We are making a special dinner which you will be having with the director of operations."

We went to the cafeteria for a late lunch of soup and goulash. The doctor rejoined us, and Yulya translated our conversation.

"Do you have a wife?" the doctor asked me.

"No," I replied, "but I have a fiancée."

The doctor asked Tim the same question.

"No," came Tim's short response.

I cringed. I knew how Yulya would interpret his reply and suspected that this one word would provoke hours or even days of brooding silence. As we left the cafeteria I overheard Yulya and Tim's exchange.

"Why you say no when he asked if you have wife?" she asked.

"Well, I don't have a wife," he replied. "We're not married yet and he didn't ask if we're getting married."

"Colin and Julie not married either, but Colin say he getting married," countered Yulya. "You make me feel like nothing!"

"Julie and Colin have gone through a little ceremony, which we haven't done yet," Tim said, trying to placate Yulya. Their voices trailed off as we went different directions.

Later that evening, I asked Tim if he and Yulya had patched their rift.

"Yup, she's good as gold," he replied cheerily. "I told her we'll be doing a little ceremony when we reach Irkutsk."

"You mean you're proposing to her?" I asked.

"Yeah, basically," said Tim. "She's nuts. If I didn't promise to marry her and to propose, she'll be broody and dark and angry for the remainder of the expedition."

The next morning, we toured the ore-processing plant with the director of operations. The rocks were first crushed to a fine powder before being conveyed in a slurry through a series of separation processes, which included a centrifuge and vibrating washboard.

"All this equipment is made in Canada," our guide proudly informed us. "We purchased this state-of-the-art machinery four years ago, and our yields are now significantly higher. As well, no chemicals are used in the separation process, since it is entirely mechanical."

Our tour of the mine concluded with a gift of three large hardback books detailing the history and background of the mining company. The colourful textbooks must have weighed a kilogram each. I groaned inwardly at the thought of lugging this extra weight over the hills.

We left the mine at 11 a.m. and waved goodbye to the administrative staff and the doctor. They had told us we could expect a road-building camp, closed for the winter but inhabited by a security guard, 40 kilometres down the road. An occupied bridge-building camp sat at 90 kilometres.

Our progress so far had been less then ideal. We were slipping behind schedule again. I suggested that we aim for the bridge-building camp, but both Tim and Yulya balked. "We're starting late," Tim said, "so we have less time."

"If we don't make it before dark, we can camp," I said. "We have the world's best camping gear and may as well put it to use."

Yulya's eyes widened. "We cannot camp," she insisted. "It is dangerous and not healthy."

"What do you mean, it's dangerous?" I asked. "We camped the night before last with no problems."

"I was very cold," said Yulya. "I do not want to camp again when we can stay in populated points."

I sighed. We could never stick to our schedule if we dawdled at every warm shelter on our route, but Tim and Yulya seemed more concerned about comfort than progress. We had all the same gear as an Antarctic expedition, yet one night of camping in cold was all our team could handle.

"Tomorrow we will do a full day," Tim promised. "Won't we, Yulya?"

Yulya didn't respond.

MID-AFTERNOON, A VAN TOOTED AND PULLED UP BESIDE US. A crowd of cheery Yakutians, en route from Ust Nera to Oymyakon, invited us in for some coffee, pickled horse meat, and other treats. After our meal, Tim and I withdrew gifts from our panniers to repay the kindness of our Russian hosts: two shining new hardback volumes detailing the wondrous history of mining in the region. Thrilled, our new friends asked us to sign the inside covers.

Shortly afterwards, we reached our destination for the day—an unlovely collection of trailers and shacks, which housed road workers in the spring and summer. Two barking dogs summoned the caretaker from the adjacent forest. He introduced himself as Gregory. He didn't receive much company and seemed pleased to have unexpected guests for the night.

"Wait here in my hut and have a cup a tea," he said. "I'll light the fire in the best insulated cabin and it will be warm in an hour." After firing up the woodstove, Gregory returned to tell us about life as a caretaker. "It gets lonely, but at least I have my dogs for company. My wife and family live in a village 400 kilometres from here."

Gregory told us about the wildlife of the region, including an animal with a name that I jotted in my notes as "caberge." This dog-sized animal is known in English as a musk deer. Instead of antlers, the male "caberge" is adorned with tusk-like fangs. At first I thought he was having us on, so Gregory fetched the frozen head of a "caberge" he had shot the previous month. It didn't look anything like a deer. Rather, it resembled a sabre-tooth tiger.

Upon saying goodnight, Tim and I crunched through the snow under the light of a full moon to our little cabin. We walked through the door to find Yulya pulling pictures off the wall and tossing them into the woodstove.

"What are you doing?" I cried.

"These pictures are dirty," Yulya replied. "They are sinful."

I peered at the few remaining pictures of women in various states of undress.

"Yulya!" I screamed. "This is a private residence. You are a guest here. It is not your right to destroy someone else's possessions. Stop right now!"

Yulya ignored my pleas. She threw the remaining naked ladies into the stove and slammed the door. "Don't you understand?" she demanded. "These pictures are used for masturbation purposes. Masturbating is one of the greatest sins. It is unhealthy!"

I tried to convince her again that she couldn't destroy her hosts' decorations, however much they offended her. "If you don't want to sleep in a cozy cottage with pornographic materials on the wall then you can sleep in the tent," I told her. But my words fell on uncomprehending ears.

"God says masturbating is evil," Yulya said with finality. "I will listen to him." Her cheeks flushed, whether from emotion or the heat of the fire I couldn't tell.

THE NEXT MORNING, after another late start, we set off for the bridge-building camp 50 kilometres away. I cycled ahead of Tim and Yulya, and waited at the top of each hill for the two of them to catch up. I was at a loss as to how to motivate our small group to put more effort into this cross-country expedition. Yulya seemed to think, because the expedition had already taken so many months, that time and speed weren't relevant any more. Our undertaking was so huge that she had lost sight of our ultimate goal. Tim didn't express views that went either way. He seemed content to move at whatever pace Yulya set. I wondered if he favoured having someone along who was even slower than himself.

As our group struggled across Siberia, I held out hope for our team dynamics. We had overcome huge obstacles already, but tension was building between us. Tim and Yulya constantly fought, mostly about Yulya's romantic insecurities. Tim and I quarrelled over expedition logistics and about what changes could speed our progress. Our casual conversations and joking banter began to disappear.

Gregory's two dogs, a Siberian husky puppy and a mongrel, had followed us down the road when we departed. As the kilometres ticked by, the dogs showed no sign of turning back for home, and I began to worry. The dogs kept pace with the front rider and lapped up snow to stay hydrated as they sprinted effortlessly across the land.

Yulya was cycling in the lead when, from our vantage 500 metres back, Tim and I watched her flag down two oncoming trucks. Each paused briefly to confer with her and then rumbled on.

"They wouldn't take the dogs back home?" I asked when I caught up.

"I don't know," Yulya said. "I didn't ask. I asked how far to bridge camp."

"You flagged down two big rigs to ask how far to the bridge camp? It's 20 kilometres."

"I know, but I wanted to make sure. It is very dangerous out here."

I looked at the poor dogs. They had eaten nothing all day. The puppy was beginning to whine.

"Why didn't you ask if they could take the dogs home?" I asked.

"I forgot."

After ascending a high pass, we dropped into a river valley and could see a scattering of shacks beside a partially completed bridge. The road traffic crossed the river on the ice adjacent to the metal structure. As we neared the bridge camp, a fight erupted between our exhausted dogs and territorial local canines. Some workers appeared, perplexed by the growling, barking fracas we had brought with us.

Russian hospitality prevailed, and we were offered a warm lodging for the night. I would share a cabin with the foreman, and Tim and Yulya were given beds in a nearby cabin with several other workers. The dogs were fed some scraps from the mess hall.

Most of the men in the camp had come from distant corners of the former Soviet empire—Ukraine, Kazakhstan, Uzbekistan, and Georgia. Motivated by poor economies in their homelands, these workers had exiled themselves to eastern Siberia to pick up where the gulags had left off. They told us that the Kolyma Highway would be ready as an all-season road in five more years. There was even talk of asphalt coming after that.

We were offered a dinner of raw fish, fish soup, and bread—bland but delicious after a day in the cold.

After dinner, a man named Kolya entered my cabin. "The *banya* is hot," he told me. "Come and clean yourself."

Kolya tutored me in the etiquette of *banya* bathing. First, you scrub yourself in a room adjacent to the sauna, using water heated over the stove. Once clean, you enter the wooden furnace, beat yourself silly with a bouquet of pine branches and needles (allegedly to promote circulation and slough off dead skin), and just when you're about to faint from the heat, you dash into the minus-40 cold and roll in the snow. You top this all off with a final scrub. You emerge from the experience with a renewed definition of being truly clean. The anticlimax, for me, was climbing back into my soiled, damp travelling apparel.

I exited the sauna to see a crowd of men standing around Tim's bike. Tim was showing one of them, a metal worker, where the plastic arm cuffs had broken off the handlebar extensions. The tall man scrutinized the problem and said, "Nyet problem."

"Looks like this nice guy, Igor, is going to fix my broken handlebars for me," Tim said.

Igor removed Tim's defective handlebar extenders and beckoned for us to watch him work his magic in the metal shop. The resourceful Georgian cut some metal from a discarded fuel tank and shaped it to Tim's broken plastic cuffs. I glanced up at Yulya and noticed that her attention was not on the metal worker but on the wall behind him. Two pictures of scantily dressed women were taped there. I cringed and readied myself to restrain Yulya if she tried to tear the pictures down. Instead, she said something in Russian to the Georgian as he laboured over Tim's handlebars.

"What did you say?" I asked.

"I told him he's disgusting," she replied.

MY MOOD DARKENED THE NEXT DAY as we cycled away from the bridge camp. We still had the dogs with us. Our food was limited and we couldn't afford to feed the hungry creatures. I felt sorry for Gregory. His reward for looking after three cyclists was to lose his porn collection and his two canine friends.

With every passing day, I felt that Tim and Yulya were living in a different reality, one that didn't jive with my own. To me, our plan seemed straightforward: we had set out to go around the world in under two years. If we continued at our present rate, we wouldn't have time to cross the Atlantic during the appropriate weather window. All three of us were physically capable of moving much faster. However, our expedition's mental focus wasn't there. I tried to motivate our team—offering pep talks, praising Yulya when she did things efficiently or with effort, clarifying our objective. Still, the speed of our progress only declined.

Five days after leaving Ust Nera, we were averaging 47 kilometres per day. Once again, we decided to aim for a populated point—a nearly abandoned village—far short of where we could be going. I felt I was losing touch with my two reasons for going on expeditions. I love to explore and challenge myself, experience exotic lands and people, to work harmoniously in a team and to be happy. The dynamics of Tim and Yulya were changing all this. I no longer noticed the beauty around me. Instead, I fussed, my mind in a constant state of frustration and stress.

Tim Cope, a good friend of mine, cycled through Russia in 1999 and 2000 with his buddy Chris Hatherly. Their relationship began to falter—a not uncommon experience in long-distance expeditions. Together, they decided that the simplest remedy to this problem was to spend some time apart. They continued cycling independently and met up several weeks later at a pre-arranged location. The "trial separation" did wonders to patch up their differences and put their larger goal back in perspective. The two later wrote a book detailing their journey (*Off the Rails*) and produced a film.

Perhaps this solution could work for us too. I could cycle the 4,000 kilometres to Irkutsk and work on the book I was writing while I waited for Tim and Yulya. And perhaps Tim and Yulya might travel more efficiently without my constant badgering to move faster. Sometimes I suspected their apathy was a subconscious form of rebellion.

I waited for Tim and Yulya a few hundred metres from the skeletal remains of the Soviet-constructed village of Kyubyume. It consisted of a scattering of windowless, cracking concrete apartment blocks and concrete houses with roofs caving in. It was the most depressing castoff of civilization I have ever seen. Thirty-five people apparently still inhabited this ghost town. Chimney smoke streamed from a few homes.

When Tim and Yulya caught up, I shared my new plan with them. We were now on the established road system of Russia. The obstacles we might encounter from now on would be far less than the hardships we had endured on the Chukotka peninsula. We no longer needed to remain together for safety's sake.

"I'm going on ahead alone," I said. "I think it would be best for the team dynamics, and there is no reason why we should jeopardize our combined goal of making it to Moscow and beyond. I'll cycle to Irkutsk and wait for you guys there." As I uttered these words, I felt relief washing through my body. I had liberated myself from a situation that had plagued my emotions for too long. "We have duplicates here of almost everything—tents, stove, repair equipment—so both parties will have enough equipment for camping and cycling."

Tim just nodded his head.

That evening, we separated our equipment. We split the

food, two thirds for Tim and Yulya and a third for me. I divided the last of my money in the same ratio. Tim assured me that his income from the articles he was writing for the *Vancouver Sun* would be enough to see him through to Irkutsk. The only two items that didn't come in pairs were the satellite phone and the video camera. The phone hadn't been working properly—there was a faulty connection with the antenna—and Tim chose to take the video camera.

Since leaving Ust Nera six days previously, we had camped only one night. From now on, I would pitch my tent almost every day to maximize my progress. The discomfort of the extreme cold would be great, but that's why we had asked outdoor companies to sponsor us with their highest-quality cold-weather gear. Besides, only by sticking to a more steady schedule could we exit Russia before our visas expired.

At seven the next morning, as the snow-blanketed land began to emit a diffused glow, I said goodbye to my expedition colleagues and began my 4,000-kilometre journey to Irkutsk. My tires crunched through the snow as I cycled westwards, alone.

I WONDERED WHETHER TIM AND YULYA, left on their own, would make better progress. What would happen if they continued to average only 40 to 50 kilometres a day? We would be too late to cross the Atlantic this year. I was also nervous about travelling through the rest of eastern Siberia alone. Hardly a soul out here can string two words of English together, so all communication would involve my Tarzan Russian and charades. As well, I had only 1,500 rubles ($60) in my pocket to see me 750 kilometres to Yakutsk, where I hoped to find a bank machine.

The future was uncertain, so I took comfort in the seemingly unstoppable progress of my bicycle and legs combined. I just had to keep pedalling. I looked at the thermometer the morning I departed: the temperature was minus 45. Ice quickly formed a shell around my balaclava, and I had to stop frequently to scrape ice from my ski goggles. The occasional ptarmigan would startle me as it transformed from a white lump in the snow to a flurry of flapping wings. Apart from that feathered disturbance, the air was still and thick. Cold air is denser than warm air, and I imagined I could feel its increased resistance trying to slow me down, trying to bring me to the speed of the land I was travelling through—a place of stillness and silence.

A roar in the distance would announce the approach of a transport truck. The din of clattering metal and the tooting horn would draw me out of the trance I'd been lulled into. By 2 p.m., the valley had narrowed, and the road now veered towards a formidable range of mountains. Tusks of granite rose skyward above spindly fins of dormant larch. The road angled between two such peaks. This must be the first of the two dreaded passes that truck drivers had warned us about. Countless rigs had lost control on the steep, slippery roads and tumbled off the numerous precipices. I wasn't too worried about falling off cliffs because my new disc brakes and carbide studded tires kept me securely on the road, but I was concerned about the steep gradient I would have to hump my overloaded bicycle up.

I ascended the first pass without trouble. The panorama I enjoyed from its summit would prove to be the most spectacular scenery I would encounter until I reached the Russian–Ukrainian border, some 10,000 kilometres away. On the west side of the col, a frozen river, blown clear of snow, glittered a sapphire blue as it contorted towards a high-sided canyon. The road performed acrobatics as it roughly paralleled the canyon in the shadow of snow-capped peaks.

It took me eight days to reach Yakutsk. After two days in the mountains, the land flattened out and made progress easier. With my westward movement and the approach of spring, temperatures warmed to highs of minus 4 and lows between minus 20 and minus 30. Road conditions worsened during the last few days, as the afternoon rays of sunshine melted the snow and turned the road into a thick soup of slush, mud, and boulders. I also worried about the deteriorating bearings in the bottom bracket of my bicycle, which wobbled with every pedal stroke. Although I carried a spare bottom bracket, I didn't have the specialized tools to swap brackets. I hoped I could remedy the problem in Yakutsk.

As I struggled over the final 100 kilometres, I realized I would have to reduce the weight on my overloaded bicycle.

The hard-packed snow had given the rough, wonky roads a finish as smooth as asphalt. Now, as the rising temperatures revealed the true nature of the road, stresses on the bike were increasing. As I crashed through deep potholes and navigated around football-sized boulders, I knew there was no way my bike could continue hauling 50 kilograms of gear across the remaining 9,000 kilometres of Russia's road system. In Yakutsk, I would rid my baggage of every single luxury or excess item. There were still 2,500 kilometres of dirt roads ahead, 800 kilometres of which were still under construction and composed of nothing other than a loose bed of boulders. Any major mechanical problem out there would be a disaster, as I was still 3,000 kilometres from the nearest bike store.

Yakutsk, with a population of about 200,000, sits on the north shore of the tenth longest river in the world, the Lena. It was founded in 1632 by Cossacks and became the capital of the autonomous state of Yakutia. Abundant reserves of gold and other resources in the region give Yakutia a more vibrant economy than some of the poorer states to the south. The main shipping corridor for Yakutsk is the Lena River itself, which can be navigated to the railway system of southern Siberia or up to the Arctic Ocean. The roads leading into this central Siberian capital are abysmal, with the Road of Bones leading 2,000 kilometres east to the Pacific, and another dirt road (with periodic patches of decayed asphalt) heading due south.

Finally, six months after reaching the eastern shores of Siberia, I reached Yakutsk, the first major city since Fairbanks, Alaska. The rigours we had endured were catching up with me, and I weaved slowly through the congested streets leading into the centre. Damp, smelly, and exhausted, I wanted only to find a hotel and clean myself and my gear. The roads had been such a quagmire that every inch of my bicycle and panniers had been spray-painted with thick diarrhea-brown mud.

The track crossing the bridgeless frozen river led straight to a beautiful Russian Orthodox cathedral. Its gold onion domes seemed to mark the centre of the city. Lada buses and new European and Japanese cars whizzed along a freeway that separated the city from the river. I felt overwhelmed by the speed and noise and exhaust.

More than half of the city's inhabitants seemed to be of Yakutian ancestry, distant relatives of Mongolians. I was directed to the Lena Hotel, a grand-looking building a few blocks from the city centre. I was nervous about entering this establishment covered from head to toe in mud. The thing that had so far struck me most about the inhabitants of Yakutia was their perfectionist ways. Everyone dressed impeccably, in suits or other stylish clothing. Shoes are always polished, all buckles on briefcases clipped, and everyone will stamp his or her feet three times when treading from the snow onto bare concrete. I found their perfect manners and attention to detail fascinating, so contrary to what you find when visiting a remote outpost in Canada or the United States.

The staff of the Lena Hotel couldn't conceal their shock as they glanced at my soiled clothing. However, they maintained their composure, and before long I was ushered to my room along with the balls of mud that contained all my possessions. My bicycle was relegated to a garage out back. After a half-hour shower, I collapsed into my bed and soon fell asleep.

ALTHOUGH YAKUTSK DOES NOT HAVE A BICYCLE STORE, there is a local bike club with a dozen members. Several months before, I'd received an email from Gavril Scryabin, project manager of the bike club, who informed me they would be happy to be of assistance when I was in Yakutsk. Now I prayed that the club members would have the tools to replace my bottom bracket and the rest of my battered drive train.

After a good night's rest and several hefty meals in the hotel restaurant, I went in search of what might be the northernmost bike club in the world (and definitely the most isolated). I marched through the busy city and tracked down the building on a quiet side street. The large log structure housed several offices, but nothing that looked very bicycle-ly.

"Velecopyet Kloob?" I asked a man sitting behind a computer.

"Nyet, nyet," said the young man, who looked like a bespectacled stockbroker. "Chass wait." He made a phone call. Within five minutes two Yakutian men in suits, along with a younger woman, arrived in a late-model Toyota Camry.

They introduced themselves as Gavril and Nikolai. The men spoke no English, but Helena spoke it fluently, the best I'd heard in months. She had spent several years studying in Finland, and all her courses had been in English. "We are proud that you have chosen to cycle through our city," she said. "Gavril and Nikolai have offered to help you with anything you need while in Yakutsk. And we have bicycle tools if you need them."

I breathed a sigh of relief. The next two days were a whirlwind of activity as I—with the help of Gavril and Nikolai—replaced my drive train, purchased various items that had broken, welded my broken gear racks, and enjoyed the generous hospitality of the bike club.

The bike club even organized a ceremony on my behalf. We went to a traditional Yakutian log home, where a shaman woman performed a ritual to bring me good fortune on my travels. As she chanted, she drew energy from a crackling fire and diverted it my way. (I could have used that magic fire over the past few weeks of Siberian cycling.) Ten members from the bicycle club turned up for the meal and we indulged in traditional Yakutian fare, including fermented mare's milk, sliced frozen raw fish, and reindeer meat.

In Yakutsk, I was unable to send the video cassettes and camera film back to Canada. The post office informed me that, by law, all the pictures would have to be exposed and Russian customs would have to view all the footage and photos to make sure that no restricted areas had been documented. They would then issue a document that would allow the material to be sent overseas. The whole procedure would take months. I had no choice but to continue carting the priceless material through Russia on my bike.

From Yakutsk, the M56 road headed due south for 1,150 kilometres before I would reach the Trans-Siberian Highway, which runs along the nation's southern perimeter. Here I would turn west and travel for 2,200 kilometres to Irkutsk. Although the M56 is more heavily travelled than the Kolyma Highway, I expected worse conditions because of spring melt. In the afternoon, the roads likely would turn to a slushy, muddy mess; by morning, that same mess would have frozen into a lumpy obstacle course. There were patches of asphalt, but I'd been told these respites were more a tease than a saving grace. The main advantage, though, would be travelling through a more populated region. I looked forward to regular meals at inexpensive truck stops.

My new friends from the bike club clustered into the lobby of the Lena Hotel and wished me well as I pushed off on my newly serviced and lightened bicycle. I had given away all my unnecessary clothing, my heavy winter boots, the seven-kilogram lead-acid battery, my reindeer hide (replaced with a thin foam mattress), my guidebook (except the pages still relevant), one thermos, and many other items. I felt my minimalist approach was the only way to make it on the road ahead.

FROM YAKUTSK, I stuck to my schedule of pedalling 100 kilometres per day and camping at night. The days blended into one another, each a non-stop struggle of forcing my bicycle through conditions that bicycles aren't built for. I'd get a flat tire almost every day, necessitating repairs under the heat of the camp stove to dry the glue. I would pass two or three diners a day, usually in remote locations, and eat hearty meals, the highlights of my day. These small restaurants, operating out of log huts or railway cars, would rarely have running water or even electricity. Heated with coal, they were an oasis from the cold as I devoured borscht, goulash, salad, and crepes with condensed milk for dessert. The babushkas who ran the cafés would fill my thermos with hot water, and I would plunge back into the cold. Between meals, I would snack on chocolate bars and *pryalnekes,* a Russian cookie. I would begin and end each day in my tent with a meal of Chinese noodles, a coffee, and cookies.

As I travelled farther south and emerged from the perpetual winter high-pressure system sitting over Yakutia, the weather began to deteriorate. Heavy snow fell, sometimes 30 centimetres in 24 hours, and made cycling treacherous. Camping off the roadside became almost impossible as I tried to push the bike through chest-deep snow and erect the non-free-standing tent in these conditions. Instead, I would have to pitch the tent on side tracks, created to service roadside logging operations. Here, the snow had been ploughed or compressed by heavy machinery. I hoped that no traffic would also plough or compress my tent and me into the ground.

On one particularly bad day, two- to three-metre snow banks towered over the road, and I cycled along the narrow windy corridor 20 kilometres beyond my usual 100, hoping that a side track would materialize so I could set up camp. Finally, when it was completely dark and I was too exhausted to go on, I ended up setting up my tent on the shoulder of the snow bank, two metres from the traffic. Through the night, motorist after motorist would pass me and then reverse, bathing my tent in their headlights, puzzling over who would be camping on the roadside in such horrendous conditions. One man got out of his car and warned me that it was dangerous to camp there. I couldn't decipher whether he was concerned about the road bandits, the drunken drivers, or the extreme cold.

Since arriving in Yakutia, I had been worried that neither Tim nor I had a *rasporyazheniye,* the special permit to travel through the state. My guidebook stated that, until recently, the permit had been necessary, and although it was no longer officially required, many officials were unaware of this fact and would still demand to see a permit. My greatest fear was encountering an expensive bureaucratic delay.

Several days after leaving Yakutsk, as I neared the town of Aldan, a police car skidded to a stop on the opposite side of the road. Three policemen, in fur hats, leapt out and yelled at me to stop. I hit the brakes and awaited their approach. It was my first encounter with the Russian police.

"Where are going?" asked a thin-lipped officer.

"I'm cycling to Moscow."

"Where are you from?"

"Canada." I shifted on my bike. This is when they would ask for my *rasporyazheniye.*

"Are you hungry?" another policeman asked.

"What?"

"We have food in the car," he said. "Come on in."

I was ushered into the car, and the three jolly policemen pulled out an assortment of pickles, kielbasa, cheese, bread, and sweets.

"Vodka?" the driver enquired.

I declined, but that didn't stop the rest of them from polishing off a one-litre bottle of home brew. Finally, after being stuffed silly and asked to autograph the ceiling of the car, I was released by the drunken policemen, who waved and hooted goodbye as they continued down the road.

In Yakutsk, I had encountered several people who had a bad flu. Seven days after leaving the city, I began to succumb to the illness. The damp and cold environment I was travelling through did nothing to stop the onset of a gurgling chest infection. In my weakened state, I also suffered a bout of diarrhea, and my health continued to decline. I staggered and pushed my bike into the city of Neryungri, a coal-mining town of 50,000, where I checked into the first hotel I could find. I spent three days lying semi-comatose in bed.

The girl working at the front desk worried that she had a dying guest, so she sent for her aunt, a kindly older Buryat woman said to be skilled in shamanistic medicine. While my memory was scrambled by the delirium of a high fever, I do remember her placing four jars on my back. Each jar contained a piece of burning newspaper that consumed the oxygen and created a vacuum, leaving big hickeys on my skin. The old woman chanted and danced, and the jars seemed to clink in harmony. The next day I felt remarkably better and hit the road again.

For a week, I seemed to tread a fine line between remission and recovery as I exposed myself to the rigours of Siberia. It wasn't until a month later that the gurgle in my chest disappeared for good.

SEVERAL DAYS LATER, I passed city of Tynda on the BAM railway line. The BAM is a major railway artery, only recently completed, that parallels the Trans-Siberian Railway several hundred kilometres to the south. About 80 kilometres past Tynda, as I laboured onto the summit of a muddy pass with heavy wet snow falling around me, I rubbed my eyes in disbelief at the sight of a woman marching up the far side pulling a cart behind her. I coasted down the hill and was filled with curiosity as the figure came closer. She was in her mid-40s, and wore long underwear and high gumboots. She was harnessed like a sled dog to a green box with two BMX-type wheels on both sides.

"Hello?" she said tentatively.

This unusual stranger, it turned out, was on a human-powered journey in the reverse direction of my own. Rosie Swale-Pope was from England and was attempting to jog around the planet, completely unsupported. Rosie pulled a closed-cell foam mat from her cart, placed it in the mud, withdrew a thermos of tea, and we sat down to chat. Apart from Tim, she was the first Westerner I'd met in months. It felt good to talk in fluent English again.

She had left her homeland almost two years ago and had been on the move ever since. She jogged about 20 kilometres a day with her cart in tow. Siberia, of course, had been the toughest part of the journey, but she hadn't let the brutal cold slow her down. Like me, she camped most nights. She described how she would dry two moisture-laden sleeping bags in cafés while she ate. From here, Rosie would continue to Yakutsk and then follow the Road of Bones through to Magadan in the summer. She was aware that portions of the road were closed in the summer, but Rosie felt confident that she could haul her cart through the bogs and across the bridgeless rivers. From Magadan, she would board a boat to Alaska and resume her six-year jog in North America.

I marvelled at the tenacity of this woman who dared to take on such a monumental challenge. Remarkably modest, she downplayed her achievements. She was a true explorer, out to experience the world and loving every minute of her once-in-a-lifetime journey. She seemed oblivious to the fame and respect such an undertaking would bring her, and couldn't remember the exact web address of the site her son had created to track and promote her expedition.

Rosie seemed equally excited to meet a fellow explorer in such a remote part of the world. I felt almost sad to say good-bye to her after an hour of chitchat.

THE LANDSCAPE VARIED LITTLE on my 1,100-kilometre journey south from Yakutsk. Rolling taiga of pine and birch stretched as far as the eye could see when I was fortunate enough to be given a vantage of the land around. A large portion of this stretch sits upon the Aldan Plateau, where the 1,500-metre-plus elevation creates a thick snow belt. In places, the snow depth exceeded two and a half metres, and the road had a tunnel-like feel, with towering banks of ploughed snow on each side.

A trucker informed me that there was little snow beyond the Trans-Siberian Railway line. I couldn't wait to reach the end of the most miserable winter I had ever experienced. The village of Bolshoie Never, a scattering of wooden shacks at the end of the M56, marked the end of my southward journeying. From here, I would turn west and continue in a straight line to Moscow.

Called by some the Trans-Siberian Highway, the road I had reached runs all the way from Vladivostok to Moscow. Unfortunately, the highway has never been completed, and 800 kilometres remains under construction. Large parts of it are a bouldery road bed that would make the M56 seem like an auto-bahn. Regardless of the road conditions ahead, the snow pack had significantly decreased, and I could see large patches of open ground. Recently the snow had been slushy enough to ooze through the floor of my tent, saturating my sleeping bag, and dampening my spirits and health. Now there might be some respite.

Months of physical exertion had taken their toll on my body. I had lost a significant amount of weight and felt perpetually tired. My joints and muscles begged for a bit of rest.

After one day on the Trans-Siberian, I took a rest day beside the first flowing stream I had seen since the previous fall. The late-April sun warmed my tired body. I spent the day washing the mud off my bicycle and panniers, cleaning my underwear, making repairs, and drying all my wet gear in the branches of a willow tree.

My course of travel now would never stray far from the famous Trans-Siberian railway. I could hear the reassuring rumble of a train following one of the world's most exotic railway lines only a few hundred metres from my tent. In the coming days, the sound of the trains both pacified me and filled me with envy. After I'd been travelling so long through a frozen, empty landscape, the Trans-Siberian seemed a link to the outside world from which I felt so removed. At the same time, the effortless pace of the electric-powered trains mocked my own two-legged efforts. At times, when the trains passed close, I could discern passengers peering out from the dining car as they dug into their meals. They reminded me of underwater explorers viewing the crushing ocean depths from the safety of a submersible.

After my relaxing day beside the stream, I returned to the road feeling refreshed. My flu symptoms had improved, and the renewed cleanliness of my gear buoyed my spirits. The road was rougher than ever, and I couldn't pedal much more than 10 kilometres each hour. After 30 kilometres of struggle, during a routine check of my load, I found that my tent had fallen off. I turned around and cycled three hours back to my previous campsite looking for my portable home. Nothing.

A motorist must have picked up the tent from the road. I was devastated. Not only had I wasted six hours of time, but I still had 1,000 kilometres—nine days if all went well—to travel on these wretched roads to reach the city of Chita, the first place I'd be able to buy a new tent. My spell of sunshine broke, and sleet was being driven horizontally across the road by a strong south wind. I cycled glumly onwards, and no longer looked forward to the evening as I normally would. Before, after a gruelling day of cycling, I would enjoy snuggling inside my tent, an oasis in which to eat, write, and sleep.

Setting up camp was now simpler, at least. That evening, I unrolled my damp sleeping bag behind a rock and listlessly lay in it while snow gathered on my face. The following day, my cough worsened, and I worried about my prospects for the next nine days.

The next night, I discovered an abandoned factory, another of Stalin's money-losing outposts. I walked through a gaping hole in the brick wall and unrolled my sleeping bag beside what looked like a 12-metre-high steel cauldron. Throughout the night, the smell of shit permeated the air. In the morning, I discovered some other vagrant had placed a cracked porcelain toilet bowl as a place to relieve himself—right beside the cauldron. I missed my tent.

Periodically, I would pass construction crews on the road working on the seemingly endless task of transforming the strip of dirt and rocks into something suitable for traffic. Although the road was too rough for transport trucks, a steady stream of late-model Japanese cars nevertheless flowed westward, bumping and banging over the boulders. Entrepreneurs would fly out to Vladivostok from Moscow, Novosibirsk, Krasnoyarsk, and other large Russian centres to purchase cheap second-hand vehicles from neighbouring Japan. Then they would wrap these cars in cardboard and tape to protect them from the brutal conditions of the road and drive them home to fetch top dollar. A heavily used Japanese car was far more reliable than a new Russian Lada or Volga. Many of the drivers, wishing to maximize their profits, would tow a second car. Others would drive Japanese flatbed trucks with a car on the back and another in tow. Another popular but extremely precarious combination involved a large flatbed truck carrying a smaller flatbed truck, which itself was carrying a sedan along with a sedan in tow. Many of these vehicles had smashed windows or ripped-out exhaust systems from being forced along such awful roads.

I rejoiced at finding a large scrap of polyurethane plastic in an abandoned road-building camp. This castoff would be my new home. In the evenings, I would remove the panniers from my bicycle, turn the bike upside down and use it as a frame to support the plastic. With rocks to hold down the corners and strategically placed sticks, I was able to create a reasonable shelter to protect me from the still-falling snow.

Three hundred kilometres from the city of Chita, I came to a fork in the road. I was unsure which way to go. I flagged down a passing motorist, who informed me they both went the same direction but the left track was better. At first, the road of packed dirt offered good cycling conditions. It went over grazing land and was nothing more than a track created from the tires of cars that wanted a reprieve from the torture of the main road under construction.

However, as I pedalled past herds of cows and sheep tended by men on horseback, the weather began to deteriorate, and it wasn't long before 60-kilometre-per-hour winds and horizontal sleet blasted across the land. The packed dirt under my wheels transformed into an intensely sticky mud that adhered to my knobby tires and caused them to grow, like a snowball rolled down a hill. Eventually my back wheel stopped turning as the thick mud rubbed against the frame. Ten minutes of scraping gave me a five-metre reprieve. Useless.

I tried pushing my heavily loaded bike, but the friction of the locked wheel against the ground was too much. I dropped my bike in dismay, puzzling what to do next. My frustration with the mud had been so great that I hadn't put on my foul-weather gear. Now I was soaked through and shivering. Too late, I put on my raingear and set off across the grassland without my bike to discover how far the adjacent road bed was. It turned out to be two kilometres away, and I dejectedly walked back to my bike and endeavoured to carry all 60 kilograms of it back to the main road across the plain.

Two hours later—exhausted, soaking, and cold—I was back on the road of boulders. The wind shrieked with such force that I had to walk my bicycle as the precipitation switched between rain and snow. I shivered profusely and knew that the tattered plastic would blow away in this treeless region if I tried to erect a shelter. I had no choice but to continue down the road. It had been hours since I had last seen a vehicle.

As evening light began to fade, a farmhouse materialized in the emptiness, the only object that gave any perspective in my two-kilometre visibility. I pushed my bike down the rutted track to the front of the large wooden building and was greeted by a young man bringing in firewood. Through gestures and sporadic words of Russian, I tried to explain my predicament and asked if I could stay the night. The gentle, quiet man seemed to understand my shivering much more clearly and gestured for me to follow him inside.

The abode was divided into two homes, with a room separating the two where dirty boots and jackets could be removed.

The women lived in one side and the men in the other, which I was led into. Instant warmth from a coal and wood fire greeted me, and a second man waved a hand in greeting. Tea bubbled on the stove. A partial dividing wall separated the sleeping area, which housed four single beds.

The man sitting down had an air of authority and looked of Mongolian ancestry. Prayer flags and statues of Buddha adorned the wooden walls. The younger man introduced himself as Tolya and the older fellow was Constantine. They poured a mug of hot, milky tea for me and some beef was placed in a pan. As the scent of sizzling meat permeated the house, Constantine beckoned me outside to the sauna. A pot-bellied woodstove had heated the wooden structure to an inferno. Bliss.

In the morning, Constantine showed me around the remote farm. It was a leftover collective project from Soviet times. I couldn't ascertain whether Constantine now owned the farm, but he was certainly in charge. About eight people lived in the farmhouse commune style, some paired up, others single. The mainstay of the ranch was 800 head of sheep, currently housed in a large barn and soon to be released for grazing once the ground turned green again. The farm also had horses, cows, and chickens. I helped Constantine milk a cow, and he chuckled as I struggled to match one fifth of his output.

I left early in the afternoon, warm, dry, and well fed, and pedalled into the still atrocious weather. Two days later, I reached a major milestone: Chita. With a population exceeding 300,000, this state capital was big enough that I knew I'd find a replacement for my lamented tent. Even more exciting than the prospect of a new home was the expectation of communicating with Julie again. The antenna connection on the satellite phone had failed completely, so I had been unable to communicate since Neryungri, two weeks earlier. Chita also marked the beginning of the paved highway. From here, all the way to Lisbon, a thin strip of asphalt stretched ahead of me. The rigours of the dirt and mud had been tough physically, psychologically, and on my bike. I was giddy knowing that they were behind me.

Busy roads, buses, trucks, and billboards dominated the scene as I passed through the outskirts of Chita. Just before entering the city, I had washed my bicycle and panniers in the water flowing through a culvert, and so the hotel receptionist reluctantly allowed me to bring my clean bike to my room on the fourth floor. The room had a TV and other amenities, yet there were still hints of the Soviet mentality that prevailed when the hotel was built. In the bathroom, a solitary chunk of soap lay by the sink, parsimoniously cut from a larger block. The scrap of toilet paper measuring from the tip of my index finger to my elbow had been torn from a "mother roll," re-rolled and placed by the toilet. These were my bathroom rations for my two-night stay.

As I settled into my new home, a knock on the door interrupted me. A man stood in the hall, bookended by two scantily clad young Russian women.

"Sex?" he enquired.

I politely declined and soon retired to my hard but comfortable bed for the night. The worst of the trip, I figured, was over.

10

SMOOTH ROADS CYCLING TO IRKUTSK

THE NEXT MORNING, I found an Internet café. I could barely contain myself at the prospect of contacting Julie again. It had been difficult being on the road, alone and with no means of sharing my experiences with someone I missed so dearly. I logged in to my email account and skimmed through a deluge of emails from Julie, as well as from Tim and Tim's family. My heart sank as I absorbed the information. None of the messages contained the warm conversation I had been hoping for. Instead it seemed a war was escalating, which I had been oblivious to while toiling through the mud, ice, and slush of eastern Siberia. My excitement about sharing my tales with Julie, and of hearing of her own news, crashed like a burning 747. I was filled with dread as I agonized over how I would deal with the latest development.

Tim and Yulya had run out of money as they travelled down the M56 highway. Tim had assumed he would find a bank machine en route. Unfortunately, none had materialized. The duo's progress had been further slowed when Tim's bicycle frame extender broke, worn down by the rough roads and heavy load. They had to stop for a welding repair in Yakutsk.

It seemed they hadn't taken weight reduction on their bicycles to heart, as one quote from Tim's May 7 article for the *Vancouver Sun* indicated: "It's difficult to keep track of Colin's well-being. The news I gather comes from drivers who spot him a few hundred kilometres ahead of us on the road. Some report his bicycle was upside down for maintenance, and others have seen him cycling at dawn. One source reported he stocked up on tools in the sunny city of Yakutsk, but discarded his heavy boots, perhaps to offset the added weight. Yulya insisted that she and I lug our boots along, and as we pitched our tent in knee-deep roadside snow in the mountains south of Yakutsk, I was quietly pleased that my feet were warm and dry. I was worried about Colin. Then came news to confirm my worst fears—he was bed-ridden with a bad case of bronchitis. I wondered if we might over-take him sooner than our scheduled meeting at Lake Baikal."

As the duo continued down the M56, their bicycles strained under the loads. Tim complained about breaking spokes, an axle, and a rapidly disintegrating frame and luggage racks. With their mechanical woes arose money problems. Tim sent Julie an email from Neryungri, the town where I'd recu-perated from the flu, asking if she could send him some funds. However, Julie was on vacation in Ontario with her family and without computer access.

When Tim didn't receive a reply within 24 hours, he sent a second, more curt letter. He described how his health was suffering because of the lack of money. He had a respiratory infection and flu—likely the same flu bug I'd picked up in Yakutsk. "The persistent hunger is less an issue than the headaches and respiratory congestion that makes it difficult to sit and type," he wrote. "Forget that my health and patience is deteriorating rapidly as we live like peasants in a dark, mouldy stagnant room; think instead of the aims of this project, and that to carry them out we need you to begin communicating and make a transfer of 10,000 rubles to the party indicated in the previous email."

Without being able to communicate with me, Julie had neither the authorization nor the means to withdraw money from my bank account. She also knew that the expedition funds generated by sponsorship had long been depleted and the cash would come from my own savings. Julie wrote to Tim and informed him that ~~he~~ she would have to wait to hear from me before lending him money from her own account. In the meantime, she offered to contact his parents, who, she imagined, could remedy the situation more quickly.

Meanwhile, throughout this correspondence, I was struggling down the Trans-Siberian Highway, proud of the tattered plastic I had found as my new home and oblivious to the rest of the world.

In a *Vancouver Sun* article, Tim described his financial predicament: "Like Russia after Perestroika, we were broke, ailing, and unsure of our allies, until Colin's fiancée, Julie Wafaei, offered some certainty. The budget I had helped generate had run dry. I hoped it had not simply been privatized."

Tim told Julie not to bother contacting his parents, as he would wait until I was in the loop. What he didn't tell Julie was that he had already been in touch with his mother, Dorothy. He had contacted her when Julie hadn't immediately answered his first email; he told her that he was starving and that Julie was ignoring him. Dorothy called Julie and gave her an earful for not sending money to her son. When Julie told her that she would have to wait for my permission, since sponsor funds were depleted, Dorothy accused her of lying and hung up.

Dorothy then sent an email to her ex-husband, Christopher Harvey, to complain about Julie's actions: "She appears not to be able to understand Tim's explanation that he is unable to access his own account because there are no bank machines," she wrote. "I think Colin would rather make a dash for Moscow, and glory, by himself now that the most dangerous part is over."

This chain of emails had commenced almost ten days before my arrival in Chita, and still, nobody had sent any money to Tim.

After reading about these unfolding events, I emailed Julie, instructing her to send the cash immediately. In a later visit to the café I received Julie's reply. She informed me that Tim's brother Crane had offered to tide Tim over. Crane told Julie he would happily mortgage his $750,000 home for his little brother if it was required. Along with his offer of financial help, he issued a threat by email and said he was advising Tim to include his perceptions of Julie's wrongdoings in his *Vancouver Sun* articles. Things were getting ugly.

IT WAS TIME FOR ME TO LEAVE CHITA and continue to Irkutsk, past the shores of Lake Baikal. I asked Julie if she could send along a budget that would clarify for Tim and his family the large amount of personal money I had paid into the expedition. As well, I sent an email to Tim's family to try to bring some peace to the table.

My purpose for exploring these remote lands was to experience exotic cultures and beautiful landscapes and to challenge myself. Suddenly, the whole experience was turning into something contentious and unsatisfying. Worst of all, I saw that Julie was being drawn into a conflict that was none of her doing. She had in fact volunteered more than 30 hours a week to complete expedition-related tasks that benefited both Tim and me.

I hoped the outrage from the Harvey clan was simply a case of miscommunication. In my letter, I tried to convey the entire story as precisely as possible.

> Dear Tim and family,
> I have just arrived in the city of Chita and it has
> been brought to my attention by Julie that all hell

has broken loose while I've been cycling the roads of Siberia. Crane and Dorothy have made threats to go to the press and have called me "selfish" and a "jerk." They have also labelled my fiancée, Julie, a liar.

I find all this hurtful and shocking, and am bewildered as to how such benign actions on my part have led to the wielding of swords and the start of a hate campaign towards me. Please allow me to explain the events from my perspective, and I hope you will re-evaluate the stance you have taken.

Here's my version of events:

On the Kolyma highway Tim, Yulya, and I travelled on vastly different schedules. This created friction for both parties. At this point I felt the best solution for the team was for us to separate and travel freely at our own paces. I would travel ahead to Irkutsk where I could work on my book while waiting for Tim and Yulya.

As opposed to being a "selfish" decision, I felt for the sake of team dynamics this would be a positive change.

With regards to Tim and Yulya's safety, I felt my absence was in no way jeopardizing their health. We passed through the difficult regions and are now on the established road systems of Russia. Dozens of cars and trucks would pass every hour, populated points were frequent, and the local people were generous and would always be happy to lend a helping hand if needed. The route we cycled could be compared to cycling in rural Canada.

With regards to finances, I gave two thirds of my remaining cash to Tim and Yulya to see them through to Yakutsk. This was more than fair, as travelling in pairs is always cheaper than single travel. As well, Yulya's dexterity with the Russian language will ensure that they would receive much more local hospitality. Tim assured me that, from Yakutsk, he and Yulya would be able to get by from his earnings from the *Vancouver Sun*.

So financially I felt confident that Tim and Yulya would have no problems. I was also aware that he has a loving family that could offer a hand if worst came to worst. There are plenty of towns where money can be accessed along the route.

So, I left Tim and Yulya feeling they were safe, that they had adequate funds, and that they had all that was needed for the journey ahead of them. I bade goodbye to my colleagues and continued down the roads of Siberia.

Since leaving Tim and Yulya I have had virtually no communication with the outside world, instead focusing my efforts on travelling the icy, slushy, muddy, and rocky roads of Siberia. After triumphantly reaching Chita I was absolutely shocked to hear of the chain of events that has unfolded in my absence.

Had I known of Tim's plight, I would immediately have sent him the money. Right now the most important thing is for the team to move forward as quickly as possible, to beat the hurricane season. I would be a fool to withhold money from my expedition colleagues.

Julie is completely undeserving of the names that have been directed her way. As "home-based coordinator" her role includes updating the website, uploading photos, and communicating with the media. It does NOT include playing mother for Tim. Julie was merely looking after my finances in a responsible manner, which means all money coming from my personal savings needs my OK. Julie has spent hundreds of hours helping the expedition, more than anyone else, and receives none of the glory that Tim and I receive. To be called a "liar" and other unsavoury names is not the gratitude I would have hoped for.

Secondly, there seem to be rumours circulating that I have run off with pockets of sponsors' cash. Ironically, the lion's share of the expedition budget is composed of my own personal cash and donations from my family. I have always been completely fair, treating Tim as an equal, spending my money on him and myself equally. Without this financial input the expedition would have ended a long time ago.

To me it is very hurtful to have spent so much of my own finances on Tim and to be called "selfish." This is disrespect beyond comprehension.

I am including a very rough budget that Julie compiled. It does not include the ongoing expedition expenses such as food, hotels, and the countless small items that were purchased before the expedition. At a time of greater convenience, I will be happy to provide the accurate budget and documentation. I hope this helps to dispel the myth that I am running around with bags of sponsor cash. Julie has informed me that Crane has offered to cover Tim's current cash-flow problem. Thank you, Crane. The expedition can sure use any financial help that is offered.

Good luck and see you two in Irkutsk.

I will be out of communication for the next 10 days
until reaching Irkutsk. A new antenna has been sent
out for the phone, so at that point I will be able to
communicate much more frequently and discuss any
problems you might have.

AFTER TWO NIGHTS AND ONE FULL DAY IN CHITA, I'd found a new two-
man tent and other miscellaneous items I needed. I packed my
bike in the hotel lobby and looked out at the wet falling snow.
Twenty centimetres of slush had fallen in the night. The roads
were a mess. I was tempted to stay another night in the hotel.
Instead I forced myself into what would be one of my most
depressing days in memory.

The air temperature was just below zero, so the slushy
water spraying up from my wheels froze onto the frame and
created an ice ball the size of a cantaloupe. Near my bottom
bracket the chain disappeared into a hole in the ice ball and
emerged on the far side. The depth of the slush on the road
meant I couldn't ride near its edge. Instead I had to remain in
the two ruts created by the busy traffic. Cars would slip and
slide mere inches from my bike.

I pedalled hard to escape from the treacherous city centre
and reach the quieter outskirts. A sudden hiss of air alerted
me to a deflating back tire. I remembered I'd forgotten one of
the chores on my list: to repair all of my holey tubes while in
the comfort of my hotel.

I pushed my bike into a concrete bus shelter closed on
three sides. It was a rough part of town, and veiled eyes
regarded me stonily as I lay my bike down beside a wooden
bench with a puddle of diarrhea at one end. I lit the camp stove
to dry and warm the inner tube. It took me half an hour to chip

the ice off my frame so I could remove the wheel. While patching the tube, I inadvertently dipped it into the not-quite-frozen diarrhea, which then worked its way onto my glove.

Finally, two hours later and smelling like shit, I wheeled my bike away from the sullen group waiting for the bus and back into the slush and traffic. I needed gasoline for my stove, so I pulled into a gas station, paid my 20 rubles in advance, and stuck the nozzle into the MSR bottle. The liquid, under extremely high pressure, ricocheted right back out of the bottle and doused me with gas. I then returned to my bike to find the gas station mutt eating the last of the *pryalnekes* cookies I had earlier purchased to fuel me through the day.

My mood was darker than black as I left the station, now stinking of shit *and* gas, and pedalled into 30-kilometre headwinds through slush and snow.

At least I had a tent. As the wet slop bucketed down through the evening, I set up my new simply designed dome tent and was relieved that, whatever had happened that day, one thing had worked out: it was waterproof.

Locals had told me that the 1,100-kilometre asphalt road connecting Chita to Irkutsk was in rough shape. I'd travelled some of the most abominable surfaces on the planet, so the potholed highway felt like heaven under my wheels. Cafés punctuated the route and allowed me to keep to my habit of two or sometimes three meals daily.

At the western end of a valley, three days from Chita, the ribbon of asphalt ascended a high pass where I was assaulted by winds and gusting snow. I warmed up and filled my belly in a snug café, a common site on mountain cols, before I rolled down the other side and into a watershed that held special significance for me: the Yenisey.

I heard the first tinkle of a stream paralleling the road. This water, I knew, would lead into the mighty Yenisey River, the fifth longest in the world. Beginning in central Mongolia, the Yenisey flows more than 5,500 kilometres through Siberia to the Arctic Ocean. In 2001, I had joined a team of three others to become the first adventurers to voyage the Yenisey's complete length. It was through this five-month journey that I first experienced the unassuming and undervalued beauty of Siberia.

Frequent villages and farmhouses were scattered across the valley, often favouring the fold of the neighbouring mountains for shelter. Unlike the construction in northeastern Siberia, largely concrete buildings designed by a central planner a continent away, here in the south the homes were almost all wooden and looked as though they had been built by the occupants. Considering the remoteness of the harsh land around, I was amazed at the pride people took in their icy homes. Almost all the houses had been adorned with brightly painted and often intricately carved shutters. The windows harboured crimson geraniums or tomato plants.

The Hansel-and-Gretel homes would invariably feature a cow or two loitering about with the chickens. In the villages, water was drawn from a well, with a handle and bucket—just as in the fairy tales—and here I would fetch my water too to fill my five-litre jug. Old babushkas would watch me uneasily as they led a cow to pasture or stooped under the weight of a bough over their shoulders with a bucket of water on each end. Their gaunt, dishevelled husbands more often than not would be gathered under a bridge or beside a dilapidated tractor drinking vodka.

Rutted dirt tracks led between the homes. I would bump along these trails searching for the main store. Inside a matronly woman would hover behind an abacus. All food items rested behind the counter, so I had to ask for each product individually in stumbling Russian. Villagers behind me stood back in amusement, as though enjoying the best entertainment they'd seen in months. Depending on what the often bare shelves offered, I would leave with my loot: a few wrinkled apples, Chinese noodles, and a hefty load (often the entire stock) of chocolate bars.

IT WAS NOW LATE APRIL. Although the weather was still abysmal, alternating between rain and snow, the land felt like a great creature about to come back to life. Fields were being ploughed in preparation for planting. The occasional mosquito harassed me with gentle whining—hinting at the nightmare to come.

Six days from Chita, I pitched my tent on the edge of a farmer's field that bordered a grove of pines. After a meal of Chinese noodles and a coffee, I fell asleep to the gentle murmurs of an irrigation channel.

I woke up in the night and felt something small crawling on my leg. Immediately I turned on my Petzel headlamp and confirmed my greatest fear: a tick. Although it hadn't yet bitten, it was a clear sign that tick season had begun. Southern Siberia harbours the most dangerous ticks in the world. One in ten carries a type of encephalitis that is almost always fatal to humans. Most Russians won't venture into the woods at this time of year, because the danger is so great. These parasitic creatures feed by inserting their watermelon-seed-shaped body into an incision they chew in the skin. They then remain under the skin for days, sucking blood, with just the tip of their abdomen sticking out.

After squashing the tick, I spent the next two hours searching every square inch of my small abode. I shook out my sleeping bag and clothes, did a grid-like search with my headlamp and felt carefully through my hair, armpits, and crotch—favourite haunts for ticks. Nothing.

I lay sleeplessly in my sleeping bag. From now on, I would have to take careful tick precautions. I would have to tuck my pants into my socks and my shirt into my pants, spray myself and my gear with repellent, set up camp as quickly as possible, and remain in the tent's tick-proof interior with the netting permanently closed.

I did another groin, armpit, and head check. A scab-like bump on the nape of my neck indicated the presence of another tick. I extricated him, along with a clump of hair, and waited for morning.

Several hours after breaking my tick-infested camp, I cycled along as the road carved down from a steep rise and an enormous river slid into view: the Selenga. I stopped my bike and admired the implacable brown flow winding through low, treeless mountains.

I had reached an interesting crossroads in my life. The Selenga River is the primary tributary of the Yenisey. Three years earlier, with Ben Kozel and Remy Quinter, I had followed this river from its source—a melting glacier in the Hangayn mountains of Mongolia—first by foot and then, when it became deep enough, by kayaks and whitewater rafts.

On our expedition, we were looking up from the languid flow of the river at the constantly changing panorama. Now, to look down upon that same river, after crossing half a world by muscle power alone, felt exhilarating. I laid my bike by the roadside and watched the river in a trance. I had earned this reward, and it felt good.

The road descended to the banks of the 700-metre-wide Selenga and continued towards the capital of Buryatia, Ulan-Ude, a city that boasts the world's largest bust of Lenin. The route to Irkutsk bypasses Ulan-Ude by crossing an enormous steel bridge and following the Selenga River's eastern shore. I remembered drifting under this same bridge in our yellow raft.

Today, almost three years later, I crossed that path. To celebrate, I purchased a one-litre bottle of beer brewed in Ulan-Ude, camped in a picturesque spot near the Trans-Siberian Railway track and just metres from the river, and toasted the Yenisey expedition. Coffee-coloured water swirled by in meandering eddies and boils. I fell asleep contentedly, despite the roar of passing trains every fifteen minutes. And the ticks left me alone.

TWO DAYS LATER, I descended the mountains between Lake Baikal and Irkutsk. I pedalled through villages and towns that slowly conglomerated into the outskirts of the city. Traffic became busy and, in another downpour, I struggled past giant billboards towards the city centre.

Irkutsk began as a fur-trading post in 1652 and was officially recognized as a town in 1686. This historically rich city has a population of more than half a million, and is located on the banks of the Angara River, flowing from Lake Baikal. It is situated on the Trans-Siberian Railway line and is a popular tourist destination for those wanting to explore nearby Lake Baikal.

Hundreds of stark five- to ten-storey apartment blocks ringed the city—the characteristically drab housing of the Soviet era. Irkutsk's city centre, however, was a stark contrast of traditional log and wood architecture along with sleek modern glass, steel, and concrete buildings. The quaint log apartment blocks, like country cabins on steroids, are devoid of plumbing, so the inhabitants gather their water in urns at public spigots on the streets. San Francisco–style streetcars ply the neighbourhood streets on narrow-gauge tracks.

I was pleased to be back in Irkutsk again, as I had fond memories of the city; this had been a major stop on our Yenisey expedition. Our team spent three weeks here converting an old, rotten Russian dory into something suitable to travel down the rest of the Yenisey River.

Here is where I would wait for Tim and Yulya while I spent a few weeks catching up on my writing and doing some filming. My arrival in Irkutsk felt like the beginning of a long-awaited vacation. I even looked forward to seeing Tim and Yulya again. Having spent so much time alone, I would be happy to have someone to swap stories with.

I hadn't bathed since wallowing in excrement and gasoline 11 days earlier, so I was equally ecstatic at the prospect of a shower. I entered the hotel lobby, drenched to the bone and splattered from head to toe in mud. The receptionist hesitantly gave me a room key and insisted that my dirty bike stay in the basement. The $20 room was comfortable and even boasted a colour TV, but there was no bathroom. After exploring the premises, I found a communal toilet and washbasin out in the open, but no bath or shower. I went back to the receptionist, who spoke no English, to inquire about the facilities.

"Gde douche?" I asked.

"Nyeto," she said.

I was filthy. Mud caked my face and 11 days of grime had built up, yet I had nowhere to clean myself properly. Eventually I asked for a bucket, filled it from the basin and sponge-bathed myself in my room. All the other Russian occupants in the hotel looked spotlessly clean and yet they never carried buckets of water to their chambers. It was a mystery to me. I flipped on the TV and watched an ad for the Sauna Belt, a miraculous invention that turns obese people into sex gods and goddesses.

The next day, after feasting on greasy chicken and hot cabbage wraps, I made my way to an Internet café. The proprietor greeted me warmly, although without recognition, and I felt the three years vanish since I had last visited his establishment.

First of all, I read Julie's email, which conveyed news about how things were going at home. She informed me that Iridium had been able to courier a new antenna for the phone and it was en route to Yulya's mother, here in Irkutsk. As well, Julie had been in touch with superintendent Denny Kemprud from School District 51 to let him know that soon the phone would be working again and we would be able to link Siberian students with the kids in Canada. Julie's own dreams of human-powered adventure were in poor shape. She informed me with disappointment that her rowing partner had backed out. So far they had been unable to raise any money for their proposed expedition, and Cathy felt it was too much of a risk borrowing tens of thousands of dollars for such a precarious endeavour.

I then clicked on an email from Tim. I read his words with growing dismay. He was still in Neryungri and flat broke. His brother hadn't sent any money. Tim didn't clarify why, other than to state, "I thought you would want me to ask you first. It would also make a better story if the cash came from within the team." He then claimed that the budget I had sent was flawed because it didn't include a large donation from his family. "You made various accounts (one financial, as useless because it ignored over $17,000 of financial input from my family, as if a memory, like a boat, can only be trusted if it leaks)."

I read his words slowly, thought about them for a few minutes, and made a decision. The $17,000 he claimed his family had donated were as fictitious as Monopoly money. It was time to break ties with someone who darkened my days with his lies. We still needed tens of thousands of dollars to get back home to Vancouver. We had raised no money for this upcoming leg. Most likely, I would need to borrow $50,000, or more, from my line of credit, credit cards, and who knew where else.

I couldn't stomach the thought of continuing to pay for Tim's journey while enduring abuse from him and his family. The solution was simple. It was time to make the big step. I began tapping out a reply.

> Dear Tim,
> I read your last email and find it disturbing—accusing me of dubious accounting and a selective memory. And then you add that your family has contributed $17,000 to this expedition. I am afraid this is too much.
> As far as I have been informed, the following (approximately) are the only financial transactions between you and your family that could be construed as being somewhat related to the expedition:
>
>   - A gift of a PDA for YOU from Crane
>   - A gift of a digital camera from your father
>   - $1,500 from your mother to buy yourself camera gear
>   - $1,500 Christmas cash from your father
>   - Your father consolidated your loans—a collection of debts including a loan owed to your mother covering your living costs in Central America, credit cards defaulted on, and your cost of living in Vancouver. You are still liable for this debt.
>
> How one can turn the above into a $17,000 donation and then accuse me of dubious accounting is beyond me. The accounting I sent through included actual cash donated to the expedition to keep it running or to buy essential expedition equipment that

would enable BOTH of us to move forward. It is not precise because I don't have the receipts in front of me, nor does it include all the costs, just the large ones on memory file. The actual money spent is in the sixties (none of this includes living costs or expedition "office" costs).

Below I am listing the facts:

A) Almost half of the cash required to move this expedition ahead has been contributed by me and my family. You can deny this all you want but it is fact. I have receipts of every item and service purchased, before leaving Canada, and bank records of all withdrawals along the expedition route.

B) Despite the fact that I am paying for half this trip, I am receiving nothing but flak from your brother and mother. This comment from Crane sums up how low he will stoop: "I told Tim that the reason the reality TV show Survivor is so popular is certainly not for the plot, but because of the dramas that unfold between the people. It's a sad reflection on society that people are captivated by this, but that's reality and it has made Mark Burnett (the founder of the show) almost a household name. Tim has a huge following of Vancouver Sun readers and I told him that they would love to read about him having to sell his thermos for cash as he was running a high fever and how an email to the expedition organizer went unanswered for five days as he felt his body shutting down, starved for food." We can all interpret things the way we want.

Your email was unanswered for TWO days (amazing how quickly the truth becomes distorted with you lot) because Julie was on vacation in Ontario and I was slogging through driving snow, weeks from being on a computer.

C) Tim, you are proffering complete fiction with your claim that your family has contributed $17,000 to the expedition. If you'd claimed the value of your gifts as $4,000 or so, okay, that's one thing. But to come up with $17,000 is ludicrous. What happened to the remaining mystery $13,000? I'm surprised you didn't dip into that to resolve your current cash crisis.

D) So far we have raised absolutely no funds for the second expedition from Moscow to Vancouver. Not one penny. I am roughly estimating costs for this leg to be $50,000. Money is already required to ship the boat, start purchasing gear, etc., which I will have to take out a loan for. Depending on how much, if any, money is raised through sponsors I may have to borrow up to $50,000.

I'm afraid the camel's back has been broken. I'm taking this shit no longer. You and your mother and brother can live your delusions, but I will not be a part of it. I will not borrow huge sums to be spent on YOU and be called a jerk, selfish and to have fairy tale contributions thrown at me. It's bullshit.

Tim, I do not wish to undermine your contributions to this expedition. You are strong and talented and together we have helped each other to get to

Moscow. I have no intentions of charging ahead and stealing the glory. But from Moscow I will continue alone. Our efforts so far have been focused almost exclusively on Vancouver to Moscow and little work has been done, or funds raised, for the Moscow to Vancouver leg. Even the satellite phone contract expires shortly.

We both stand on equal footing to make it back to Vancouver from Moscow. There is nothing stopping you from continuing on your own and I will wait for you before Vancouver if you make it across the Atlantic before this upcoming hurricane season and if it is before Jason Lewis completes his circumnavigation. I would ask that you do the same if you are ahead.

Speed is essential to beat hurricane season so I will be continuing from Irkutsk in a few days. I will skirt Moscow and continue on towards Portugal. Please keep me informed of your progress and I will return on public transit so we can complete our journey into Red Square.

I will ask Julie to send through Yulya's final two months' pay. If you require her services for longer you will have to foot the bill yourself. This money should be enough to see you through to Chita where you will have access to a bank machine.

I'm sorry it's come to this. It would have been so much easier doing this second leg together instead of splitting our efforts. Your strengths and talents were a huge asset on the Vancouver to Moscow expedition. But there's a limit to how much shit I will take.

When bullies raise their fists, I choose to remove
myself from the room.

Shashliva,
Colin

I hit Send and leaned back on my chair. That was it. Like
a spouse breaking free of a troubled relationship, I suddenly
looked forward to creating plans for a new reality. I would continue solo to Moscow. There, I hoped I could find a new travel
partner. I suspected Julie might be interested, having just lost
her own expedition partner.

THE NEXT DAY, IT FINALLY FELT LIKE SPRING HAD ARRIVED. The temperatures were in the high teens, and the Russians were shedding
their fur hats and heavy clothing. I rode my bicycle 12 kilometres to Yulya's mother's house. It took almost four hours to find
the apartment block in a distant suburb. I ascended the concrete stairs to the fourth floor and looked for apartment 141. A
large brown door near the stairwell had the numbers 141 and
142 beside it; 142 was written neatly in felt pen while 141 was
scratched into the wall with a blunt object. I wondered if
Yulya had inscribed those numbers. Both apartments shared
the same entrance corridor, which had a locked door. Yulya's
mother's doorbell had wires hanging out, so I dinged the neighbour's at 142.

A blonde woman in her early 40s, hair in rollers, came to
the door. In my broken Russian and beckoning towards the
broken doorbell, I asked if she could fetch Natalia Fedchenko.
The woman informed me that Natalia was at work. If I came
back the following evening, she would be at home.

I cycled back to my hotel, disappointed by my unsuccessful mission. Almost $9,000 of my equipment was with Yulya's mother, including my summer clothes, camera film, iPod, the bicycle trailer to lug my gear across the remainder of Eurasia, bike tools and inner tubes, and the PD170 video camera. Just as important were two packages that Julie had sent me. I longed to read the letters she would have included.

The next day, I visited Trial Sports, a store that specialized in bicycles. Mine needed a new drive chain and a few minor repairs. The mechanic completed the job in an hour and a half, and I was able to find other items I needed: a bike pump, summer sleeping bag, new pedals, and a water bottle. When I went to settle the bill, the manager shook his head.

"We are proud of what you are doing," he said. "It will cost you nothing."

With a bike like new, I went back to work at the Internet café. A voice interrupted my thoughts.

"Is that your bike?" a man in his late 20s asked with an American accent.

"Yeah," I said.

"I was just admiring your Axiom stainless steel racks," he said. "I want to do some bicycle touring around here, but you can't buy racks anywhere in town."

Dave Chebalin of New England was living in Irkutsk while he studied Russian at the university. It was a great way to learn a foreign language, he explained, with a cheap price tag. Tuition and accommodation for the year added up to just over $1,000.

Dave, an outdoors enthusiast, revelled in the natural splendour surrounding Irkutsk. In the winter he would cross-country ski across the ice of Lake Baikal; in the summer he would ride his mountain bike through the mountains. Dave was interested in learning more about my long-distance cycling, so we agreed to meet the following day for a coffee.

That evening I made the long ride back to Yulya's mother's. Once again I rang the neighbour's bell. This evening, her friendly manner had vanished and her eyes wouldn't meet mine.

"Natalia is not in tonight."

"When do you think she will come back?" I asked. "I can wait."

"She is working very, very late."

Two other doors opened. Women peered from darkened interiors.

"Does anybody know when Natalia will be in?" I asked.

Eyes darted back and forth. Shoulders shrugged. I was at a loss. Natalia didn't have a phone, and I desperately needed my equipment to continue my journey. The woman was about to shut the door when a man came up the stairs with a FedEx package in his hands.

"Is Natalia Fedchenko here?" he inquired.

I peered at the package and saw that it was from Iridium. Inside, I knew, was the satellite phone antenna and batteries. Julie had told me in an email that she had spent hours on the telephone wrestling with FedEx and Russian customs to get the antenna cleared. She also had to pay an exorbitant duty with her credit card.

I pointed to the package and wished more than ever that I could speak better Russian: "Mine. Mine."

The man shook his head sympathetically. Natalia would have to receive it. According to her neighbour, she wasn't here.

The satellite phone and antenna were more important than everything else combined. It would allow me to hear Julie's voice again on the road, and we could continue our communication with School District 51. I considered snatching the package and making a dash for it. However, I didn't fancy doing hard time in a Siberian prison.

I rode home in the dark and formulated a new plan. Perhaps I was just being paranoid, but Yulya's mother seemed to be avoiding me. Had someone instructed her not to hand over my equipment? Since she had no telephone, I had no choice but to keep going back to her apartment, a two-hour bike ride. Perhaps I could persuade my new friend Dave, with his knowledge of the Russian language, to translate for me.

Julie and I had been communicating almost exclusively by email, because of the challenge and expense of long-distance phone calls. I fired off a note to ask her to redirect the Iridium package to my hotel before it disappeared into the black hole of Natalia's apartment. If I just got that antenna, I would be happy.

The next morning, I got good news from Julie. She had been in touch with FedEx and the parcel should now be delivered to my hotel. I breathed a sign of relief.

Then, as I was still at the computer, a message from Tim arrived in my inbox. It was a three-page response to my decision to end our partnership. Tim said that he felt I was making a big mistake based on misunderstandings. He justified the mysterious $17,000 contribution with the following statement: "Its ridiculous to argue about accounting, maybe you will say that because I will, one day, repay the bank, that my mother's $15,000 of generosity isn't a valid contribution. But it's my business whether I pay the bank back and when, and the fact is that the cash came to me, and thus us, as we partnered up and needed to kick off our expedition preparations, so suddenly I could access $15,000 over several months and I did—every cent of it and thus made everything possible."

So that was it. Mommy lent him money for his extravagant lifestyle in Vancouver, so Tim could avoid waiting tables in the evening. This loan in his mind had transformed into a donation that should have been included in the budget for running the expedition. His arguments certainly weren't doing anything to make me change my stance.

DAVE ARRIVED AT THE INTERNET CAFÉ and we rode back to my hotel to have some food and coffee. The FedEx package hadn't yet arrived and the workday was almost over. I was worried. Dave agreed to join me on another attempt to track down Yulya's mother. At the front door of the building, the manager stopped us.

"We are looking for Natalia Fedchenko," Dave said in smooth Russian.

The fat woman shook her head. "Natalia is away for several weeks. She is on a work vacation in Krasnoyarsk."

Dave chatted her up, trying to ascertain whether she was telling the truth, while I trotted up the stairs. The woman yelled for me to stop and then lumbered in pursuit. This time, I didn't bother dinging the neighbour's bell and instead thumped on the heavy wooden door leading into the hall separating the apartments.

A thin, hoarse voice called out: "Who is it?"

"Colin."

Silence.

Finally, the manager arrived and shooed me down the stairs.

"She says nobody is home," Dave translated.

I felt sick. I would never get my equipment back. Thank god the phone antenna had been redirected. I pondered going to the police, but I knew this approach wouldn't achieve much. I was in a foreign country and didn't speak the language. Anyway, I had to go. Dave gave the apartment manager his cellphone number and asked if Natalia could phone him when she came home.

I had hoped to leave the next day, but that was no longer

an option. I was still waiting for the phone antenna and I now had to purchase some rudimentary equipment to replace what was at Yulya's mother's.

The phone antenna still hadn't arrived, so I decided to track down the mysterious FedEx agent of Irkutsk, a man whom the mother company had no information about. I spent four hours marching through town to locate the UPS office, where I hoped they could help me locate their competition. A young man who spoke English made some enquiries for me.

"The package has been delivered," he finally said, the telephone pressed against his ear.

"Where to?" I asked.

"Natalia Fedchenko signed for it 7:30 yesterday evening."

I was devastated. The package had arrived 10 minutes after Dave and I had left the building. Now it was gone, and there was nothing I could do.

Dave offered to continue to try retrieving the gear. If successful, he promised to forward it to Moscow. He also offered a solution for sending home the videocassettes and camera film I had lugged halfway across the country in my panniers. I had tried several times to mail or courier them to Canada, but had been told each time that such material was restricted from leaving the country. I constantly worried about carrying such valuable footage through a country renowned for its crime. If the footage was destroyed or lost, our entire documentary would be ruined.

Dave had a German friend from the university whose parents were coming to visit. They were reliable people whom he felt sure could smuggle the cassettes back to Germany in their suitcases and then courier them to Canada. It sounded risky. However, the alternative—keep cycling with them—was even more dangerous. I had heard a story about a cyclist who was robbed of everything outside Moscow.

I handed the cassettes over to Dave.

I LEFT IRKUTSK THE NEXT MORNING, May 21, feeling low. Tim now had both of my video cameras, so I would have no way to film the upcoming stages of my journey. Without new gear, I was wearing my soiled and ripped winter clothes. My broken pannier rack would have to continue to bear its load held together with baling wire and duct tape. I continued to lug the satellite phone in my pannier, even though now it was dead weight.

I stopped one last time at Yulya's mother's apartment. The manager stopped me at the front door and again insisted that Natalia was still on vacation.

I stared into her eyes. "I don't believe you," I said.

My Russian was abysmal, so I pointed behind her, toward the apartment. "Natalia," I repeated.

The fat woman shrugged and returned to the building. It was time to leave Irkutsk and move on from my frustrations here.

Weeks later, Dave would write to explain that his efforts to free my gear were in vain. Natalia finally phoned him, apologized for her actions, and said that she had been ordered by Tim and Yulya not to hand over any of my equipment.

I had feared that Tim might take vindictive action. A week later, I found out that I was right. In his next article in the *Vancouver Sun,* he seemed to have taken his brother's advice and turned our expedition into an episode of the *Jerry Springer Show.* "On an expedition your partner's well-being is as valuable as your own . . . a partnership transcends expediency and applies an unbreakable code," he wrote. "Had Colin Angus broken the code?"

He even twisted my own words until I didn't recognize them: "But as for cash he [Colin] wrote, I had better ask my family—after all they had yet to contribute a thing." This was not what I had expressed, I knew—because I had saved all our email correspondence.

I had said goodbye to Tim. I had hoped to remove him from my life and my thoughts. Over the following months, I would discover that withholding my gear and defaming my character would only be the beginning of Tim's vindictive campaign. He felt he had been wronged by me.

11

SIBERIAN SOLILOQUY

A BRIGHT SUN WARMED ME as I cycled away from Irkutsk. The road was a four-lane divided highway, the first freeway I had encountered since the Coquihalla Highway back in Canada almost a year ago. I knew the quality of the roads here would soon degrade. For now, though, it felt like I'd put the rigours of Siberia behind me. Europe seemed like it might be just around the next bend.

Moscow was still a staggering 5,400 kilometres away, but the prospect of reuniting with Julie in Russia's capital buoyed my spirits and my legs. I had sent her an email asking if she would like to join the expedition from Moscow back to Canada. It seemed almost serendipitous that both of our expeditions were foundering simultaneously, and our joining forces seemed to be an obvious solution. Julie wrote back immediately saying yes. It was a massive undertaking—a bike ride across two continents and a 10,000-kilometre row across the Atlantic Ocean. Few people would be able to cope with the mental and physical challenges of such a journey. But I was confident that if anyone could, it was my wife-to-be.

As I cycled along the smooth pavement, I thought about the last few weeks. I felt confident I had made the right decision in changing expedition partners. The qualities I loved about Julie were her determination, her strength, and her ability to solve problems in a rational and intelligent manner.

These strengths would help us travel halfway around the planet. As well, we have a relationship devoid of jealousy and competitiveness; each of us wants the other to succeed in all situations. These two traits are fundamental to the survival, let alone the success, of any team.

The outskirts of Irkutsk disappeared, and soon boreal forest bordered the road, interspersed with small industrial towns and villages. The road followed the broad Angara Valley. The mountains to the south lay beyond the horizon and out of sight.

I quenched my thirst at a *kvas* kiosk. These drink stands are usually located in or near urban centres. A yellow trailer would support a metal drum, like a fuel barrel or a container for hazardous chemicals. In fact, the drum housed *kvas,* a deliciously refreshing drink that had quickly become my favourite beverage on the journey. Made by fermenting rye, *kvas* tastes vaguely like a sweet non-alcoholic beer. Russians claim that it is good for one's health and aids digestion.

For 10 rubles, the babushka handed me a half-litre cup of goodness. The last time I had been in Russia, the *kvas* vendors all supplied reusable glass cups. Consumerism had infiltrated the country since then, and now the drinks were doled out in disposable plastic containers that litter the highway shoulders.

Back on the road, my mind returned to the steps ahead to get back to Vancouver. Julie and I would need to raise more funds, buy an ocean rowboat and make it seaworthy, and work out the cycling logistics for the remaining 20,000 kilometres overland. It was daunting to say the least. How could I manage all this organization from the road, while exhausted and with limited means of communication with the world beyond my bicycle? Internet connections were virtually impossible to find along the edges of the highways. Using public telephones was an extremely complicated, expensive, and often frustrating exercise. I had faith that Julie would be able to take care of most of the business while I focused on closing the distance to Moscow; otherwise our Atlantic departure would be in jeopardy. If we didn't leave from Portugal in our rowboat within the next four months, we risked running into the stormy season off the European coast. Meanwhile, 11,000 kilometres of road remained between me and the port city of Lisbon.

THE SUN BAKED THE BACK OF MY NECK and the asphalt skimmed by at a steady 18 kilometres an hour. Occasionally, my expedition worries were interrupted by Russians who stopped their vehicles to extend gifts of chocolate bars or fruit and request a quick photo session. They would hand addresses to me and insist that a home awaited me should I ever pass through their city. The generosity I encountered in this sparsely populated land did wonders to heal my frayed nerves. In roadside diners, patrons and proprietors would gather to hear my tales of cycling through their country. I would often wolf down meals of barbecued chicken, buckwheat, salad, and tea, and then be told it was all on the house.

The landscape flattened out, and the days passed in a blur of taiga and occasional settlements. Two hundred kilometres of road, still under construction, proved to be achingly devoid of asphalt, but the rest was decently paved. I never had the chance to examine the meteorological records for this part of Siberia. I had imagined it would be a dry climate, due to the flatness of the terrain and distance from any oceans or large water bodies. I was wrong. Two days after leaving Irkutsk, the rain fell in sheets, soaking through my raingear and flooding the land around me. Strong west winds always accompanied these torrents, sometimes reaching speeds of 60 kilometres per hour. Three times, the winds blew so strongly that I had to dismount and push my bicycle. I would take long breaks from the weather in roadside diners and try to forget about the miserable conditions outside.

Eight hundred kilometres from Irkutsk, Krasnoyarsk is a stark industrial city situated on the Little Yenisey River, a major tributary into the Yenisey River itself. With almost a million inhabitants, Krasnoyarsk is Siberia's third largest city. During Soviet times it was a closed city, and nearby were several underground uranium processing facilities. Its present vibrant economy includes aluminum production and forestry. Its position at the junction of the navigable Yenisey River and the Trans-Siberian Railway offers economical shipping for resource extraction.

I had originally planned to take a rest day in Krasnoyarsk. But as I approached the city's grey skyline, arranged against the horizon like a frown of broken teeth, memories from a previous visit there made me reconsider even such a brief stay.

In September 2001, I'd completed the first descent of the Yenisey River and said goodbye to my expedition mates in Dudinka, near the river's mouth. From Dudinka I flew by Air Krasnoyarsk to its mother city. In Krasnoyarsk, I would wait for the train to Beijing, from where I would fly home at last to Canada. The train didn't leave until the next morning, so to save money, I decided to stay the night in the station rather than book a hotel room I wouldn't need for long. As is typical in Russia, the station was a magnificent piece of architecture.

It was also where homeless people, drawn to its comfortable opulence, could turn a steel chair or bench into a bed for the night. In Russia, the homeless are less prominent than on North American or Western European streets. However, the ones who do exist are truly desperate, as there are few soup kitchens and almost no social assistance in the post-Communist state.

A thin man in his mid-40s sat down beside me and placed a duffel bag between his feet. At first I thought he was waiting for a train, as he was well dressed in a wool sweater and tweed pants. However, his slightly rough edge—several days of facial growth and tousled, greasy hair—hinted that perhaps he had been away from home for more than just a few days in the train.

"Are you from America?" he asked in good English.

"North America. I'm Canadian," I replied.

"My name is Anatoly," he said, extending a hand. "I'm from Krasnoyarsk, and the only travelling I have ever done is up here."

Anatoly tapped his head and explained that he had dreamed of exploring Africa and the United States. But during Soviet times, travelling abroad was impossible for political reasons. Now it was poverty that prevented him from travelling.

He told me how he had lost his job teaching in a high school because of a conflict with his superiors. His wife then kicked him out, and his family, with whom he'd been locked in a long-simmering feud, refused to take him back. Unable to find another job, he now lived at the train station and did whatever he could to survive.

"Life isn't easy any more," Anatoly reflected glumly. "My dreams used to be about exploring. Now I just yearn for the basic comforts of my own home and enough food to eat."

He explained matter-of-factly that his main income came from killing people for the Russian mafia. He would be given a name, address, photograph, and $100. Within a few days, a human life would vanish. My train-station companion showed no remorse. He had to do what it took to survive.

Perhaps he was lying to impress or scare me. All the same, the cold killer he described is a real part of the new Russia. Easy death has always featured in the nation's troubled history; the Siberian gulags and their ruthless overlords have been replaced by hit men for hire, who do the deed at point-blank in broad daylight. Russian newspapers barely have enough space to list the numerous contract killings of influential or wealthy people, let alone the anonymous underlings gunned down in tit-for-tat chess moves by rival mob bosses.

The problem is nationwide, but Krasnoyarsk is especially well known for its mafia-controlled business. My conversation with the man in the railway station made this criminal underworld seem all the more real.

Approaching the giant city of belching smokestacks, loading docks, freight train terminals, and clusters of apartment blocks, I decided to give it a miss this trip. Instead, I cycled the labyrinth of roads towards the city outskirts.

I wasn't worried about mafia. They would have little interest in stealing the soiled gear of a long-distance cyclist. But I did worry about letting my guard down in a city where a life is valued at $100. I had that much money in my wallet alone. The cold eyes watching me from darkened alleys as I passed likely knew this, too.

The city sprawled for miles. Darkness descended while I was still within Krasnoyarsk's seedy limits. Now the architecture was composed exclusively of the concrete eight-storey apartments serviced by enormous pipes that ran above ground. I turned into a large vacant lot of tall grass, meandering pipes, and litter. I was exhausted and needed to pitch camp somewhere, anywhere. But then I noticed a group of people huddled around a fire not too far off and so I decided to move on. A few kilometres farther, I found a plot of land where nearby apartment residents grew vegetables. Here, I erected my tent behind a four-metre-high steel pipe that transported the city's heating water, distinguishable by the layers of insulation covering it. Relatively hidden, I cooked a quick meal and fell asleep.

I broke camp as fingers of sunlight slanted through the gaps of nearby apartment blocks. Similar to Irkutsk, the highway immediately outside of Krasnoyarsk was in excellent shape, and I made good time on a four-lane freeway. As I cycled under an overpass, I heard a wild racket coming from above. I've always been wary of hooligans dropping rocks or cinder blocks onto passing traffic, so I glanced upwards as I emerged from the cover of the overpass, prepared to dodge any fast-falling missiles. But I wasn't prepared for what I actually saw.

Two slim men in suits, each gripping a wrist, dangled a third man—balding, plump, not nearly as well dressed—over the side of the 15-metre-high overpass. The victim made the most horrible sobbing, screeching sounds—like an animal caught in a trap—as he squirmed fruitlessly. It seemed clear to both of us what fate his two antagonists intended for him. I pedalled slowly, unsure what to do, unsure what I *could* do. I felt sick. I couldn't believe I was about to witness this man's last desperate moments, before he was hurled with a splat in front of an oncoming car.

Finally, the two men in suits pulled their terrified victim back from the precipice and tossed him roughly into the back seat of a shiny car. They quickly drove off. I considered going to the police, but I knew it would be a fruitless exercise. I couldn't describe any of the men, or even the car, with accuracy. And likely nobody would speak any English. I could only hope the thugs had finished their scare tactic and hadn't instead gone to a more discreet location to finish the job.

KRASNOYARSK SOON DISAPPEARED BEHIND ME, though memories of the grim city would take far longer to fade. It wasn't long, however, before another disturbing sight lurched into view. A transport truck had slammed into two cows. The bloody animals now lay on the road, their eyes frozen open in terror. The damage inflicted upon flesh and bone by the transport was tremendous. The truck, with a dented fender and broken headlight, was parked on the side of the road, where the driver haggled with the farmer over compensation.

Hundreds of such trucks rushed past me every day. On the narrow roads, they were my greatest fear. It was too easy for my imagination to transform these crushed and bleeding bovines into a human body—my own. Just two days later, my premonition nearly came true.

The road from Krasnoyarsk to Novosibirsk is fairly flat. It passes over low plateau before descending gradually to the plains on which the capital of Siberia is situated. The unlovely scenery alternates between vast fields of grain and great stretches of taiga. Enormous cities appear where one would imagine little villages looking at the dots on the map, with names like Kunsk and Kemerova.

On May 30, still 500 kilometres from Novosibirsk, I continued through the relentless rain that had been chasing me westwards nearly every day. A rattle from the far side of the road drew my attention to another passing big rig. Suddenly, out of my control, my bicycle swung 90 degrees to my line of travel. No longer on its saddle, I sailed through the air before skidding to a halt across the pavement.

I checked myself, but seemed no worse for wear beyond my bleeding, skinned hands. What had happened? I looked around and discovered that a 10-kilogram chunk of leaf spring, part of a truck's suspension system, had struck my front pannier. The steel chunk of road detritus must have popped out from under the truck's wheels like a bar of soap and rocketed towards me. Inside the pannier, my SLR camera had been shattered, the battery ripped out of the Iridium phone, and even the charging cord for the phone had been severed. Still, I considered myself lucky. If that random projectile had caught me on the leg or head, road rash would have been the least of my concerns.

The rains continued for the next four days, only letting up as I neared Novosibirsk. Again, I had planned on taking a one-day rest in this city of 1.5 million. However, the weather was finally shifting for the better, and I couldn't resist the prospect of cycling under more pleasant skies for a change. I decided to push on. I'd put 1,800 kilometres on my odometer since Irkutsk. Moscow felt more of a reality, only 3,600 kilometres beyond the horizon.

I passed through the city quickly. From my vantage on the major throughways I saw little more than concrete and cars—a bleak urban Anywhere. Five hours later, after traversing the largest city I'd yet encountered, I stopped in a restaurant nestled by a forest to celebrate this fact.

A tall man entered the establishment and smiled. His eyes darted over the patrons before resting on me.

"Where are you cycling to?" he asked in fluent English.

"Moscow," I replied. The man pulled up a chair, and I outlined my journey for him.

"And you're going down this road?" he asked.

I nodded. He explained I must have made a wrong turn in the city—four hours back. "This road leads straight down to Kazakhstan," he said.

I felt deflated. It was now late evening and I would have to venture back through Novosibirsk to get on the main road. It would be morning before I could find an area suitable to camp.

The man introduced himself as Alexei and laughed warmly. "Come and stay at my place tonight," he insisted. "I live right along the route you will be going. You can have a nice hot bath and we have a washing machine to clean all your dirty clothes."

I relished the thought of such comfort and accepted gratefully. The last shower I'd had was more than a month ago, in

Chita. Since then, the bucket bathing I had done in Irkutsk barely scratched the surface of the grime that covered my body.

A friend was coming to pick Alexei up, and he suggested we take the ride together. I declined and explained that my journey had to be done entirely by human power. However, I did accept his offer to ferry my heavy panniers. Our brief conversation had provided clues that Alexei was someone who could be trusted. Shortly after, his acquaintance arrived, and we loaded my bags into the trunk of his Toyota Corolla. The duo then drove slowly back into the city while I gave chase on my much-lightened bicycle.

An hour later, I was cocooned within the two-bedroom apartment of Alexei and his wife, Lena. Typical of Russian homes, the interior harboured a jungle of potted plants and was comfortably furnished. Lena greeted me warmly in similarly fluent English. She began readying a hot meal while Alexei drew the bath.

"Please use as much water as you want," he told me. "I don't know how things are in Canada, but I remember in Europe everyone had showers lasting milliseconds. Here in Siberia, as you probably noticed while cycling, we have lots of water. Too much water! And it is free for us, including hot water."

After a one-hour soak, I drained the brown water, finished off with a shower, and emerged cleaner than a Persian princess. Alexei handed me a crisp set of clothes to wear while my own grimy rags were being throttled in the washing machine.

Alexei was a warm soul whose ever-present laughter and smile conveyed his laid-back attitude to life. His eyes twinkled as he explained his own travels. Alexei had spent several years hitchhiking through Europe. During this time, he obtained his captain's licence in England, and he had crewed on a Russian boat that sailed through the Mediterranean. Now anchored back in Novosibirsk, he fulfilled his passion for sailing by crewing on local racing yachts that plied the hydro-electric reservoir during the two ice-free months of the year.

Alexei and Lena, both in their mid-30s, were in excellent health and shunned the too-common Russian fondness for heavy smoking and drinking. They enjoyed a diet of organic fruits and vegetables, and kept fit by hiking in the nearby Altai Mountains. They were both university educated, but found it hard to obtain good work. Alexei worked as a paint salesman. Lena had recently started a pet-grooming business.

I settled down to a meal of homemade borscht, salad fresh from the family dacha, and a raspberry milkshake. I asked my gracious hosts whether life was improving since the fall of communism.

"Not at all," admitted Alexei. "The rich are getting richer and the poor, which is 95 per cent of the population, are staying the same. There is far too much corruption for any of the new wealth to reach the hard-working folk. At least communism looked after everyone. Although it is a flawed system, and I don't agree with its principles, the fact of the matter is people were better off."

Alexei couldn't help but notice as I glanced around at their comfortable, yet simple, apartment.

"Yes, people get by," he replied before I could even ask my next question. "But that is still off the back of communism. These apartments were given to us free when the empire collapsed. The infrastructure in place to deliver our hot water and electricity was built by the Soviets. Even much of our food comes from our dacha plots, dished out by the old government. Most families get by on $100 to $400 a month."

"But," continued Alexei ominously, "this, of course, can't continue. Children are growing up and will never be able to afford a new home. Already many two-bedroom apartments house two or three families."

Alexei and Lena's generosity was typical of Russians. I felt guilty that they were probably spending half a month's wages to make a stranger's visit special. Lena disappeared to the market and returned with armfuls of tasty foods. They also purchased a card for the computer so I could access the Internet. They refused to let me contribute a penny.

The next morning, Alexei and Lena, along with some of their friends, took me on a tour of the city. They pointed out a monument marking the geographical centre of the Soviet Union, and the world's largest technical library. Afterwards, we visited the zoo, home to the world's only "liger" cub—a cross between a lion and a tiger. During our tour, Alexei stopped at a specialty map store and bought me a gift that I would soon find to be worth its weight in gold: two road atlases to guide me through the maze of asphalt ahead.

Later, Alexei tried to solve my problem with the satellite phone by finding a replacement antenna. In this city of 1.5 million, though, we couldn't track down a single satellite phone antenna. Nevertheless, Alexei talked to a technician who felt confident he could fix the problem. We dropped the phone off, and I prayed for success.

In the evening, I caught up with my email and learned that Tim was in Irkutsk. He had made a roundabout trip there by train from the region of the BAM railway. His Xtracycle had broken to pieces, and he had made the 4,000-kilometre round trip to pick up my BOB trailer from Yulya's mother. The BOB company had given us three bicycle trailers to use in Russia. However, Tim had elected not to have his BOB sent over because he felt the Xtracycle cargo hauler would be up for the job. As I continued through Russia with broken bicycle racks, wishing I had my trailer, Tim only had to fetch my cargo hauler from Natalia's in Irkutsk. I read this news in an email from Dave, the friend I had made in Irkutsk, who had been in communication with Natalia.

Later, the technician Alexei had commissioned to fix the phone delivered another piece of bad news: he was unable to repair it. In fact, in his futile attempt, he had damaged the antenna receptacle and rendered the phone useless, even if I did find a replacement antenna.

Julie posted an update on my progress on the website. The update stated I would be leaving Novosibirsk the following day. I felt apprehensive about disclosing my precise location, in case the announcement motivated criminals to track me down. I quickly realized I was being paranoid. Really, what were the odds that Siberian thugs would be reading a Canadian-based expedition website in search of an easy mark?

AFTER TWO ENJOYABLE NIGHTS and a day in Novosibirsk, I said good-bye to my new friends. My bicycle was overloaded with fresh produce, dried fruit, and other treats they'd given me for the coming days of my trip. Just before my departure, Alexei placed a yellow cord around my neck.

"It has been blessed by a lama and will protect you on the journey ahead," he said.

With a wave goodbye, I teetered through the parking lot and was off. For the next 2,000 kilometres, all the way to the Ural Mountains, the road would be flat. I would be able to clock my fastest speeds yet. A rare tailwind boosted my speed as I zipped across the monotonous lands of taiga, grain fields, and occasional marsh. On my second day, after logging a solid 172 kilometres, I camped in a farmer's field, under the shade of some birch trees, just within sight of the road. The green of my tent blended into the land.

The temperature was about 28 degrees, and I kept the mosquito netting closed. Hordes of mosquitoes, blackflies, and horseflies buzzed hungrily outside. Safely inside the tent, I sat naked, sweated profusely, and wrote in my journal.

A sudden thump against the outside of the tent jolted me from my thoughts.

Occasionally, curious locals would tug on my tent strings or tap on the tent to get my attention. However, there was something about the force of this blow that conveyed a more urgent tone. I glanced at the tent-wall pocket to make sure my knife was within easy reach. So far, my experiences with Russians had been positive. But I had heard the rumours, knew the statistics and remembered the poor guy being dangled from the overpass.

Then a voice in accentless English rang loudly: "Colin, get your ass out here!"

I pulled on my underwear and climbed out of the tent. Outside, Tim stood with Yulya by his side. About 30 metres off, two stocky men wearing sunglasses watched me silently.

"You didn't do a very good job of hiding your campsite from the road, did you?" Tim said.

"I didn't think I had anything to worry about," I said. "I guess I was wrong."

I tried to remain calm. I could see a car parked by the roadside, so Tim and his posse had driven 2,100 kilometres from Irkutsk to locate me at this remote roadside campsite in central Siberia. So what were his intentions?

"I want to discuss some business with you, mainly regarding the videocassettes," Tim said. "Earlier you mentioned that you owned the video camera."

I nodded. "That's right," I told him. "I purchased both cameras on my credit card, and the money to purchase them came from my own funds, some of which was a gift from my brother."

"Exactly," said Tim, "and earlier in the budget you provided, you included this money as a donation to the expedition—which embodies you and me."

Colin cycling along the Cassiar Highway in northern B.C. on a heavily loaded bike.

Tim rowing the *Bering Charger*—the sailboat he and Colin converted into a rowboat—down the Yukon River toward the Bering Sea.

Colin in the stern and Tim in the bow of their decrepit canoe, purchased for $200. It came with a hole the size of a grapefruit.

This photo of Tim was taken in mid-Siberia.

Yulya in the mountains shortly before reaching the village of Konergino.

A bitterly cold campsite in Siberia.

Colin in Siberia in the Fall, when the weather is still relatively warm. Eventually it got too cold for beards.

Kindergarten kids in Siberia.

The three Siberian policemen who invited Colin into their car for borscht, pilmenny, and, of course, vodka.

Colin decked out for Siberian winter travel.

A Chukchi man and his son.

Julie on her bike at the Guatemalan border.

Dorado fish drying in the sun in the mid-Atlantic.

Before and after photos. The one on the left was taken for Colin's Russian visa before the expedition started. The one on the right was taken minutes after Colin stepped from the rowboat onto land by someone from the Canadian Consulate in Costa Rica for an emergency passport.

Julie and Colin finishing the expedition in Vancouver after almost two years on the road.

I knew where this line of reasoning was going. Tim's father was a lawyer and Tim was well versed in the legalities of ownership of the footage from the camera. Generally, in situations of dispute over ownership, the footage is deemed to be the property of the producer, or the person who owns the filming equipment. Tim wanted to ensure he had a stake in the footage we'd shot so far.

In reality, the money my brother had donated was only a small portion of the total cost of the recording equipment. Tim had come onto the expedition with no filmmaking experience and no money to put into the recording equipment. Yet here he was in middle Siberia stretching legal loopholes to become an equal shareholder in the film.

"So my brother's donation is how you justify the withholding of both video cameras?" I said angrily. "How does the rest of my equipment factor in—my BOB trailer, my clothing, my packages from Julie, my iPod, and everything else?"

"Calm down," Tim said. "Yulya and I have both been extremely distraught about the fact that you've been unable to collect your belongings. You see, Yulya was merely worried that if you were allowed to collect your own things, perhaps you might steal some of her stuff in the process. In fact, the reason why we have driven all the way here is to deliver your property."

Tim nodded at a bulging nylon backpack that Yulya had set on the ground in front of her. I stepped towards the bag, but Tim held up his hand.

"One little thing we need to do before you get your stuff back. I've drawn up a contract that I would like you to sign. I'm sure you will find it reasonable. It's merely an effort to prevent any future misunderstandings between us."

Tim handed me two crisp sheets. The contract stated the PD170 video camera and the footage taken with it was jointly owned by Tim and me. Tim would continue to use the camera until Moscow, at which stage he would forfeit rights to the equipment and return it to me. After handing over the camera, he would be allowed to make copies of the cassettes.

I sighed. I was in Russia and there weren't any other options. To solve my problems through the legal system would be impossible while on the road. My choices were to sign the document and have my gear returned, or to never see it again. Purchasing a new PD170 wasn't possible, not now. At this point, I didn't have enough money to make it back to Canada, let alone purchase expensive recording equipment. If I didn't sign the contract, I would have no means of recording the second half of the expedition. I felt sick.

I read the document carefully and finally signed with a pen that Tim held towards me. He looked pleased as he slipped his copy into a plastic folder.

"Now there's one last piece of business I'd like to tend to," Tim said. "Since we both own the footage, it really doesn't matter who is safeguarding the cassettes. I would feel much more comfortable if they were stored at Yulya's mother's."

"I already informed you by email that they've been delivered back to Canada by a German couple," I said.

Tim was looking at my bike, locked to the tent without its front left pannier. I always keep this pannier, home to all my valuables, in the tent.

"I don't believe you," Tim said.

"Believe what you want. You'll have copies made when my video camera is returned."

"I wouldn't mind taking a look through your front left pannier," Tim said.

"I'm afraid not. It's private property, and without a warrant I'm not going to let you go snooping through my gear."

Tim chuckled. "Out here I don't have a warrant, but I do have two big guys with me."

The two Russian men sauntered closer.

I stepped back and allowed Tim to enter my tent. After several minutes of rustling, he emerged empty handed.

"Tim, you work so hard for film. You must get cassettes," Yulya said. "Maybe they in other bags."

Tim searched through every pannier, emptying bags, opening pots and even peering under the tent. Yulya looked crestfallen. The burly men stood emotionless.

"Well, I guess it looks like you did send them after all," said Tim. "Lucky for you."

I thanked heaven that I had entrusted the cassettes to two total strangers. I recalled one of Tim's favourite expressions: "Possession is 90 per cent of the law." I was learning quickly how true this was. If I had tried taking my own property from Yulya's mother, I would have ended up in jail. If Tim had succeeded in acquiring possession of the cassettes, it could have been years before I received them back through the legal system—if I ever did. Often in such cases, it comes down to whoever has the best lawyer.

I looked through the nylon backpack Tim had returned to me. It contained only some of my gear—used clothing from the summer before but none of the new clothing.

"Where's my BOB trailer, the new clothing, and the tools?" I asked. "And how about the little video camera since you're hijacking the big one?"

Tim shrugged. "I can't believe you're whining. We've driven over 2,000 kilometres to help you out of the bind you've gotten yourself in, and all I receive is flak. How's that for gratitude. Anyway, we need to hit the road now. These guys need to get home soon."

The quartet climbed into the shiny car and departed. Apart from the rustling of leaves above my head, a silence filled the air. The sun slipped down below the horizon, and I returned to my tent to have my evening meal.

I couldn't believe what had just happened. Did I make the right choice by signing the contract? In return, all I'd received was a pile of dirty clothes, the iPod, some film, the satellite phone antenna, and the promise that the big video camera would be returned to me in Moscow. Nothing really had changed. Tim still possessed both of my video cameras. I was still unable to document my unfolding journey. Nothing had changed for the better, that is. According to the contract I'd just signed, Tim was now a co-owner of all the footage. I wanted to scream.

I plugged the antenna into the Iridium phone and confirmed my suspicions. The attempted repair, just three days earlier in Novosibirsk, had destroyed the antenna socket. Even after all I'd gone through to get the new antenna, the phone was now useless.

It was a bitter irony that such angst and hostility had motivated Tim's 4,400-kilometre motorized round-trip journey in the midst of our zero-emissions expedition. One of the main objectives of this project was to provide positive examples in how to reduce greenhouse-gas emissions. Tim's recent actions certainly didn't abide by this concept. He would never mention this side trip in his website updates, but later he would make a point of noting how much fuel was consumed in my life-saving trip back to Canada from Anadyr (without giving the purpose of the journey). He stated on his website: "A motorized side trip isn't against the conventions of a modern expedition, but it was against the spirit of mine . . . Canadian adventurer Colin Angus flew roughly 50,000 kilometres by jet airplane during his recent 40,000-kilometre expedition (on aircraft that burned about 4 litres of gas per second)."

THE FOLLOWING MORNING, I loaded my extra gear into my panniers. My rickety racks jiggled precariously as I continued along the flat roads. The heat of late spring brought out the bugs, and enormous horseflies easily kept pace with me. These irritating creatures, the size of large wasps, numbered in the hundreds, and their drone was like a disturbed beehive.

From now on, I would make sure all my camping spots were out of view from the road. I had been getting slack in my vigilance. Tim's visit was a reminder that the success of the expedition relied on more than just doing miles on the road.

Four days after leaving Novosibirsk, I skirted the large city of Omsk via a southern route that bypassed the industrial megalopolis. Beyond Omsk, the road enters the southern end of the world's largest wetlands. The Western Siberian Lowlands—between the Yenisey River and the Ural Mountains, bordered to the north by the Arctic Ocean and stretching as far south as Kazakhstan—comprise a total area of almost 2 million square kilometres—larger than France, Spain, and Germany combined. It is a birdwatcher's paradise and a bug hater's nightmare. My time spent in the Amazon basin, in northern Canada, and in Alaska did nothing to prepare me for the bugs in the world's biggest swamp.

The 700-kilometre stretch of road within the swamp was a nightmare to build. Fill for the roadbed often had to be trucked in hundreds of kilometres. For large sections, a type of red clay, not an ideal substance, was used as the base. Such an unstable foundation results in ruts in the asphalt, sometimes 30 centimetres deep, as it sags under the weight of countless transport trucks.

The positive side of such a landscape for a bicyclist is a flatness so complete it almost feels like you're riding down a slight but perpetual slope.

In their attempts to colonize Siberia, the Soviets deemed

even this endless swamp habitable. I passed small settlements that seemed to be sinking into the mud. Brief stops in these Mudvilles were visits to the world's most depressing communities. Muck was everywhere. Babushkas waged a never-ending battle to mop muddy footprints off the floors and keep the swamps at bay. Even the roads and sidewalks, a relative sanctuary from the mud they passed over, were painted brown with a thick layer of grime.

Another element at war with the people was the bugs. Fly screens, fly paper, bug sprays, mosquito coils, and fly swatters were everywhere. Still, the insects remained, buzzing unperturbed over the corpses of their fallen comrades.

A man smoking a cigarette on the muddy steps of a store proclaimed he couldn't wait for winter. During this season, the bugs disappear and a clean coat of snow smothers the filth of the land. I chuckled. This truly was a living hell. Where else in the world are minus-40 temperatures and short days considered a period of bliss?

I would camp in the occasional forests where the land was better drained, a prisoner in my tent, as the insects waited outside. The words *hum* and *drone* don't adequately describe their collective buzzing. It is a smooth sound that resembles the roar coming from a packed hockey stadium when Wayne Gretzky scores the winning goal.

In the cool mornings, the horseflies lacked energy and could be squashed as they waited on the tent for the sun to rejuvenate their bodies. Once the air had warmed to 20 degrees or so, they were back in action and would chase me down the road, hour after hour. There were times, I'm sure, when motorists could barely see me for the cloud of insects enveloping me—a buzzing cloud with two wheels poking out the bottom.

On occasion, my cloud of insects could be put to practical purposes. A Lada passed me, and the shirtless driver honked his horn and saluted me with his middle finger. Shortly after, seeing the same man filling up with gas at a service station, I pulled up beside him and asked if the road continued on to Chelyabinsk. He scowled and shrugged, so I departed— leaving him with my day's collection of horseflies. I glanced back and saw him dive into his car.

The swamps passed in a blur of mud, bugs, depressed alcoholics, and the fastest speeds I had clocked to date. The sunshine and tailwinds allowed me to coax my overloaded mountain bike to cover 205 kilometres one day. I was averaging about 170 kilometres.

The fair weather ended at about the same time that I emerged from the wetlands. Again, I was exposed to heavy rain and headwinds. In these dismal conditions, I passed one big city after another, first Kurgan and then Chelyabinsk, a flash of concrete in a land of vast monotony.

The Ural Mountains offered a reprieve after traversing almost 4,000 kilometres of relatively flat land. These smoothly contoured hills and ridges of pine and rock offered a refreshing change in scenery. Even more appealing was the sudden disappearance of my entourage of winged vampires.

The spine of the Ural Mountains, which runs from the Arctic Ocean down along the northern border of Kazakhstan and into the Kazakh steppes, marked a political boundary as well as a major milestone I had been looking forward to. This line divides Asia and Europe, and announces the end of Siberia.

This portion of the Urals appears more hilly than mountainous. Still, the elevation losses and gains on the road felt more akin to the Himalayas. I summited three ridges before finally ascending a pass that was marked by a giant obelisk. I stopped at the sky-reaching monument and deciphered the Cyrillic letters at its base. One side said "Europe," the other "Asia." I was ecstatic. One year and 17 days after leaving Vancouver, I rolled into my third continent. At times Siberia had seemed so vast, so impenetrable, and so harsh that it was impossible to entertain the belief that I would ever reach the other side. The whole focus of the expedition had become nothing other than traversing this expanse of ice and bugs. Now it was behind me.

I freewheeled down a hill that seemed to go on forever. Down into Europe! The air blew through my shaggy hair, and the sun dappled the road through the pine trees. In two weeks, I would be in Moscow and see Julie again.

Sporadic lakes and small villages dotted the wilderness. Villagers would sell merchandise along the roadside—rubber boats, air mattresses, fishing rods, and berries picked from the adjacent forests—to tourists from the larger centres of western Russia. I purchased a bag of wild strawberries from a young woman. She wore a pair of standard university-issue sweatpants. Across the buttocks, instead of advertising the name of her college, large letters spelled out "COCK." She spoke not a word of English, and most likely was oblivious to the obscene advertisement on her backside.

At the base of the mountains, I met a Ukrainian in his 60s riding a bicycle en route to the Siberian city of Yekaterinburg. He had come all the way from Ukraine on his dilapidated 10-speed and used burlap sacks for panniers. His clothing was in line with his equipment: he wore cut-off sweatpants, tied around his waist with a rope, and a tattered shirt. The man spoke a little English and explained that he was just satisfying his wanderlust while his wife waited for him back in Ukraine.

"Just because we have no money doesn't mean we can't have adventures," he said with a wink.

Before departing, he gave me his home address and said that his wife would welcome us if Julie and I came by.

ALMOST 1,800 KILOMETRES REMAINED to Russia's capital, and it took all my emotional strength to continue my non-stop push from Novosibirsk. European Russia didn't appear much different from Siberia apart from an increase in population: rolling hills, and a checkerboard mix of agricultural land and forests. After the Urals, the weather deteriorated. Once again, I faced torrential rain, which would continue all the way to Moscow. The roads would alternate from beautiful four-lane highways with wide shoulders near the large cities to narrow rutted lanes in the country.

In some stretches, the roads were so narrow that 30 centimetres of space remained when a semi-truck's wheel ran against the centre line. When two trucks passed each other, there simply was not enough room for a cyclist. In these situations, the trucks would either slow down to my speed and wait until the adjacent lane was clear or give me a blast of the horn—that was my signal to make haste and veer into the ditch or face the consequences.

At the end of each day it seemed a marvel I was still alive. Russians are aggressive drivers, and I passed the aftermaths of numerous fatal collisions, with bodies still waiting in bags to be carted away. These accidents would leave me feeling more vulnerable than ever. Seeing the volume of vodka quaffed in the truck stops did nothing to steady my nerves.

I spent hours in my tent poring over my road atlas, trying to determine the most direct route into Moscow. A maze of highways led into Russia's capital, all interconnected by a spider's web of ring roads. I opted to cut over from the M5 to the M7 via a country road, the P239, which looked relatively straight on the map. In reality, this shortcut took me though the hilliest terrain in my memory. While the land appeared flat, the road somehow undulated over countless tiny but steep hills.

On one particularly steep hill, I stopped for a breather. Some farmers were scything their hay and loading it into a horse cart—a common sight at that time of year. Two of the men approached me, smiled and asked where I was riding to. We chatted and I asked about the scythe that one of the men carried.

"It has been in my family for 220 years," the stocky man said proudly, holding the scythe forward for me to examine.

I pointed to the blade, which had been whittled away to almost nothing from countless sharpenings.

He nodded. "We must replace the blade every twenty years, and the handle gets changed every five years."

There was nothing more to the scythe than a handle and a blade. I wondered whether they'd ever changed the two simultaneously. That was the way with Russia; their history not only lives in their books and museums but is woven into the world around them. Stories from their forefathers are tied to tangible objects such as their tools and land. If the house burns down and is rebuilt, it is the same family home it has always been, and the fire merely another story of perseverance to be added to the family history.

MOSCOW DIDN'T ANNOUNCE ITSELF with the bang I expected. Instead, its periphery seemed to arrive unnoticed, simply a conglomeration of villages that had expanded into suburbs. Even the sign marking the official city limits, 20 kilometres from Red Square, was small and set to the side.

It was here at the city-limits sign, in the pouring rain, that I dismounted from my bicycle and felt how I imagined Neil Armstrong must have felt upon bounding onto the surface of the moon. Pure elation. Thirteen months after departing from Vancouver, I had finally reached Moscow, halfway around the planet, only using my arms and legs. My elation was tinged with anxiety. This city was as far from home as I could go, and a long, potentially dangerous journey still awaited me.

I took some photographs in front of a sign with "Moskva" written in Cyrillic, but I didn't venture past it. My bitter feelings towards Tim remained, but I had promised that I would refrain from completing the Vancouver-to-Moscow leg of the expedition until he had arrived. Instead, I backtracked to the ring road around Moscow until I reached the M2, the freeway that leads to Ukraine. When Julie and I departed from Moscow, we could intersect with my path of arrival. I then flagged down a taxi-van and broke my chain of human-powered travel by motoring several hundred metres over the city limits. After unloading my bicycle from the back of the van, I resumed my ride towards the city centre.

Moscow is the sixth biggest city in the world, and I felt as if I was entering an entirely new country. Shopping malls, big-box stores, and American fast-food chains litter the suburbs. However, as I drew within a few kilometres of the centre, more traditional architecture began to dominate the scene. Russian Orthodox churches were frequent and beautiful, with their traditional onion-domed turrets.

I had no idea where I would be staying for the night, although I prayed I would be able to follow up on an offer I'd previously received. Carole Paquette, a Canadian teacher in an ex-pat school in Moscow, had read about our adventures in the media. She kindly sent an email to our team and offered accommodation in the nation's capital.

When I finally reached Carole, calling from a payphone in the pouring rain, she was as gracious a host as anyone could hope for after a 22,000-kilometre journey.

"I'm heading out to see a play at Theatre Bolshoie," Carole said. "It's right across the street from Red Square, so I can meet you there in half an hour and give you keys and directions to my flat. In one hour, you'll be soaking in the tub."

Bless her precious heart. Without Carole, I am sure I would have spent a miserable night in a park. I could be accused of arriving ill prepared in Moscow, with no reservations, local knowledge, or even a guidebook. It wasn't because of laziness or disorganization. The task of travelling around the world by human power is so enormous that tasks must be prioritized in order of importance. Organizing my arrival in Moscow had been at the bottom of the list.

Carole Paquette saved the day. The thirtyish, outdoorsy-looking Vancouverite met me at the fountain in front of the Grand Bolshoie Theatre, the only person in the area wearing raingear instead of carrying an umbrella.

Half an hour later, as she had promised, I was splashing merrily in the bathtub of a spacious two-bedroom apartment. Finally, I felt the first leg of my journey was truly over.

12

THE POWER OF TWO

I WANTED TO RELAX IN MOSCOW, but there was no time. Julie would be arriving in two days, and we would have two weeks to raise $50,000 and organize the logistics of the journey home: cycling across two continents and, in between, rowing 10,000 kilometres across the Atlantic Ocean.

The physical efforts required to complete the journey ahead would be incredible, but even more overwhelming were the logistical components. I tried not to dwell too much on the seeming impossibility of what we were attempting, and instead I focused on the small jobs on an endless to-do list. Julie had been working hard on logistics for the past few months, but she had not been able to procure any financial support. Some of the work still needing to be done included purchasing a row-boat suitable for offshore rowing; having the vessel shipped to Lisbon, where we would start our row; acquiring and shipping all the miscellaneous items we would need for the row, including a life raft, emergency beacon, and electronics; researching the ocean currents and winds to determine the most suitable route; having new bicycles transported to our destination in North America; and creating a new website.

Julie was close to completing a stylish website, and was in discussions with a couple of British men who were looking to sell a rowboat for $35,000. The men had wished to row across the Atlantic Ocean themselves but bailed out when they realized just how difficult this would be. On her way out to Moscow, Julie would make a pit stop in Scotland to examine the vessel. If it was suitable we would make an offer, pay a deposit and then continue our quest for cash and hope we could pay the rest.

We expected the unsupported trans-Atlantic row from Lisbon to Miami to take four to five months and knew we couldn't take the preparation lightly. Once we figured out where the cash would come from, we would get the boat shipped to Lisbon, where we hoped it would be waiting for us when we finished the cycling leg. If we pedalled extremely quickly across Europe, we would have maybe two weeks to ready our boat for sea—provisioning it, painting it, and making numerous repairs. If we didn't stick to this schedule, we wouldn't get away before the onset of stormy season in early October and would have to wait another year.

My one-hour soak in Carole's tub proved to be the extent of my vacation in Moscow. After I dried off, it was time to get down to work in front of the computer.

The efforts of executing our expedition so far had left little time for Tim and me to keep tabs on the progress of our competition in the round-the-world quest. Using Carole's high-speed Internet access, I surfed the websites of both Jason Lewis and Erden Eruç. Jason was making good progress and had succeeded in pedalling his boat, *Moksha,* from Australia to Indonesia; he was accompanied on this leg by the builder of the boat, Chris Tipper. Currently he was crossing Indonesia, an archipelago of islands, by kayak and bicycle, along with two other friends. He had now completed three quarters of his global circumnavigation and only needed to cross Eurasia to reach his starting point again.

Erden Eruç had not moved since we had last checked his progress, almost seven months previously. In January, he had completed his Seattle-to-Miami bike leg and returned home to Seattle. From Miami, he had planned on boarding his rowboat and rowing to Panama in Central America. However, on his website he wrote that it was getting too close to hurricane season and he would wait another year to continue this voyage.

At this point, though, hurricane season was still more than four months away. I suspected that he had actually learned that the contrary currents and winds he would face for such a row would make his route next to impossible. The Gulf Stream runs past Miami heading due north at almost two knots. Additionally, the west-pushing trade winds would drive his boat towards reef-strewn shores as he tried to row along the coast southwards. Potentially this journey could be done in a light paddle craft with little windage, such as a canoe or a kayak, but not in an unwieldy 800-kilogram rowboat. Most likely, he would have to re-evaluate his mode of travel from Miami and perhaps go by bike instead.

Halfway around the world I had slipped into second place. Erden Eruç, sipping cappuccinos in Seattle while he drew up new plans, was no longer a threat. Jason Lewis, though, was still a long way ahead. And he would soon learn of my own real plans to be first around the world using only human power. That news would likely motivate him to move faster.

It would have been best to continue the expedition without publicity. However, in order to obtain sponsorship and funding for the second half, Julie and I had to promote our circumnavigation attempt through the news media. In a few days, we would fire off a press release that revealed we would be continuing from Moscow and that I would attempt to complete the first human-powered circumnavigation.

A fourth competitor might also complicate our race around the world: Tim. Although I was now almost 5,000 kilometres ahead of him, more than 20,000 kilometres remained to Vancouver. My lead could evaporate with a minor injury, financial problems, or maritime woes in the rowboat.

I had promised Tim months earlier that, should I arrive in Vancouver first, I would wait for him: "I will wait for you before Vancouver if you make it across the Atlantic before this upcoming hurricane season and if it is before Jason Lewis completes his circumnavigation. I would ask that you do the same if you are ahead." Even though we had our differences, it would be the most sportsmanlike ending to the expedition. We had both started the expedition together, and I could see no reason why we couldn't finish together, even if we could no longer travel as a team. At the time, Tim agreed by email, "I promise to do the same should I be ahead (as I trust I will be)."

Considering Tim's actions throughout the expedition, I felt the best way to ensure that each man stick to his word was to draw up a contract. The agreement would stipulate that each of us would wait for the other prior to arriving in Vancouver, and this clause would be conditional on the slower party making it across the Atlantic before the upcoming hurricane season—that would increase our chances of finishing before Jason Lewis completed his journey. If either of us forfeited, the contract breaker would be liable for a large sum of money.

I figured Tim had no intention of carrying on past Moscow. He was riddled with debt and had acquired a bad credit rating, and it seemed unlikely his family would lend him any more money. Perhaps he could find new funding, but drumming up willing sponsors is difficult at the best of times, even more so when you're on the road. He kept insisting, in his frequent emails, that he *was* planning to continue—in a July 3 email to Julie he wrote, "Now that my agents at home have found a publisher for my book, and I've got the world's first round-the-world, and first continuous, to

shoot for, I'm surprised Colin thinks I'm heading home!!!"—
but that only made me more skeptical. He seemed to be trying too hard to convince me that he was still in the race, as
though he took pleasure in my thinking he was hot on my
heels. Just in case, though, I felt now was the time to put the
details of our earlier agreement into writing.

On July 8, I sent Tim an email proposing that we create a
contract to solidify what I had earlier proposed. "We need to
have a contract drawn (I'd prefer to have it done by a lawyer to
make sure it holds water) that states each will wait for the
other or be liable for a substantial sum. This needs to be signed
quickly. If I do not have legal confirmation of this agreement,
it will leave me with no choice, but to continue going as
quickly as possible . . . I do NOT want to go this route. I want
to spend time filming, doing media, writing, etc."

Carole arranged for a van from her school to chauffeur
me to meet Julie's early-morning flight. Clean-shaven and
adorned with a bouquet of flowers, I couldn't wait to see my
wife-to-be. It had been almost six months since I had seen
Julie. It felt like I was in a dream as I spotted her tall, slender
figure walking towards me. For such a long time, I had struggled through a world of solitude. Now, once again, I would be
part of a team—a team that I knew in my heart would survive
the hardships that lay ahead.

We embraced.

"Honey, I can't believe it. No more long days of waiting for
Colin to return," Julie said, caressing my head.

It was surreal having a figure that had been in my imagination for so many months standing in front of me again.
Despite spending many hours in the airplane, Julie looked as
fresh as if she'd just stepped out of a beauty salon. I inhaled
her lovely scent, praying I wouldn't suddenly wake up alone in
a tent. I ran my fingers through her corkscrew curls.

We walked hand in hand, like a couple infatuated, towards the exit. I was excited that we would soon be leaving this metropolis as a new team.

JULIE HAD BEEN WORKING DOUBLE TIME in Vancouver to prepare for the upcoming challenge. She had quit her full-time job to focus on creating the expedition website, researching the logistics of the ocean row, finding a boat, and drumming up sponsors to support this leg.

The latter task, to Julie's surprise, had been the most difficult. We had received reasonable support for the Vancouver-to-Moscow leg and had assumed we could count on the same for the second and even more dramatic half of the journey. Our expedition promised the chance for any organization to be associated with many exciting firsts, including the first woman to row across the Atlantic from mainland to mainland, the first man or woman to row from continental Europe to mainland North America and, of course, the first human-powered circumnavigation of the planet.

The main objective of our journey was to use the adventure to promote self-propulsion as a fun and healthy alternative to internal combustion engines and to highlight issues tied to global warming. We felt confident that a progressive company with a record of social responsibility would be happy to align itself with our endeavour. For an organization seeking positive publicity, we could promise continued coverage by Canada's largest national newspaper, CBC Radio, international magazines, and countless other outlets, including a future film and book.

Unfortunately, our search for new sponsors proved futile. A bitter cloud now hung over our expedition and my character following Tim's rant in the *Vancouver Sun*. Several reporters, looking to sensationalize the story, focused on our split and often distorted the facts.

Shortly after Julie arrived, we received word from *The Globe and Mail* that they were interested in announcing our circumnavigation attempt. Their Moscow correspondent, Graeme Smith, visited us at Carole's apartment to conduct the interview. Until now, we had been keeping our quest top secret, so we were pleased that Canada's national newspaper would be the first to announce our historic plans.

Graeme had been stricken by the Southeast Asian flu. He looked pale and haggard as he sprawled on the couch and took notes. His questions were almost exclusively about the split between Tim and me, and he asked almost nothing about the journey itself. Later that evening, we all visited the Canadian Consulate, where the Canadian ambassador, Christopher Westdall, hosted a function to celebrate our past and upcoming efforts. Also present was Canada's ambassador for climate change, Jacques Bilodeau. Graeme slumped in a chair and asked a few more questions. He felt like crap, he complained, and had only two hours until deadline.

The next morning, from coast to coast in Canada, the weekend edition of the newspaper hit mail slots and sidewalk boxes with a front-page article headlined provocatively: "Expedition Splits in Sheer Disgust." The article focused on the break-up of the team and said little about the expedition and its objectives. Worst of all, it contained factual errors, which were passed through by Tim. These were stated not as quotations but as fact.

One of these errors was a statement that Tim had learned of my intentions to travel independently of him via the press.

"That's when Mr. Angus started giving interviews to the news media, saying he would be finishing the second half of the journey without Mr. Harvey. The first his teammate heard about the change of plans was when his translator noticed an item in a local newspaper."

Tim had actually learned that I would be travelling without him in an email I sent to him, to which he replied two days later—long before I mentioned the incident to any media.

Graeme Smith's article also stated that Tim instructed Yulya's mother to withhold my gear after Julie "declined" to send him money. "Soon afterward, Mr. Harvey called ahead to a city where Mr. Angus was due to pick up some equipment, and instructed the person holding the items to avoid handing them over."

In reality these instructions were given to Yulya's mother from the moment we began travelling apart, almost one month earlier than Smith indicated. This was supported by an email Tim had sent to me June 1: "If Yulya's mom was operating under those instructions, they were sent right after Colin took off like a racehorse in Kerbume back on the road of bones." Obviously Tim had told the reporter otherwise, feeling that "not receiving money" would be perceived as more credible justification for his action.

The article gave a skewed version of what had really happened and portrayed me in a bad light.

When I emailed Graeme to ask how such a misrepresentation of the truth came to be in the face of undeniable evidence, his reply was: "Eeesh, sorry. That's what Tim told me. Have to admit, as I was pawing through my notes it was sometimes hard to figure out the 'he said, she said.'"

I didn't get it. What was the fascination with the split in our team? Why did a reporter from the most respected newspaper in Canada zero in on the personal dispute like a tabloid on the trail of a bickering celebrity couple? Tim and I were incompatible as teammates and were unable to continue together—that was it. This same scenario appears every day in the workplace, in ill-suited marriages, in sports teams, and even with old men playing chess. Why did the press so doggedly harp on an aspect of our expedition that was both common and impossible to portray with accuracy? Was two men circumnavigating the planet by rowing across oceans and trekking across frozen wastelands not enough of a story?

Roughly three quarters of long expeditions suffer major rifts in or complete splits of the team. This fact isn't surprising considering the close quarters, life-and-death decisions, and the stressful environment. I had been lucky, so far, as the dynamics on all my previous expeditions were relatively harmonious. At the beginning of this journey, I had believed that Tim and I would be able to work together to the end. I was wrong. And because of this error, reporters seeking juicy gossip would irrevocably change the rest of our expedition.

The *Globe and Mail* article was a speed bump that almost ripped out the undercarriage of our expedition. We were on the verge of closing a deal with a company that wanted to become a lead sponsor. However, after reading Graeme Smith's words, the company's representatives changed their minds. They said that they weren't looking for the kind of spotty publicity seen in the *Globe* profile. Even some of our existing gear sponsors seemed swayed by the report, and our relations with them became increasingly strained.

A flood of hate mail also arrived from Canadians who had read the story. They said we were an embarrassment to Canada or gave their own analysis of our shortcomings, with hurtful comments such as "immature representatives for Canada. Disgraceful. The press/media has portrayed the optics of this situation—this trip is not only poorly managed, but also a joke to our national credibility as idiots like you travel the road under my flag. The way you represented this country makes me sick to my stomach."

FALLOUT FROM MY SEPARATION WITH TIM looked like it would continue to haunt me. There was nothing Julie and I could do except focus on our own upcoming challenge. Regardless of how the world perceived us, we would soon be travelling through the renowned architecture, forests, vineyards, and mountains of Eastern and Western Europe. We would follow that up with an epic crossing of the Atlantic Ocean.

The biggest obstacle now was cash. Julie had put down a $5,000 deposit on the rowboat, and we needed to come up with the remaining $25,000 by August. We were going nowhere in the sponsorship quest, and we needed big bucks very soon. It looked like we would have to go into debt—we each had access to about $15,000 through lines of credit and credit cards. This was still $20,000 shy of the $50,000 we figured we'd need to get home. I doubted the banks would be able to loan us more money. Ocean rows most likely fall in the category of "high risk" investments.

It was time to ask my brother, George, for a loan. I had never borrowed money from my family before, but I was look-ing at a disintegrating dream that I had longed for so many years to realize. The entire journey was in jeopardy for lack of funds. My brother was our last hope. If he said no, we would have no choice but to quietly pack our bags and go home.

George, who worked as a successful bond broker in London, replied immediately to my request. "Of course I can lend you the money," his email said. "And don't worry about the interest."

And that was it. Julie and I would go into massive debt, and the expedition would continue. It was a daunting prospect to sink so much borrowed money into such a risky venture.

With so many pitfalls, we could easily be forced home in the red with the expedition incomplete.

I received an email from Erden Eruç congratulating us on our success of getting to Moscow and wishing us luck on our continued journey back to Vancouver. He also asked for Tim's email address so he could get in touch with him directly. I thanked Erden for his encouragement and gave him Tim's address.

A few days later, I received an email from Tim responding to my proposal to wait for each other on the outskirts of Vancouver. Surprisingly, he had suddenly changed tack and stated that he was not carrying on with his expedition. Again, though, it seemed he was trying far too hard to convince me of this change of plans. He concluded the long email with the following: "But, given that you will feel compelled to rush hard and fast if I don't sign the document, I sure as hell won't be signing it. Something about knowing you would abandon a comfortable pace for a mind frame of anxiety and paranoia tells me I'd better not sign as this will likely prove my point about achieving less if you go through life like your hair is on fire, as well as making it a more amusing expedition to follow."

As I read through Tim's email, my pulse quickened. Was Tim in fact carrying on? If this was the case, and he was not signing the contract, it seemed obvious that his intent was to beat me. Tim sent four more emails. In each, he reiterated that he was not carrying on and would be flying home from Moscow. I felt nervous. If Tim did become an additional competitor in our race around the world, what tactics might he deploy to capture the lead?

13

FROM RED SQUARE TO THE DANUBE

O N JULY 19, JULIE AND I STOOD beside our bicycles in front of Saint Basel's Cathedral in Red Square. The drizzle had momentarily stopped, and the colourful architecture defied the grey skies above. The striped onion domes seemed like an image from a fairy tale—they'd been imprinted upon my brain from a young age but seemed stored in the files of fiction rather than reality. Ivan the Terrible, after commissioning this beautiful cathedral, had the architect blinded so he could never create such a masterpiece for anyone else.

Arguably the world's most beautiful city square, it seemed a fitting spot for Julie and me to begin our 22,000-kilometre journey home. Our farewell crowd was small: a reporter and cameraman from Channel One, a Russian television station. Behind them, hundreds of tourists milled about on the cobblestones of Russia's most famous landmark.

Our tight timeline to leave the Portuguese coast made it impossible for us to remain in Moscow and await Tim's arrival so he and I could officially complete the Vancouver-to-Moscow leg together. Instead, I had asked him to keep me posted on his progress and promised to return by public transportation so we could cycle into the city together and proclaim the expedition complete. A train ran from Kiev, Ukraine, to Moscow, parallel to our route, so a return visit seemed fairly straightforward.

Julie's bike was a new Norco touring bike, much lighter than my own. We expected the roads from Moscow to Portugal to be well paved, so she shouldn't need a bike as robust as mine. My own bicycle had again been overhauled by the kind folks of Trial Sports, which also had an outlet in Moscow, and I felt confident it would be good for the remaining 5,500 kilometres to the Atlantic.

We waved goodbye to the film crew and rolled through the busy streets towards the M2 highway, which would lead all the way to Ukraine. For me, it was just another day in the saddle; for Julie, it was the beginning of a long, exciting adventure. Like the nervous apprehension that begins a new romance, our departure from Moscow represented, for Julie, an entrance into an exciting and volatile new world far removed from her office job in Vancouver. Julie's eyes were wide as she absorbed her new surroundings: busy markets, unusual Russian vehicles, tooting and waving motorists, and strange traffic signs inscribed in Cyrillic. Even the daring fashion with which Russians darted between traffic to cross the street was a contrast to the more cautious attitudes of home. Old babushkas would cross the four-lane freeway by simply traversing one lane at a time, pausing on the dividing lines and, as cars whizzed by, waiting for the next lane to clear.

Julie kept a strong pace. Upon reaching Moscow's outskirts, we pulled into a café to satisfy our appetites. I dug into the food that seemed mediocre compared to the home cooking I'd sampled at the more remote diners.

"Wow!" Julie exclaimed as she began eating a tomato, cucumber, dill, and onion salad. "This food is absolutely gourmet. When you told me you ate in cafés, I imagined coffee shops selling packaged sandwiches. This food is delicious."

The waitress fought to find room on our table as she unloaded bowls of steaming borscht, bread, barbecued skewers of chicken, steamed buckwheat and vegetables, followed by tea and crepes with sour cream.

"It only gets better," I promised, "and at four bucks a meal, it certainly fits the budget."

I was pleased that Julie was more than happy to continue the tradition of eating two meals a day in restaurants. For me, these culinary breaks had become the highlights of my cycling days. In between diners, we would keep our bodies fuelled with a regular supply of fruit, chocolate, chips, and more exotic junk foods that we would buy from small stores along the way.

After eating in the café, we entered the adjacent store to pick up some snacks. Julie was transfixed by the layout of the shop, so different from what she was used to. A plump lady in a tunic, with dyed red hair, stood behind an oversized abacus. All items sat behind the counter, and I had to ask for each thing I wanted individually. The clerk placed the products on the counter and tallied them up with firm clicks of the abacus.

It seemed like an awkward, laborious system. Still, it is light years ahead of the old three-part Soviet system. Back then, you first had to queue to tell the clerk the items you wished to purchase. She would write a list, along with the prices of each item. Then you proceeded to the cashier to pay in advance for the goods. This cashier issued you a stamp so you could return to the first clerk and finally go home with your desired goods.

We passed the point where I had entered Moscow and continued southwest along the excellent freeway. It had a wide breakdown lane that gave us plenty of room to cycle. Kilometre markers along the road's edge slipped past rhythmically as our bikes devoured the straight, fast asphalt.

WE COVERED THE 550 KILOMETRES to the Ukrainian border in five days. Our long days of cycling were often broken up by Russians stopping their cars to offer words of encouragement, almost always followed by gifts: chocolate bars, cakes, fresh apples, spring water, or cookies. One man, in a rusting Volga, excitedly told us he had seen us on TV. He took two pictures of us and then peered into his car and frowned: he had little to offer us. Finally, he handed over all that he could—a half-empty but still cold sports drink—and bade us goodbye.

After almost a year of struggling across Russia, I felt both elated and sad to reach the country's far border. Here, still on the Russian side, sat a tiny village, its name forgotten and lost in my notes. This community, in my mind, became a final symbol of the vast, proud, and compassionate nation we were about to leave. Julie and I planned on slipping past the hamlet, just off the main road, to continue to the border crossing. A vanload of geriatric men weaved along the road and intercepted us. The ringleader of the pensioners, Constantine, a bald man in his mid-70s, invited us to join his buddies for a feast in the village. He spoke German, so Julie, with her fluency in that language, could chat easily with the old man.

We followed the dilapidated van into a village composed of two concrete apartment blocks along with some smaller wooden buildings. The vehicle swerved to avoid the livestock wandering on the road. We were led to a café with several tables and chairs out back. The tables were loaded with fresh foods that the old men's wives had prepared.

Constantine informed us that all the food was homemade and homegrown (as is often the case when one has to live on a $50-per-month budget), coming from the local gardens, chickens, and cows. Rich, creamy scrambled eggs, cheeses, fresh salads, pancakes, sausages, cakes, tomatoes, and fruit compote were spread across the table. Plus, large plastic bottles of homebrew.

"Sit down," our hosts offered.

Julie and I feasted. A few shots of moonshine subdued our niggling concerns about how this region was situated squarely in the fallout path of the Chernobyl nuclear disaster. The Russians were unperturbed by this fact, and I felt my concerns petty, considering we were only eating one meal here. Undoubtedly, one super-sized, high-fat meal at the golden arches would do more harm to our health.

Constantine explained that all of the men at the table were veterans from World War II. Each week they would gather to eat, drink, and shoot the breeze. The oldest member of the club was Dmitry, a mischievous-looking man of 96 years.

"Dmitry may be getting on," Constantine said with a wink, "but he is still the best dancer in town."

Dmitry verified Constantine's claim by standing up and gyrating his arms to demonstrate his prowess. The rest of the men clapped and hooted, and then he sat down, beaming from ear to ear.

"We're all secret communists," Constantine said. "The new Russians all talk about the wonders of capitalism. But for old geezers like us it does nothing. Russia has forgotten about us, and all we can do is exist until we die. At least we have our drink, though."

He held his freshly filled glass, containing six ounces of moonshine, high in the air, and the rest of the group followed suit.

"Here's to peace and happiness throughout the world. We have two foreigners at our table and we welcome them to our circle and wish them good luck in their continued travels."

Julie and I departed the village satiated—and drunk. A rusty Lada with four young guys stopped opposite us. The driver leaned out the window. He smiled like a prankster and declared in broken English: "Watch out for Russian mafia. Me gangster—bang, bang!"

His back-seat audience roared with laughter, and the car rattled down the road towards the village.

☙

IT'S HARD TO BREAK THE ENGLISH HABIT of saying "the Ukraine." The citizens of Ukraine prefer not to have their nation referred to with a definite article. As, no doubt, would my compatriots if people began referring to our country as "the Canada."

After a straightforward border crossing, we entered Europe's second biggest country. From here, Julie and I pointed our bikes towards Kiev, the nation's capital, 200 kilometres distant.

Ukraine seems like a rebellious child trying to break away from his parents. Once part of the Soviet Union, it still has a Russian flavour. The main language spoken remains Russian, Russian cars are everywhere, the food is similar, and even the countryside looks almost identical. Despite its Soviet connections, or no doubt because of them, Ukraine is trying to break away from the rubble of communism and increase its ties with Western Europe.

It is easy to see why the nation looks so longingly westwards. Poverty is widespread. After decades of being used to wipe Russia's ass, the country has been left with little. Most of the rural population lives at subsistence level, a way of life that most North Americans would believe is restricted to a few colonies of Doukhobors.

As we cycled down our rutted concrete highway, past fields of grain and sunflowers, I was amazed to see how few tractors and cars were used by the local residents. Instead, horses pulled carts loaded high with hay or dragged iron ploughs across the black earth. The hay itself would be cut with long scythes, as families worked in unison to cut fodder for their livestock.

Despite the rustic nature of their work, many of the younger women wore clothing more suitable for a night out in the city, with miniskirts or tight shirts and pants clinging to bodies well toned by this manual labour. The young men dressed more plainly.

We stopped to photograph a mother, father, and daughter pitching hay into the horse cart. In their loose wool and cotton clothing, the parents could have been teleported from the eighteenth century. By contrast, the girl, in her late teens, was dressed in a miniskirt and a tight floral lace blouse.

The two women walked over to us and smiled, while the father continued piling the hay. They carried an urn of spring water, from which we drank before filling our own bottles.

"We are almost finished getting our winter supply of hay for our cows," the mother said. "It has been a good season with lots of rain."

The bountiful food that the country folk reap now is a stark contrast to how things were during Soviet times. The Soviet government greedily eyed Ukraine's fertile fields and imposed massive, impossible-to-meet quotas on the collective farms. Almost all produce and grain was shipped eastwards while Ukrainians starved in their own gardens of plenty. Between 1932 and 1933, millions died of starvation, more than all the Ukrainians lost fighting in World War II. The great Ukrainian famine, or Holodomor, has been recognized by several governments worldwide as a form of genocide, recognizing that the Soviets had engineered the famine in order to weaken the country and its people.

Ukraine's weak economy means that all locally produced goods and services are inexpensive. Julie and I were able to eat hearty meals in roadside restaurants for next to nothing, and we even treated ourselves to two nights in a hotel. The comfortable, clean room in a castle-like building cost ten dollars a night. Another treat we discovered was Ukrainian ice cream.

Even better than the Russian variety, the Ukrainian creamy treats taste better than Häagen-Dazs, at about one tenth the price. Our favourite flavours were vanilla with real raspberry swirl, coated in white chocolate, and vanilla with caramel, coated with chocolate and nuts.

Three days of cycling brought us to Kiev. It proved hard to admire the scenery, however, in the picturesque, ancient city. Traffic on the narrow roads demanded our undivided attention. If our attention drifted from cycling, our soft bodies could get squashed between large, fast-moving objects. Our stay here would be brief, just long enough to find an Internet café and tend to business. We needed to transfer money to purchase the boat and organize its delivery from Britain to Lisbon.

ORGANIZING THE OCEAN ROW had begun to feel overwhelming as we cycled across Europe at the same time. A good friend, Dean Fenwick, volunteered to be our Vancouver-based logistics manager—work that amounted to a second, and unpaid, full-time job. Over the next few months, Dean helped oversee the complicated shipping process, transferred funds, updated our website, and ordered dozens of expedition essentials, such as charts, pilot books, electronics, and underwater camera casings. My brother, George, assisted us with ongoing research and gathering information for the ocean leg.

I had always hoped that the success of my previous expeditions would eventually allow me to focus my efforts 100 per cent on the physical challenge of the pursuit while a team took care of all other aspects: a cameraman for the film, a logistics crew at home, and perhaps a support squad to ready our boat for the ocean, so all Julie and I would have to do is step off our bikes and start rowing.

My dream of Team Angus wasn't to be. My filmmaking experience has followed the same formula. My previous two documentaries, each produced on a budget of under $5,000 have won eight awards at international film festivals and been aired worldwide on National Geographic Television. This publicity, however, wasn't enough to garner a penny of support for our most exciting project yet, and our present film was being financed by dregs scraped from our lines of credit. An average documentary involves the labour of four or five full-time professionals for several months with a budget of several hundred thousand dollars. For Julie and me, the work of creating our film was just another full-time job to squeeze into our already full work day. We were the producers, directors, sound crew, camera operators, stunt doubles, and subject material. What we lacked in resources we made up for in determination. We intended to make this film the best ever.

A couple of email notes had arrived from Tim. It sounded as though he was struggling to reach Moscow before his (and my) visa expired on August 19. However, he was doing his best to assure me he would make it on time: "You may anticipate a later arrival by me than the estimate of August 15 as I gave you earlier, but of course, we both know I am much faster than you are," he wrote. "If you travelled from Novosibirsk in 24 days, then I should travel from Omsk in little more than two weeks. Even Yulya is faster than you are." In another email he asked, "Was 170 kilometres on June 8 (at that point your longest day) your longest day yet recorded? I don't ask simply so that I may make your high mark a distance to beat, I wanted to let you know that Yulya cranked out 180 kilometres the other day putting you solidly in third place, if I'm not mistaken."

Tim said he would not hand over the video camera unless I came to Moscow in person. It was obvious he knew I would be having second thoughts because of our expiring visas. The question was, why did he care? It certainly wasn't because he was harbouring warm feelings towards me and wanted us to share the glory together. If I didn't return to Moscow, the loss would be entirely mine, and I would never be able to say I officially completed the Vancouver-to-Moscow expedition since I hadn't ridden my bicycle across the city limits.

I pondered my options. If Tim could cycle 170 kilometres a day for 17 days straight, he would arrive in Moscow on the final day of our visas. Although it was possible he could maintain this speed, any injury or mechanical problem—or countless other unpredictable delays—could undermine his tight schedule. When I had planned on doubling back to complete the bike leg into Moscow, I had always assumed Tim would arrive well before our visas expired. Russian officials would not look kindly on a tourist who had overstayed his visa, and it was not a mess I wanted to place myself in. If I was going to go back, I would need to apply for a new visa at a Russian embassy somewhere outside Russia (an existing visa cannot be extended within Russia). That process that could take up to two weeks. In all it would cost me at least three weeks of precious time.

Could these anticipated delays be the very reason Tim so badly wanted me to return to Moscow? I reread his emails carefully: "Otherwise maybe you're still paranoid that I'm chasing you down, trying to be first. I told you before, I did find it entertaining that you were driven by this fear, but not to the point that I want to see you undermine your career, and make things difficult for me by ducking out of our meeting . . . Try seeing it from my angle—with so much to gain from going on tour while B.C. and Alberta are hot following my newspaper series, why would I let that slip away? . . . So don't let paranoia over my plans stop you from meeting me in Moscow."

Was I paranoid? There seemed to be something desperate in Tim's attempts to persuade me to return to Moscow.

My gut instinct told me not to go back. I decided there and then that I wouldn't. Regardless of what Tim was plotting, stormy season would soon be hitting the west coast of Europe. I simply couldn't afford to take three weeks off from the expeditions without putting Julie's and my own safety in jeopardy. I wrote back to Tim and told him I would not be coming back to Moscow and that I would be making alternative arrangements to pick up the camera. "It looks like you will be pushing extremely hard to make it by August 18," I wrote. "Since this is the day before both our Russian visas expire, I am afraid I cannot take the chance of flying into Russia when a slight mechanical delay or any other problems would render my trip fruitless. I wish you and Yulya an enjoyable conclusion to this journey."

"Honey, check this out," Julie said, gesturing towards her own computer screen.

She had been checking Erden Eruç's progress on his website when an update caught her attention. Erden had written about a frenzy of work he had been doing on his offshore rowboat. One of the points he detailed was the fact that he was mounting a video-camera system that could film non-stop for 90 days.

"How long will he be out at sea rowing from Miami to Panama?" Julie asked.

"Against those currents, probably forever," I said. "But I'm sure he expects to do it in a few weeks."

"So why would he need to film non-stop for 90 days?" Julie wondered.

It was a mystery. Was he planning a longer row that he wasn't revealing? Or were Julie and I just becoming paranoid wrecks from days of baking in the sun?

UKRAINE PASSED BY QUICKLY. We were impressed by the quality of the main highway to Hungary, after hearing contrary descriptions of its state. Most of the countryside was flat and agricultural, dotted by small lakes and ponds. We were puzzled by the frequent sight of gigantic bird's nests—on top of chimneys, disused smokestacks, basketball hoops, and telephone poles. I figured they were homes made by giant, mutant, glow-in-the-dark Chernobyl starlings. Julie shattered my theory by spotting the storks that used the metre-wide nests.

It was late July. Temperatures soared into the high 30s, probably in the low 40s on the asphalt. I felt sorry for the baby storks in their shadeless nests. On the road, we weren't faring much better. Sweat saturated our clothing, and mild headaches hinted at impending heatstroke. Whenever we could, we would stop at the roadside lakes and briefly splash in the water next to truck drivers unabashedly scrubbing their sweaty bollocks.

The Carpathian Mountains were the final barrier before Hungary, and we were relieved to find the inclines reasonable to bike. The mountain vistas are spectacular, and I felt as if I were visiting Switzerland 300 years ago. The slopes stretched skywards, a combination of pine forests and pastureland. Cows and sheep wandered the slopes, bells ringing, tended by shepherds. Towering hay stacks, constructed by scythe-touting families, dotted the fields. We filled our water bottles from the crystal-clear streams that burbled off the mountainsides.

We glided down the far side of the mountains on a smooth new road, with a good shoulder for bikes.

"Wow," exclaimed Julie. "These roads are getting good. And just think, they're only going to get better."

Or so we thought.

We negotiated the Ukrainian–Hungarian border easily— only to enter the least bike-friendly country in Europe.

Hungarian roads, we discovered, are extremely narrow, with no room for cyclists. Busy traffic hissed past inches from our bicycles. We noticed frequent signs that depicted a stylized cyclist within a red circle—a warning to motorists to look out for bikes. These signs were at least a token effort to support zero-emissions travel, we figured—that is, until an angry motorist informed us that the signs actually meant no bikes allowed. There were no alternative roads, so we had little choice but to flout Hungary's anti-cycling law.

Hungary was also the most monolingual European country we encountered. Almost no one spoke Russian, German, or English, which made communication incredibly difficult. Prices for prepared food were much higher than in Eastern Europe, so Julie and I had to start buying ingredients for our meals from supermarkets to stay within budget.

Our biggest disappointment in Hungary came upon reaching the first autobahn. During my Siberian ordeals, I had fantasized about the European freeways. I imagined the flat, smooth asphalt and wide shoulders as the safest and speediest route across Western Europe. Our dreams of speedy travel were short lived. Two hours after merging onto the Hungarian autobahn, we were escorted off by the police. The disgruntled officer led us to a potholed, narrow, busy side road—complete with No Cycling signs—and said we would be safer there.

Hungarian motorists had taken their country's signs to heart. They helped get across the no-cycling message using middle-finger salutes, aggrieved honks, and, most frequently, fingers angrily pointed towards yet another No Cycling sign. The occasional cycling path seemed to justify their hostile actions in the minds of the drivers. However, Julie and I learned to hate the cycling paths almost as much as the signs. Numerous times an inviting paved side lane marked for bicycles would lure us off the road. Invariably these paths would lead away from the main road and end in some remote village or become impossible to follow as they merged with a labyrinth of country lanes. Every time, we had to retrace our route back to the main road, losing hours of progress.

Still, Hungary did have highlights for road-weary cyclists: clean bathrooms, well-supplied service stations, well-stocked supermarkets, and one uncharacteristically friendly motorist who stopped to give us hot fried chicken, made fresh by mama.

AFTER FIVE DAYS IN HUNGARY, we slipped across the border into Austria. The hard-working, perfectionist national character of the Austrians became immediately apparent. Litter was non-existent. Every stone house looked as though it was maintained as a museum showpiece. Flower borders were weedless. Peeling paint was a foreign concept. I have never experienced such widespread cleanliness and precision. The villages with their ancient stone buildings on narrow cobbled streets could have been plucked from the pages of a fairy tale, placed amongst fields of grapes or sunflowers. Ornate churches, usually in the town square, would sport fountains, stone benches, immaculate flowerbeds and shrubs. Behind the villages, amongst the sunflowers, modern windmills churned out environmentally friendly electricity. All that was missing were the Austrians, as many of the scenes were eerily devoid of people, like movie sets after the film crew had gone home for the day.

Although the highway we travelled on was still narrow, the asphalt was brand new, black and smooth. Motorists gave us plenty of room. There were—hallelujah!—no more No Cycling signs.

A local in his 40s, out for some exercise, pulled up alongside us on his racing bike and began chatting. Julie translated the German for me. The man informed us that the world-famous Danube River cycling path commenced just ahead in Vienna. The paved trail paralleled our direction of travel and might offer a picturesque respite from the busy roads. We could intercept the trail in Vienna, a day away, and follow it all the way into Germany.

We camped at the edge of an impeccably symmetrical corn field, next to a windbreak of poplars. The following morning we followed wide bike shoulders as we cycled through the outskirts of Austria's capital. Once in the centre we became hopelessly lost and spent hours bumping along cobbled streets and narrow alleys.

Finally we reached the Danube, Europe's second biggest river, which historically has been one of the main supply routes into Vienna. The river is dammed for electricity. Rather than allowing the backed-up flow to inundate the surrounding land, as a typical hydro-electric reservoir in North America would do, the Austrians conserved their limited land by building extensive dikes along the river's course. These dikes allow the Danube to rise considerably without spreading outwards.

Then the progressive-thinking Austrians had another brainstorm. They decided to use the flat, utilitarian surfaces atop the dikes to create an 800-kilometre bike path. The cycling route traverses some of the most picturesque alpine landscapes in Europe.

In Austria, the Danube has carved huge gorges in its passage through the northern Alps. Along the river's banks, medieval villages and castles make it easy to forget you're in a technologically advanced sophisticated nation. Best of all, for a cyclist, the path is almost completely devoid of hills, even when the river flows through the heart of the mountains.

Near Vienna, we encountered long-distance cyclists and locals out for exercise on bikes or rollerblades along the three-metre-wide path. After about 20 kilometres, most trail users were touring cyclists lugging bulging panniers. But our weather-battered and travel-worn equipment still made us stand out next to the shiny bicycles and new equipment the Austrians enjoyed. We also lugged far more gear on our bicycles, as we were camping instead of staying in the lush, and likely expensive, bed and breakfasts and hotels along the route.

Even without these creature comforts, our cycling leg along the Danube River would be the most enjoyable part of our European tour.

14

VIENNA TO LISBON

T HE SOLITUDE, THE PLEASANT CAMPING alongside the Danube River, and the break from the heavy traffic all gave us the feeling of having a vacation within our larger expedition as we cycled from Vienna. The town of Passau, on the German border, marked the end of our 800-kilometre riverside idyll. Here Julie and I found an Internet café.

I opened an email from my mother and froze. "Could you call me ASAP," she wrote. "There's something regarding my health I need to discuss with you."

I knew it had to be serious, as my mother would never bother me with a minor ailment. I picked up the public phone and dialled her number. I prayed I wouldn't hear the news I dreaded. But I knew I would. Tears welled up in my eyes.

"Hello?" My mother's voice came to me from a world away.

"I got your message," I said. "Is everything okay?"

I wanted her to tell me she had broken her leg. Maybe she had fallen on a hike. Or maybe she was getting anemic again. Some heavy-duty iron pills could fix that. Instead she said with a heavy voice: "The cancer is back. I discovered a lump under my arm and a biopsy determined it is malignant. I'm afraid it's metastasized."

I didn't know what to say. What does one tell someone who has just found out she has terminal cancer? And it was my own mother. I felt like I'd just been kicked in the gut. Tears dripped down my cheeks. "You'll beat it," I finally said. "There's nobody tougher than you are. If anybody can win this battle it's you."

My words reassured nobody, but they were all I could offer.

After I hung up, Julie wrapped her arms around me, and we walked in silence to the bikes. The night air seemed oppressive as we searched for a spot to camp on the town's outskirts. At last we found a vacant industrial lot and set up our tent in the inky darkness.

Four years earlier, weeks before her seventieth birthday, my mother had discovered a lump in her left breast. This growth had been removed with a lumpectomy and was followed up by radiation therapy. The odds of non-recurrence were in my mother's favour. Generally, if the cancer hasn't come back in five years, recovery is considered complete. With each passing year, the entire family breathed another sigh of relief. At four years, all of us felt the nightmare might be over. Our mother was tough, and she would emerge a survivor. But now it turned out this wasn't the case.

I couldn't stop thinking about my poor mother. She was living all alone in the Comox Valley on Vancouver Island, and suddenly she'd been handed a death sentence. Happy images of my childhood flashed through my mind: family trips to Sproat Lake or the Pacific Ocean, hiking trips in the mountains. Strangely, one image that kept repeating was that of my mother frantically pulling me from the back seat of the car, when I was about four years old and helplessly peeing my pants. Throughout my childhood, my mother had always seemed an unstoppable force that we had taken for granted. The prospect of her being taken from our lives by cancer was incomprehensible.

Suddenly my expedition seemed trivial, and I was at a loss about what to do next. Should Julie and I take a hiatus from the journey and fly home? If we did that, we would have to put off our ocean row until the next year because of the approaching stormy season. If Tim were to continue, he'd be able to take the lead, but I could not allow this concern to influence my decision. At the end of the day, my ambition to be the first to go around the world was purely a selfish pursuit. I couldn't let it prevent me from being with my mother in her time of need.

We had planned to be on the ocean in less than six weeks' time. I feared being captive in the rowboat. It would take up to five months to row across the Atlantic, and once we began, there was no way to get off the ocean without instigating a deep-sea rescue. I was haunted by the possibility of my mother's cancer progressing rapidly while we were in the boat and never having a chance to see her again.

Julie's compassion and rational thinking steadied me through this turmoil. We decided to keep cycling to Portugal, about three weeks distant, and then decide whether to continue once we reached Lisbon. My mother would be undergoing a series of tests over the next few weeks, which would give everyone a clearer idea of her status.

I would call her every day from the road and try to give her support and mild distraction. France is one of her favourite countries. I knew she would enjoy hearing our experiences.

ALTHOUGH THE DANUBE RIVER TRAIL continues along the German section of the river, the route is poorly maintained and hard to follow, so we were forced to return to the roads.

Long-distance cycling in much of Western Europe can only be described as harrowing. Unlike in Eastern Europe, where cyclists are allowed to travel on the primary road systems, which often sport wide breakdown shoulders and make for safe cycling, countries such as Germany, France, and Hungary strictly enforce their no-cycling rules. This leaves cyclists on narrow, busy secondary or tertiary roads where there simply isn't enough room for a bike.

Many places in Europe do have bicycling lanes (such as the Danube River trail) and special bicycle throughways. However, these routes are only in areas of geographical or historical significance where tourism is promoted. Many people had told us how much we would enjoy our "peaceful" cycle through Europe and described their own pleasant experiences touring through wine-growing regions or the Alps. Unfortunately, these meandering routes don't interconnect across the continent.

We cycled quickly through Germany and tried desperately to reach better roads before the cramped and dangerous roads got the better of us. Our pace through Europe had been fairly brisk, and it had taken us just under a month to reach the middle of Germany from Moscow. We stopped for a day in a small town called Tuttlingen, snuggled near the banks of the Upper Danube, to catch up on business.

We found an Internet café and settled down to work on some of the hurdles we faced. The owners of the boat we had purchased had not delivered the vessel to the shipping company, as they had promised, because, they admitted, "we didn't think you'd make it across Europe on your bikes." After they finally made the delivery, the shipping company proved to be inept. The boat was supposed to be in Lisbon at this point, yet it was still sitting at a shipping yard in Nottingham, England.

While in Tuttlingen we received another piece of news—a shock and yet not entirely a surprise. Tim had reached Moscow and announced he was continuing by human power to Vancouver. He explained on his website that Erden Eruç had suggested a partnership and had offered the use of his ocean rowboat. Erden's wife had volunteered to cover the costs, which would be close to $100,000. Tim also noted that he and Yulya were now engaged.

Erden's website had a similar update. Erden made it clear that he felt I'd left Tim in the lurch. "I had talked to Julie prior to Colin's announcement, suggesting that Colin and Tim should get over their differences and bring this journey home to Vancouver together . . . How will Tim cross the Atlantic?" he mused. He felt he was duty bound to rectify what he saw as an injustice. It would take a year out of his own schedule, and cost his wife tens of thousands of dollars, but Erden felt it was only fair. He noted that in his own travels through Canada, many Canadians had displayed generosity towards him. Aiding Tim was his way of repaying the favours.

Apart from exchanging a few emails, Erden barely knew Tim. However, he was obviously a devoted fan. In an interview with ExplorersWeb, an online magazine that offers live coverage of major expeditions, Erden summed up his positive feelings: "In Tim I saw hints of a man who will struggle to keep his team together, wait for the weakest member of the team and have compassion in the face of insurmountable challenges; the kinds of qualities which make us still talk about [Arctic explorer Ernest] Shackleton today." High praise indeed.

Erden was in the final stages of readying and provisioning his boat for an ocean crossing. The boat would soon be shipped in a container from Seattle to Lisbon, where it would be ready the moment it was unloaded.

Julie and I were suddenly a long way behind Tim in the round-the-world race. Geographically, we had a 3,000-kilometre head start. But a motivated cyclist could cover this scant distance in two weeks. When we reached Lisbon, Julie and I still had to ready our boat for sea. This work would include fixing hatches, painting the hull, reinforcing weak areas, fibreglassing, anti-fouling, rebuilding the water maker, checking the electronics, ordering new gear from around the world, and obtaining and packing five months of provisions. Any missed item, such as a spare set of rollicks or wheels for the rowing seat or spare O-rings for the water maker, could spell disaster. Historically, people spend months or even years preparing for an ocean row. If we stood any chance of staying ahead of Tim and Erden, Julie and I would have to do it all in a couple of weeks.

Tim, on the other hand, would not have to lift a finger to prepare for the Atlantic. By the time he reached Lisbon on his bicycle, Erden would have the vessel ready to go with all the logistics smoothed out. Tim would merely need to step off his bike and into the boat.

Tim must have known he had the tactical advantage. Why else would he be so unwilling to agree to cross the finish line in Vancouver together? I felt increasingly nervous.

An email from Tim arrived in my inbox. The subject line: "Great News." Now that he had arrived in Moscow, he was unwilling to hand over the video camera to Carole Paquette. Instead, he insisted that he would deliver it to me in person in Lisbon. "You'll be thrilled to hear the great news I'm now able to share with you," he wrote, "that I'll be able to meet you in Lisbon before your October departure. I'll be there in about 30 or 32 days . . . See you there."

I'd had enough of Tim's games. I replied that if he didn't hand the PD170 video camera to Carole Paquette immediately, he was in breach of our agreement. I would be forced to purchase a new $7,000 camera and seek compensation through the legal system. I sent a copy to his father the lawyer, and hoped he would steer his son on the less costly path.

JULIE AND I COULD DO LITTLE MORE than push forward and hope we wouldn't see Tim in Lisbon. If our boats did leave simultaneously, there was no saying how Julie and I would fare in a sprint across the Atlantic pitted against two strong men.

Our entry into Switzerland offered immediate relief from the stress of navigating the German road system. An island in the midst of the European Community, Switzerland could boast cycling lanes attached to most roads and courteous drivers who didn't flip us the middle-finger salute that was so common in Germany. We were in the southwest corner of the nation, away from the major mountains, but the scenery still pleased the eyes as we travelled along the forested banks of the Rhine River. Unfortunately, we only experienced a tiny part of the country. Two hours after entering Switzerland, we passed through the city of Basel and entered France.

Although our passage through part of Germany, through Switzerland, and into France in a single day illustrated the compactness of many European countries, France is Western Europe's largest country and would take us more than 10 days to traverse. We chose a route that would lead us through the centre of the nation and into Spain in the Northern Pyrenees.

Near Switzerland, the French villages sported the Germanic beam-and-plaster Alpine architecture. Masses of flowers—from roses to lilac trees—adorned the villages, usually cared for by retirees with an eye for floral perfection. Many of the homes seemed to be owned by British or Americans, who had been lured to the tranquil French countryside.

As we pedalled deeper into France, the rural architecture became more predominantly stone. Around the villages spread lush crops of sunflowers, corn, lavender, mustard, and grapes. Some farmers had planted their fields with hardwood trees, a crop whose yields would benefit their grandchildren.

The roads in France were generally better than what we had experienced in Germany and Hungary. They alternated between quiet country lanes and busier, still shoulderless highways. At one stage, when the roads became intolerably dangerous, Julie and I sneaked onto the motorway and spent 20 blissful minutes cycling on three-metre shoulders before we were escorted off by the local *gendarmerie*. As we neared the south of France, the highways began to sport more cycling lanes and offer brief respite from our nervous cycling.

Although it was mid-summer, the weather remained cold. Threatening clouds, which occasionally burst into downpours, tracked us across France. Only later did we learn that we had been experiencing the perimeter of an immense system that caused disastrous floods in Germany and Austria and inundated towns and villages along the Danube River. The floods made front pages around the world, and the news worried our friends back home who thought we were still in the region.

THE BORDER OF FRANCE AND SPAIN runs along the spine of the Pyrenees Mountains, an impressive cordillera that stretches across Europe from the Atlantic Ocean to the Mediterranean Sea. We chose to cross the mountains on a route that paralleled the Camino de Santiago.

The camino is a pilgrimage route that has been used for more than a thousand years. The final destination is the Spanish town of Santiago de Compostela, the final resting place of the Apostle James. Trails from all over Europe merge at the Pyrenees and then the route continues for another 700 kilometres. Every year, thousands of modern-day pilgrims follow this route. The camino has become a world-renowned adventure trek for people looking for a personal challenge with a spiritual element.

Our own journey merged with the Camino de Santiago on the western side of the Pyrenees. Trekkers, stooped under heavy backpacks, were a common sight. We enjoyed the company of these fellow travellers, who would nod or wave as we passed. The camino itself sometimes followed a paved road; at other times, it would continue on dirt tracks that crossed the scenic countryside. Our road switchbacked, taking us higher and higher through landscapes of pine forests and pastureland. Stone farmhouses and outbuildings blended into the rocky landscape.

Eventually, we reached the Spanish border, which I had assumed was at the summit of the Pyrenees. Spain's membership in the European Union had ended all border formalities, so we cycled past the now-unused border station into a new country. We were mildly disappointed to discover that, at the border, the road didn't descend down the far side of the mountains. Instead it pushed upwards at an even steeper incline. For hours, we struggled up the sinuous road until we were enveloped in a thick, wet fog. The farmland lay behind us; now only thick forests bordered our highway to heaven.

Finally, as dusk settled in, we crested the summit of the Pyrenees. A ghostly temple, shrouded in thick fog, marked the high point of the pass, Ibaneta. We descended several hundred metres on the other side before spotting a meadow where we could set up camp.

Our entrance into Spain marked a sharp transition from the naturally irrigated landscapes of France. Spain lies in the rain shadow of the Pyrenees. After two hours of cycling, we found ourselves in a very hot and dry land. The rolling hills were almost devoid of greenery, except for a few patches that farmers kept watered.

Spain surprised us with the quality of its roads. They weren't just marginally better for cycling; it was night and day over the rest of Europe that we'd experienced. Suddenly, all the roads offered broad shoulders and ideal cycling conditions. The four-lane divided highways were also open for cycling, as long as cyclists wore safety vests and helmets. Even the drivers seemed more laid-back, tooting merrily or waving as they passed.

Why was it that Spain had developed both infrastructure and attitudes so much more conducive for cycling? We pondered this question as we cycled through the blazing heat and stopped worrying that a speeding motorist might hit us.

Although the land was dry, we were able to fill our water bottles with cold water that burbled from the depths of natural springs. In village squares and sometimes on the roadside, the ancient Spaniards had built beautiful stone catchment basins to dispense these aquatic riches. Usually a stone figurine stood over the basin, and the water would gurgle from an outstretched hand through a copper pipe, corroded green with time.

As we traversed Spain and neared our final European country, I received more bad news about my mother's health. The CT scan had revealed a lump in her lung. I immediately called my brother, George. He been in contact with the oncologist and told me the prognosis wasn't good. The lump almost certainly indicated the presence of lung cancer—the oncologist put the odds at 95 per cent. However, it wasn't certain whether the lump in her lung was a new cancer or had metastasized from her breast. Since my mother was a non-smoker, it seemed much more likely to be the latter. If this diagnosis were the case, my mother's life expectancy was six months to a year.

With troubled hearts, Julie and I cycled towards Lisbon. It would be almost exactly six months before we would reach the far shores of North America. If we pursued our journey as planned, I risked never seeing my mother again. Unless there was a drastic change in my mother's prognosis, we would have to fly home from Lisbon and put our ocean row off until the next year.

After entering Portugal, we were disappointed to discover the roads were more typical of what we had found in the rest of Europe. Once again, we were banned from the main high-way and relegated to a potholed, narrow road that meandered vaguely in the direction of the capital.

A multi-year drought had parched the land. We were told that fires raged out of control in other parts of the country and had consumed much of Portugal's last remaining forest land. Cork trees seemed to be surviving the dry weather with no problems, though, and we examined the leafy deciduous trees with fascination. Thick sheets of the spongy bark, perhaps five centimetres thick, were peeled off the trees for the winemak-ing industry. A local farmer explained that it took nine or ten years for the bark to regenerate to a state that it could be rehar-vested. A freshly harvested trunk, with its deep red cambium layer exposed, looked like an arbutus tree, so familiar to me on Vancouver Island.

Portugal has an ideal climate for cork trees, and the coun-try supplies half of the world's cork. Although there isn't enough cork available to supply the world's winemaking industry, even the cheapest wines we found in Europe were stoppered with genuine cork. In North America, more expensive wines often rely on synthetic substitutes.

A few more days of cycling through cork forests, rolling hills, and picture-perfect villages brought Julie and me to the outskirts of Lisbon. Forty-nine days had passed since we left Moscow. It had been nearly a year since I had arrived on the far side of Eurasia in a rowboat. Over that year, I had cycled on frozen rivers, trekked through some of the remotest areas on the planet, endured cold beyond comprehension, and—worst of all—pedalled along nightmarishly dangerous highways that seemed to stretch into eternity. Suddenly, all that was behind us, and only an epic journey across the Atlantic Ocean lay between us and the final chapter of our journey.

LISBON WAS A FITTING PLACE to end our Eurasian traverse, a jewel on the Atlantic coast far removed from the dangers now behind us. The crime rate is low in Portugal, and we felt safe entering this large city. The population of Europe's most western capital is often given as 600,000, but this is because the city's boundaries are so close to the historical city centre. The population of metropolitan "Greater Lisbon" is closer to 3 million, and that mass of humanity gives the city a vibrant, cosmopolitan feel.

Upon reaching the city centre, Julie and I found an inexpensive hotel in which to temporarily end our nomadic lifestyle. We had camped almost exclusively all across Europe, and so a soft bed felt like a decadent luxury.

Then we received some astounding news. Further tests had revealed that the tumour in my mother's lung was a false alarm. The odds had only been one in twenty that the test result might be a smudge on the image or scar tissue in the lungs. My mother had beaten those odds.

I couldn't believe it. A dark cloud had chased us across Europe. It had been mentally taxing to maintain my previous discipline and move at a high speed, especially when it looked like we might have to pull from the race. My mother's new test results indicated that the cancer hadn't metastasized to other organs. The doctor revised the estimate of my mother's life expectancy: it was now anywhere from two to ten years, maybe longer.

My mother's new lease on life would allow us to carry on

with our journey, confident that she would be in reasonable health when we reached the far side of the ocean. Our enthusiasm restored, Julie and I resumed our efforts to ready our boat in two hurried weeks.

Even more of an impetus than the threat of Tim's being close on our tail was the fact that stormy season was rapidly approaching off the west coast of Europe. Our research had suggested that the best time to be off the Spanish and Portuguese coasts is between April and the end of September. During this period, the calmer summer weather prevails. More importantly, the winds blow more consistently and steadily from the north. These "Portuguese Trades" combine with a south-flowing current to create ideal conditions for our enterprise. We would first need to navigate southwards, off the coast of Africa, to enter the trade-wind belt. These currents would then help to sweep us across the Atlantic.

In October, though, early-winter storms arrive, and the otherwise reliable Portuguese Trades begin to falter. A low-powered vessel, such as an ocean rowboat, near land in variable winds is a dangerous scenario. A sudden onshore blow can quickly spell disaster if the rowers are overpowered and the vessel is pushed into the cliffs. We needed to leave Lisbon by mid-September at the latest.

The weather off Europe was only one of the variables in determining the ideal launch date for this ocean leg. We also had to consider the hurricane season in the lower latitudes. Hurricanes form throughout the hot season, generally between April and November, and peak in August and September. By departing in mid-September, we hoped to reach the hurricane belt as it tailed out towards the end of November.

We arrived in Lisbon on September 5, so we had very little time to get organized. Julie and I had to cram four months of labour into 10 days.

A bigger problem: our boat had not arrived. Our shipping company had assured us that our boat would be delivered weeks before we reached Lisbon. We had also been calling their representatives almost daily as we crossed Europe. Nevertheless, they had fallen short on their promise. Our pleas and screams through the long-distance line fell on deaf ears. Our vital shipment seemed no more urgent to them than bags of topsoil. After prodding them unsuccessfully for months, I was at the point of booking a flight to England so that I could bring back the boat myself. That's when we received word that the boat had been loaded into a truck and was on its way south.

While waiting for our vessel to arrive, we began the formidable task of wrestling other shipped items out of the iron grip of customs. Many of our sponsors had shipped us key equipment, including freeze-dried food from Mountain Foods in the United States, new oars from Croker Oars of Australia, a life raft and EPIRB—Emergency Position Indicating Radio Beacon—from Liferaftrental.com, and some packages sent from our friend Dean that contained dozens of miscellaneous items we wouldn't be able to find in Lisbon.

Although Lisbon has the appearance of a modern city, some antiquated systems exist beneath that veneer—and foremost among these artifacts of the past are the customs procedures, which constitute a quagmire of bureaucracy. The easiest items for us to free were the oars, which were shipped directly from airport to airport. Unfortunately, it still took eight hours of intense work and $300 in brokerage fees—the actual duties were waived—to get these. Other items, such as the life raft and freeze-dried food, looked almost unobtainable. Our most formidable barrier was the law that prevented foreigners from receiving goods shipped from abroad.

Fortunately, Miguel Leal, an old Portuguese-Canadian friend of mine, came to the rescue. He directed us to a Lisbon acquaintance. Mario DeAlmeida, a graphic and design artist who had spent several years in Toronto, became our guardian angel. Not only did he take on the gargantuan task of retrieving our equipment but he also insisted on helping us out with the rest of our work for the duration of our stay in Lisbon. We would soon find that his local knowledge combined with a broad range of skills would be just the ticket to keeping to an otherwise impossible deadline.

Julie and I visited the municipal marina, Doca De Belem, beneath the giant red bridge. We asked if there was room in the dry-dock compound. The manager assured us it would be no problem, and they would be pleased to sponsor us by waiving all charges. We could use the marina crane to lift the boat from the truck when it arrived. Additionally, we had use of a vacant shop on the premises to live in and store our gear free of charge, and use of the telephone and computer in the office.

We had no time for any sightseeing but still got a feel for Lisbon as we went about our preparations. We stopped to refuel in the city's inexpensive restaurants and savoured exquisite meals—especially Lisbon's world-renowned seafood. The city reminded me of San Francisco, with its great April 25th Bridge spanning the bay—which, I discovered, was designed and built by the same company that completed the Golden Gate. Even the dry, marine landscape surrounding the city reminded me of Marin County north of San Francisco.

WHILE OUR PREPARATIONS PROCEEDED SMOOTHLY in Lisbon, we had a chance to check the progress of the other teams circumnavigating by human power.

Jason Lewis, the Briton, had spent months sea kayaking through the tropical waters of Indonesia and had almost completed his Australia-to-Singapore leg. From Singapore, he only needed to cross the Eurasian continent, a distance of perhaps 15,000 kilometres, to complete his expedition. Julie and I still had approximately 18,000 kilometres of land and ocean to traverse. Jason was still clearly in the lead.

Erden Eruç seemed to have bowed out of the picture, as he had allocated his time and resources to assist Tim on his return trip to Vancouver.

And, of course, our third and newest competitor, Tim Harvey, was a real threat. He stated on his website that he was planning to cross Europe in 30 days, "possibly overtaking Colin Angus en route," which meant he could arrive in Lisbon within a few days. Erden's most recent posting indicated that the boat was fully prepared and en route to Lisbon. The vessel was expected to arrive in September, and he and Tim were striving to depart by October 3.

It was a tight race. An adventuring website that detailed human-powered feats stated that Jason Lewis "expects to win the race in 2007 and become the first human to circumnavigate the globe." At this point, we were hoping to reach Vancouver well before 2007. Who knew? The only thing we could do was to keep pushing as fast as we could, and that started with getting our boat seaworthy and equipped with provisions.

Our boat arrived three days after we did. I was finally able to lay eyes on the quarter-inch-plywood vessel as it was gently unloaded from the transport truck by the marina crane. We were relieved that the boat hadn't been damaged in transit and excited that our most important item had arrived.

At 24 feet in length, with a double-chined hull—composed of four flat planes of plywood—the vessel was built according to the design of British boat builder Phil Morrison. Morrison had catered to the growing demand for offshore rowboats by designing a vessel ideally suited for this purpose. His boats incorporate plywood with fibreglass joinery, one of the easiest and lightest boat-building combinations to work with.

Two minuscule cabins bookended the vessel. We would use the forward cabin as a storage compartment and the aft as living quarters. The buoyancy of these cabins, combined with ballast placed low in the vessel, would ensure that the boat could right itself should it capsize. Two heavy-duty aluminum hatches sealed the cabins from the elements.

The central portion of the boat, where the rowers sit, was open. Two sliding seats with matching oarlocks would allow two people to row simultaneously. Beneath the rowing area, the deck was sealed, and eight watertight round hatches provided access to the lockers below. We would use these compartments primarily for food storage. Ballast for the 350-kilogram vessel would be provided by 180 litres of emergency fresh water stored in jerry jugs, 70 litres of stove alcohol, and our stores of food. The fresh water could always be drunk in an emergency and replaced as ballast with salt water.

More storage was available in the aft cabin in compartments under the bed, the easiest to access storage area. Living space in the cabin consisted of little more than a tiny vinyl bed, a foot and a half wide at one end, four feet at the other. A St. Bernard would find the cabin claustrophobic. There wasn't even enough room to sit up straight.

A simple wicking alcohol stove was situated just outside the cabin entrance. This bare-bones cooker is unbreakable since it has no moving parts—it's just an alcohol reservoir with a wick under the burner. The cook could sit on the end of the bed and tend to the culinary chores outside. Toilet duties would involve balancing over the side of the boat.

Our boat had been used twice before to row from the Canary Islands to Barbados, and so it had a well-worn appearance. The dark blue paint was chipped and faded, decals were peeling, and the various components needed some TLC. Julie had only had several hours to examine the boat in Scotland, so we had paid a marine surveyor to assess the vessel. The survey results presented a daunting list of needed repairs. Most troubling, the surveyor claimed that the water maker would not be suitable for the trip because it had been stored in standing water. He ended the report with the following statement: "The boat needs a fair amount of work before she can be used."

Despite the gloomy report, we still felt it was the right vessel for the job. Besides, with our budget, we had no other choice.

NOW, AS OUR OCEAN ROWBOAT SETTLED DOWN on the asphalt, with her rusted trailer as a cradle, I began to appreciate the full amount of the work we still had to do. If the boat were unloaded into a fully outfitted shop with tools and equipment that I was familiar with, it would be one thing. But Julie and I had only just arrived in a foreign city on our bicycles with nothing other than what we carried in our panniers.

The first step would be to acquire a complete set of hand tools. We would need tools not only to fix the present problems but also to have the means to solve any malfunctions at sea. This toolbox must include not only the basic wrenches and screwdrivers but also a hand-operated drill, various saws, fibre-glassing tools, voltage meters, caulking guns, and other devices. At a builders' supply depot Julie and I laid down $1,000 to buy tools and supplies. We were ready to overhaul our vessel.

The most pressing task was to ensure that the boat would remain watertight—an important detail when crossing the Atlantic. First, we sprayed the vessel with a high-pressure hose and then inspected the compartments for leaks. We found several cracks in the plywood, some leaking hatch gaskets, and fittings that had been improperly caulked. Julie made a trip to a distant factory to have new O-rings and gaskets custom made for the hatches. I set about recaulking fittings and fibreglassing areas of dubious integrity.

Once we had properly sealed the boat, we set about repainting it from top to bottom (which inhibits marine growth). This was more than just for cosmetics, as it is essential to seal the wood from moisture. We covered the under-hull with a coat of primer and anti-fouling paint, and then anointed the topsides with red and white paint in the design of the Canadian flag. Our new friend Mario designed and printed vinyl logos with the boat's name, *Ondine* (named after my sailboat), and our web address—though we doubted we'd meet many Internet surfers in the mid-Atlantic.

We overhauled the electrical system, replaced the lead-acid battery, installed new electronics (including a deck-mounted GPS), and designed a means to recharge our array of self-contained electronics.

If anything broke while out at sea, it would have to be fixed or replaced. We made sure to pack redundant systems for all our most important electronics. That strategy meant we had three GPS units, two VHF radios, two Iridium satellite telephones, and three additional water-making systems—a hand-pump reverse-osmosis desalinator, a homemade distillation system that worked in conjunction with the stove, and a rain catchment system.

We tested our main electric desalinator with a solution of water and salt purchased from a nearby supermarket. The system works by pumping sea water at extremely high pressure against a semi-permeable membrane. Through reverse osmosis, fresh water is drawn through the membrane and expelled through a small hose. Our water maker had a thirst for electricity, and was powered by an array of solar panels that adorned our vessel. Julie and I watched in disappointment as the outflow tube failed to eject any fresh water. Perhaps the surveyor was right, and the unit should be replaced. Unfortunately, the $5,000 units were unavailable in Portugal. We still hadn't received much of the gear that had been sent weeks ago, and didn't want to jeopardize our departure date by having a water maker stuck in customs. Additionally, our budget was falling towards zero. We had no choice but to fix our existing unit.

I spent an entire day disassembling the machine to its last bolt, exposing worn O-rings and defective valves. Luckily, the unit came with spare valves and gaskets, so I was able to replace the worn parts. I reassembled the unit, and Julie and I leapt with joy as fresh water spurted from the hose. We would have water after all.

Mario finally rescued from customs our life raft, EPIRB, and other packages. Our freeze-dried food, however, had been sent from the United States and wouldn't be released, so we would have to make do with whatever non-perishable food we could find in local supermarkets.

We also finally received the big video camera. After I had threatened Tim with legal action, he finally handed the camera over to Carole Paquette, who immediately couriered it on to us. Through Europe we had been filming with an inferior camcorder that Julie had brought from home, and we were looking forward to using the professional camera again.

In two full days, we bought five months of provisions in the biggest grocery store splurge of my entire life. Julie and I lined up cart after cart filled with bags of rice, flour, sugar, dried beans, powdered milk, dried fruits, cereals, and other items we would need on the journey. We panicked at one supermarket when, after loading our carts with almost $2,000 worth of food, we learned that the store didn't take credit cards. An emergency call to Julie's bank in Vancouver allowed her to increase her daily withdrawal limit, and we were able to extract the cash from an ATM.

Julie and I had moved out of our hotel and were sleeping on the concrete floor of the vacant shop, metres from our boat. It was uncomfortable, but we wouldn't have to waste time travelling back and forth each day. While we were slightly behind schedule, finally, on September 18, we could settle on a departure date: September 22. The weather forecast promised reasonable conditions with some northerly winds. It seemed an auspicious day to trust our lives and our relationship to the sea.

JUST A COUPLE OF DAYS BEFORE OUR DEPARTURE, we received an email from Kenneth Crutchlow, the president of the Ocean Rowing Society. The O.R.S is an organization based in Britain that compiles ocean-rowing statistics and relays news about ongoing expeditions. Given our tight schedule, we'd never had time to inform the society of our pursuit. Nonetheless, Mr. Crutchlow had become aware of our efforts and had briefly corresponded with Dean Fenwick in Vancouver.

Crutchlow had been trying to sell us a $5,000 Argos electronic tracking system. We didn't need the device, since we already had a system—and one we felt was more effective— that would use our GPS and satellite telephone. In case of emergency, we carried the EPIRB unit recommended by the U.S. Coast Guard. This device, which can be switched on manually or turns on automatically when immersed in water, broadcasts its GPS coordinates on an emergency frequency. These are relayed by satellite to the maritime search-and-rescue authorities. When Dean declined the tracking system on our behalf, Kenneth replied with a pointed email.

Hello Dean

Today I read the website of your guys . . . It says Julie
wants to be the first woman to row mainland to
mainland. Does she have any idea just how hard that
will be and how long it will take? The site says

" . . . is extremely important to time the 3–4 month
crossing of the Atlantic during the appropriate
weather windows and to avoid the hurricane season
while voyaging the lower latitudes" . . .

The fact is they can leave anywhere from October
to March, this is when trade winds are expected. We
do not know each other, it is my style to be direct and
not beat about the bush.

What your crew is suggesting doing is way out
there at the limits of physical endurance.

I do not get the feeling they really know what
they are getting into, it seems they are prepared to
arrive in Portugal, load a few tins of beans on the
boat, and away.

I have not ordered Argos.

You mention other systems ALL of which rely on
the electrics on the boat working. No electrics, no
systems. EPIRB lasts 48 hours and only the crew gets
picked up, the boat is left.

To be honest I do not get the feeling the row is
well planned and properly equipped.

I always get an uncomfortable feeling when some
artificial deadline is named and there is a rush for
departure.

What we much prefer to hear is "departure will
be when the boat and crew is ready and properly
equipped."

I know you will say "they have no money to stay

in a hotel and they have to get going," we have
heard it many times before. Have they named a
destination yet?

My answer has to be, if you are not properly
funded and equipped don't leave. Go home, get funding and come back another time.

Crutchlow had no information about our expedition's
finances, the state of our boat, or our preparations, so it was
astounding to read his assumptions. The most ridiculous statement was that we could leave any time between October and
March. Every pilot book we had read argued that these were the
exact months that one should *not* be leaving the European coast.

It was a worry, though. Rowing across an ocean is dangerous no matter how well prepared you are. If something did
happen to Julie and me through bad luck, some critics in the
media might throw Crutchlow's I-warned-you comments back
in our faces.

To stick to our scheduled departure on the morning of the
twenty-second, Julie and I had to work through the final night.
We had timed our departure to coincide with the falling tide,
so the two-knot current would assist us in leaving the harbour.
Mario, his wife, and a friend arrived at the marina at 5 a.m. to
bid us goodbye. Mario pressed two bottles of wine into our
hands and insisted that we celebrate our birthdays in style.
Our small departure crowd waved as we untied our lines and
rowed out of the marina under the slanting rays of the rising
sun. We still felt sleepy, exhausted beyond belief, and yet our
trans-Atlantic row had only begun.

15

TO SEA IN A RED ROWBOAT

A S WE ROWED PAST THE BREAKWATER, a strong current gripped our heavily laden vessel and swept us towards the open ocean several kilometres distant. At this time of day, the Tagus Harbour was devoid of the usual flotilla of sailing yachts, dinghies, and powerboats. Apart from a solitary tug pulling a barge on the far side of the sound, Julie and I were alone.

My gentle strokes on the long carbon-fibre oars increased our speed to four knots, and we glided noiselessly under the shadow of Lisbon's famous landmark: Monument to the Discoveries. This 52-metre-high concrete sculpture displays the stylized bow of a ship, on which stand famous Portuguese explorers. The stony gaze of Ferdinand Magellan, the captain of the first expedition to circumnavigate the planet, cast us a final farewell.

After we'd been rowing for about 20 minutes, a dark grey boat approached us. As it drew closer, we could see it was the harbour police. Julie was now at the oars.

"Don't make eye contact," I joked. "Maybe they'll just pass on by."

We shouldn't have anything to fear, as Julie had already contacted the authorities and inquired about departure protocol. We were surprised to learn that we required no departure clearance and were allowed simply to row away without contacting customs and immigration. During my years of sailing, arrival and clearance procedures had been standard protocol in every country I had visited.

The powerful ship pulled alongside, and a uniformed crewmember threw us a rope. I felt nervous. Perhaps there had been a mistake in communication and we would now get drawn back into a multi-day clearance procedure. When Julie had asked about departure protocol, she hadn't actually mentioned we'd be leaving in a rowboat.

"Where are you going?" the captain asked.

"Miami, Florida," I said.

The eight or so crew on the invincible-looking steel ship looked at our tiny vessel with widening eyes. A few chuckled. The captain glanced over our boat and asked us a few questions about our safety equipment. He then asked for our passports and disappeared into the bridge for a few minutes. Finally he returned to the rail.

"You are free to leave," he declared. "Good luck."

I breathed a sigh of relief. We had an ideal weather window for departure, and there was no saying how long it would last. Soon the Portuguese trade winds would falter, and we hoped to be much farther south when that happened.

Red-and-green navigational buoys marked the deeper water, and Julie hugged the northern shore. Our GPS indicated that the current was diminishing, and our speed had dropped to 3.5 knots. We were in the lee of a large peninsula, which jutted 20 kilometres into the ocean and protected us from the brunt of the northern swell and wind.

We passed brightly coloured open fish boats with crews of three or four tending their nets. The crews would look at our boat in astonishment as we rowed towards nowhere, and they yelled words of encouragement in Portuguese. At least we assumed it was encouragement.

We wanted to get as far from land as we could as quickly

as possible, to reduce the risk of being smashed on the rocky shoreline if the winds changed. Four hours after leaving Lisbon, we cleared the tip of Cape de Roca and were exposed to the full force of the open ocean. Twenty-knot winds generated a choppy sea, and our stomachs rose and fell along with the boat on the enormous swell. Since we were rowing due west, the waves hit the boat on her side and made rowing difficult. It was like trying to juggle while on a mechanical bull. Every so often, when a large wave struck us broadside, we would be thrown off the sliding seat and into the lifelines which would prevent us from going over the side.

Our boat was overloaded, so the decks were constantly awash in water. If we dared to open any of the food hatches, the compartments would instantly be swamped. I swallowed uncomfortably and hoped there would be enough calm weather over the next week that we could replenish our accessible food supplies. What if the seas were always this rough, and we could never safely get at our stored food? I cursed Portuguese customs for withholding our lighter freeze-dried provisions. If the boat didn't weigh so much, we wouldn't be having this problem.

Julie and I took turns at the oars, switching each hour. The vector of forces on our boat—our westward rowing, combined with south-pushing winds and current—gave us an overall southwest direction at 2.5 knots—about 4.5 kilometres an hour.

The low mountains of Portugal teased us from the distance, like the closing credits of a memorable movie. Land would soon be just a memory, and Julie and I would become very well acquainted with our new water world. It was surreal, as my fatigue-addled brain tried to comprehend spending three to five months on the sea. We had been too busy on land worrying about logistics to spend much time considering the psychological aspects of the journey ahead. Now, as we struggled at the oars, on a rough ocean, exhausted, sleepy, and seasick with land fading in the distance, I began to feel seriously scared.

The waves would crash into the side of the boat and drench the rower. At the same time, water would gush through the scuppers—small openings that allow water to drain off the decks—swirl up to the rowing seat, and slowly retreat. Unlike a sailboat, which is stabilized by both its deep keel and the force of the wind in its sails, our vessel had no anti-roll mechanism, so the rocking motion was incredible. Both Julie and I were extremely nauseated and could eat only cheese and crackers for dinner, even after hours of physical exertion.

At 8 p.m., the sun reached the horizon. The ocean and sky briefly displayed a psychedelic array of red and orange before being swallowed into velvety blackness. The near-blindness we felt on our small, precarious vessel only increased our unease. We looked longingly back towards the electric glow of Lisbon, slowly fading in the distance. The only other retinal stimuli were the navigational lights of freighters and fishing boats on the horizon. Julie switched on the tiny incandescent light in the cabin and plotted our position on the chart while I pulled on the oars.

"We've gone 36 nautical miles," she announced. That was roughly 65 kilometres.

I was pleased. Tidal current had contributed to our speed, and that would only affect us near land. Still, it was a good start for our first day. I was also thrilled to see how well Julie was coping with her introduction to the ocean. She had never before been offshore. Landlubbers have trouble imagining just how terrifying it can be. Even though Julie remained sick from the relentless rocking, she showed no fear and voiced no complaints.

Even though the boat was fitted with two rowing stations, we would almost never row in tandem during our Atlantic crossing. Generally the boat moved at about 2 knots with one person hauling on the oars and about 2.5 knots with two (although the difference was more pronounced in adverse conditions). Therefore, it seemed more efficient to conserve our physical energies and double the rowing hours by taking shifts. The only time we'd need dual propulsion would be if our boat was dangerously near a rocky shore or oncoming vessel, and we suddenly needed extra power.

The oars, though 11 feet long, were made of carbon-fibre and feather light. They were custom made by Croker Oars of Australia, a company whose oars, more often than not, propel the winning boats in the Olympics. The sliding seat and relevant hardware were made by Pocock, a Seattle company that produces high-quality gear for world-class rowers.

As we struggled with the oars on the choppy cross-seas, we felt like anything but world-class rowers. The oars repeatedly caught on the waves or skipped across the surface. Still, we were moving forward slowly and, for now, speed didn't really matter. The most important thing was just to keep on going.

By 11 p.m., we were absolutely exhausted, having worked almost non-stop for the previous 41 hours. We were out of the main shipping lane and boat traffic seemed light, so Julie and I both retired to the tiny cabin for some much needed sleep. We set our stopwatches so we could check every 15 minutes for shipping. While the rowing station was untended, the boat would simply free drift in the winds and current. With present conditions we were moving at about one knot southwards.

Unfortunately, our cabin was so tightly packed with gear that there was only room for one person to lie on his or her back, while the other had to squeeze in sideways. Any shifts in position required a coordinated effort of verbal negotiations and physical manoeuvres. It wasn't exactly a Holiday Inn.

I felt as though I were packed into a small coffin, awaiting my watery burial. Inside the cabin it was inky black and hot, as the boat lurched in all directions. Without seeing the world outside I had an uneasy feeling that we would be dashed onto the rocks or hit by a freighter. Despite our exhaustion, we barely slept that first night.

THE FOLLOWING MORNING AT FIVE, Julie resumed the already monotonous toil of rowing while I tried to prepare our first breakfast. I heated a gruel of oatmeal, raisins, and water on the alcohol stove. Neither of us had much of an appetite, so most of my efforts went overboard for the fish. Coffee would have been a welcome pick-me-up, but the effort of searching for the various ingredients among our overpacked compartments in the lurching cabin proved to be more than I could stomach. Instead my glazed eyes looked past Julie's pistoning figure at the turbulent seas beyond.

The stiff winds continued to blow from the north. One couldn't yet consider the weather stormy, but the seas were certainly rough enough, and the swell had risen to about eight feet.

After my blistering hands took over the oars, Julie readied the water maker for its first sea trial. We both held our breath—a malfunction could mean the end of our voyage, or worse. We had back-up systems, but they are labour-intensive, and would reduce our rowing. Julie flipped the switch, and the electric motor started humming. Shortly after, the corroded unit began dribbling fresh water into a jerry jug. Two and a half hours produced 10 litres of water. I felt relieved when the jerry jug was full and we could turn the unit off. If our precious water maker could work its magic once, I reasoned, perhaps it could do it 150 more times.

We hoped to use no more than 10 litres of fresh water a day, for drinking and rehydrating our food. Cleaning ourselves, washing dishes, even brushing our teeth would all be done with sea water.

Our seasickness and fatigue began to sap our motivation. Even after several days into the crossing, it felt virtually impossible to do anything more than the bare minimum to survive. We forced ourselves to nibble on crackers and cookies throughout the day so that we would have the energy to keep rowing. Our destination, so many thousands of kilometres across a massive ocean, seemed on the far side of the galaxy. Our future looked so bleak—endless days of rocking and rowing—that at times I just wanted to turn the boat back towards Europe before it was too late.

I admired how well Julie was able to carry out jobs that required concentration, such as navigating or note taking, even though I knew she was feeling as awful as I was. Although she had never before been on an extreme adventure, Julie had displayed a pattern throughout her life of successfully completing any task she set for herself. Whether she was striving to complete her master's degree or run a marathon, Julie would push herself until the job was done. Interestingly, her motivation seems driven by something other, something deeper, than competition. Competitiveness is completely absent from Julie's character, and I've often wondered if it's because she is an only child.

As we prepared for the expedition, I think people often misinterpreted Julie's humble attitude towards the massive undertaking she was embarking on. Beneath her charming looks and casual banter was a brain that ticked with intelligence and determination. Both Kenneth Crutchlow, president of the Ocean Rowing Society, and the previous owners of our boat seemed to dismiss Julie as just another pretty face with dangerous delusions about what she could accomplish. Fortunately for me, however, over the years I had the privilege of discovering Julie's extraordinary character. When she'd told me six months earlier that she would be interested in travelling from Moscow to Vancouver, I knew I had a partner who would never let me down.

Now that we had embarked on the most treacherous part of the expedition, I knew that our combined optimism, hard work, and teamwork would carry us to the far side of this ocean.

OUR FIRST THREE DAYS AT SEA passed in a nauseous blur. We developed a routine of rowing 18 hours a day in two-hour shifts. While not on the oars, we would busy ourselves with navigation, cooking, cleaning, running the water maker, and inspecting the boat for problems. Small tasks that would be simple on the stability of land became nightmarishly awkward in the rolling sea. When we refilled the stove, we'd usually spill just as much as we managed to get in the reservoir. Any mechanical jobs would result in screws and bolts disappearing as the boat rocked. Often the cook would wear the food instead of eating it. Sometimes I just wanted to scream at the swells with frustration.

The weather remained constant, with continued stiff winds from the north. We still hadn't been able to access our deck hatches to get more food, and hoped that a calm day would arrive soon. When we departed Lisbon we had packed enough food for 10 days into the main cabin. If the weather stayed rough for more than two weeks, we would start to go hungry.

We made solid southwest progress, which was a good thing, and by day four we were about 300 kilometres from land, just below the southwest corner of Portugal. However, the winds intensified to 40 knots and the ocean became an angry monster. The waves towered higher, breaking around and across our small boat, and often threatening our vessel. On occasion the breaking waves would launch the boat forward at such speeds that she would carve down the face of the wave like a surfboard.

Eventually it became too difficult and dangerous to row, so we put out the drogue. A drogue is a funnel-shaped piece of durable cloth held open by a series of straps. A longer rope of about 100 metres then leashes the drogue to the bow of the boat. When lowered into the ocean, it acts like an aquatic parachute and creates immense drag as it is pulled through the water. The resistance keeps the bow of the boat pointing into the wind and waves and slows the boat's rate of backwards drift.

At least that's the theory. As the storm grew more menacing, we were about to discover how well it worked in practice.

LARGE WAVES CRASHED OVER THE BOAT as I struggled to the bow to secure the drogue. The boat pitched and heaved while I fumbled with the knots with one hand. My other hand clung, white and cold, to the safety rail. My Helly Hansen raingear shed the chilled water that dumped over me by the bucket. Suddenly, just as I had finished tying the bowline knot and had tossed the drogue over the side, a wave disproportionately larger than the rest reared above our vessel like a fist and then broke. The seething whitewater slammed our boat like a stick of dynamite, and *Ondine* rolled onto her side at the brink of a capsize. Instinctively, I hooked my arm around the lifeline to avoid being washed out of the boat. The water slowly drained out of the scuppers, and our vessel righted itself.

After all that, the drogue system didn't work as well as I had hoped. Unfortunately, because of the unique shape of our hull, the boat refused to point straight into the waves. Instead it sheered at about 60 degrees. At times it almost turned broadside to the swells. There wasn't much that we could do, though, other than huddle in our salt-and-pepper-shaker cabin and wait out the storm.

The cabin was damp, hot, and smelly. In these high seas, it lurched wildly like a broken carnival ride. We had to keep the hatch sealed to keep out the breaking waves and to prevent the cabin from flooding in the event of a capsize. If the aft cabin filled with heavy water, the boat would not be able to right itself.

Hours ticked by as Julie and I lay compressed against each other, with gear from both sides encroaching on our limited personal space. A snarling hiss announced the imminent arrival of each breaking wave and gave us time to brace before an almighty explosion would toss our vessel. Periodically, we would remember to open the hatch for a few seconds to replenish the oxygen in our sealed quarters. Without this manual ventilation, we would suffocate in about 12 hours.

As we lay in the cabin waiting out the storm, we called Dean Fenwick on the satellite phone so he could relay the latest weather forecast. He checked online and told us that conditions looked promising. We could look forward to calmer weather in about three days. In the meantime, the winds would continue blowing from the north and gradually diminish in intensity.

Dean also gave us an update on our competition. Erden had arrived in Lisbon. He was now clearing his vessel through customs, and it sounded like he was having far less trouble than we had in retrieving a few packages.

Tim had arrived in Salamanca, Spain, about a three-day cycle from Lisbon. He obviously had had no problems crossing the Russian border even though he had overstayed his Russian visa. He had told Carole Paquette that he planned on bribing the guards to get over the border. From Salamanca he had posted an update on his website stating that he and Erden would be racing Julie and me for the title of being the first to row non-stop from mainland Europe to North America. Strangely, perhaps after consultation with Erden, he soon changed this posting with a new update. "This is no longer a race," Tim emphasized, explaining that because Julie and I had left in an unseaworthy boat— "skipped standard boat preparations to save time"—he and Erden didn't want to put undue pressure on us by labelling their own attempt as a race.

Julie laughed when I told her this. "That's so kind of them," she joked. "I already feel safer now that I know they're not trying to pass us."

Dean went on to read out Erden's latest update:

"Colin Angus, Tim's former partner, left Lisbon rowing with his girlfriend Julie just before my arrival here. It is my understanding that they rushed their departure, and that their ocean rowing boat still needed another two weeks worth of work when they took off. Cutting corners in this endeavor is dangerous. I hope that they will be all right. Any call for rescue at sea by these two, should they need it, will give all ocean rowers a black eye, bruising the respectable status that we maintain with the respective Coast Guard units in host countries. I would like to think that Colin is not racing Tim back to Vancouver . . . Continuing this journey with the wrong motives will be misguided. Such a mindset will poison the four-month crossing, creating undue misery."

Erden seemed to have been networking with Kenneth Crutchlow of the Ocean Rowing Society. Julie and I were the only people aware of the condition of our boat, so I was surprised at how much speculation about *Ondine* was flying around. Stranger still, they all felt compelled to broadcast this gossip as widely as possible.

"So don't sink," Dean said as he concluded our long-distance chat. "No matter how seaworthy and well prepared your boat is, with all these rumours circulating, a lot of press will portray you as the disaster waiting to happen."

We were determined to follow Dean's advice. However, we were also aware that, due to the unpredictability of the sea, part of the success formula had to include good luck. If, for example, sustained heavy winds started blowing from the northwest, we would be unable to prevent a collision with Africa. We would have to call for help in the form of a tow. And then our armchair critics would really have something to gloat about.

AFTER A DAY AND A HALF, the seas calmed enough for Julie to attempt making breakfast. While she struggled to light the alcohol stove, I remained stuffed into the cabin, my feet towards the hatch, and rearranged our equipment to create more living space.

Julie released a shriek of pure terror. She was staring wide-eyed and skywards to the left of our boat.

"What is it?" I yelled, frantically trying to turn myself around.

Julie was too terrified to reply. She is normally calm and rational, so I knew something was seriously wrong. I turned around in time to see a huge wave rearing off the port side of the boat. Behind the wave a wall of dark blue steel rose as high as my limited line of sight allowed.

We were about to be hit by a freighter.

As I braced myself for the impact, a hundred thoughts flashed through my mind. We were hundreds of kilometres from shore on a cold, stormy ocean. Would we be sucked under the vessel and pulled through the enormous threshing machine of its propeller? Or would our boat just be crushed to matchsticks beneath our feet?

I had once seen a beautiful photograph of dolphins leaping out of the face of the wave cresting in front of a freighter's bow. Now, an identical scene appeared before us. Except there were no dolphins. And a 180-metre-long ship was about to mow us down.

Julie continued to shriek, and the foaming bow wave slammed into our vessel. *Ondine* was tossed like a cork to the side. The thrust barely pushed us out of the path of collision, and the steel hull passed within 30 centimetres of our own quarter-inch-plywood walls. This distance increased to an arm's length. All we could do was watch the awesome sight of 26,000 tonnes of steel sliding by for what seemed like an eternity. Finally, the transom of the tanker passed. We looked up and could make out the ship's name, *Norca*.

Julie and I looked at each other in wordless shock. I felt more vulnerable than ever. Despite out boat's radar reflector, which helps make a larger signal on a ship's radar, and brightly painted colours, nobody in the freighter had seen us, even in broad daylight. And although we had kept a vigilant watch, somehow this monster of the deep had been able to sneak up on us. Towering waves often obscured our vision. Clearly, these swells were obscuring our boat from others, too.

"I have never been so terrified in my entire life," Julie announced. "I can't believe it didn't hit us—it was a direct collision course."

Only the powerful bow wave of the freighter had saved us as it pushed our boat aside. A nagging thought haunted me. We had the drogue in the water and 100 metres of rope connecting it to our boat. Fortunately, the bow wave had tossed us *towards* the drogue, so there was no resistance. But what if we had been just slightly forward? The bow wave might have launched us *away* from the drogue, towards the other side of the freighter, but the braking effect of the drogue would have stopped us dead in our tracks—quite literally. Caught in the path of the *Norca,* we would have been crushed. Or, what if we had been 30 metres farther ahead and the freighter had run right between our boat and the drogue, snaring the connecting rope?

These were questions I hoped I would never have answered.

WE SKIPPED BREAKFAST, ate more crackers and cookies, pulled in the drogue and began rowing again. The freighter incident was terrifying, but it wouldn't stop us from rowing.

As Dean had predicted, the seas gradually calmed. On day 10, the ocean was the calmest we had encountered. For the first time, Julie and I no longer felt seasick. Long, gentle swells rolled in from the north. With the veil of lethargy, seasickness, and constant unease suddenly lifted, I felt a euphoria and renewed vigour take over. We had braved the ocean for 10 days and had travelled almost 800 kilometres. Soon we would be level with the top of Africa, and that was reason enough to celebrate. Additionally, we would finally be able to get at food secured behind the deck hatches. Julie wrote a list of provisions we would need for the next 10 days, and we took a break from rowing to embark on the delicate task that we dubbed "going shopping."

We plugged the scuppers with foam to reduce the inflow of water and gently eased open each of the eight deck hatches. There is a subtle technique to shutting the hatches without cross threading the corresponding grooves of the hatch lid and base. Unfortunately, it seems we hadn't quite mastered that skill in Lisbon. Julie opened the second starboard hatch and found it full to the brim with water. Cans and bags of food floated around. "Oh my god, the pasta has been ruined!" she said, and pulled out one soggy bag after another.

There was nothing we could do but empty the packets over the side. The other items of food were all sealed, but the 20 kilograms of pasta was a huge loss. We had extra bags stored in a different compartment, but the lost pasta still amounted to a large portion of our carbohydrate supply. We inspected the remaining compartments and were relieved to find them all dry.

With calmer conditions, our appetites returned and we put more effort into cooking. Breakfasts usually featured oatmeal, cream of wheat, rice, or tapioca pudding, along with liberal doses of powdered milk and raisins. This meal would be washed down with sweet and milky instant coffee. We were hauling 200 litres (in its reconstituted state) of powdered milk, so we used it abundantly in our cooking. We had also packed pancake mix for special occasions.

For lunch, we filled up on dried bread or crackers, cheese, cured meats, or tuna and canned sardines. Throughout the day, we fuelled our efforts with cookies and candies.

While I was assigned to be breakfast boy, Julie used her imagination to create an array of dinners from our limited ingredients. In our first month at sea, she somehow managed not to repeat the same meal twice. Some of these culinary delights included macaroni and cheese (made from fresh Portuguese cheese, butter, tuna, flour, milk, and pasta), chili (onions, garlic, beans, spices, corned beef, and rice), omelets, stew and rice, Moroccan curry (chick peas, raisins, caramelized onions, garlic, cinnamon, and couscous), and Thai curry (coconut milk, pineapple, tuna, green Thai curry sauce, canned vegetables, and rice).

OUR THREE-DAY SPELL OF CALMER CONDITIONS soon came to an end. The blue skies faded, although the temperatures remained warm and muggy. The winds began to blow from the south-west, the exact direction we didn't want them from. It came as a sudden shock to row into the wind and waves. The oars were harder to pull and strained our joints to their limits. Over the course of eight hours, even as we hauled hard, our speed gradually decreased until we were stationary.

The only thing more frustrating than rowing on the spot is going backwards while exerting every bit of energy. And this is what began to happen as the southwest winds reached 20 knots. I laughed ruefully as I thought of a friend from my distant past who told me that he preferred kayaking to rowing because he couldn't see where he was going while on the oars. If only I could teleport him onto our boat, he would have his wish: he could row his heart out and still see exactly where he was heading.

Finally, we abandoned the oars and threw the drogue over the side. Even if it didn't point us into the waves, at least it would slow our backwards drift.

For three days, the wind blew hard from the southwest and our boat drifted slowly back towards Europe. It was disheartening, but there was nothing we could do but wait for the weather to relent. We did, however, keep a more vigilant watch to avoid another close encounter with a passing tanker.

16

HURRICANE VINCE

WE SCRUTINIZED OUR BRITISH ADMIRALTY PILOT CHARTS, which compile weather data from thousands of ships. Our charts covered the North Atlantic, with 12 versions, one for each month of the year. The charts display the mean water temperature, air temperature, frequency of storms, average winds directions, and other essential information. Pilot charts are the best source of comprehensive weather probabilities for a given region. It was by studying these charts that Julie and I were able to determine the time of year we should depart and the route we should take to catch the best currents and winds.

From the charts, we could see that the southwest winds we were experiencing were not common, so they were unlikely to remain indefinitely. We were also reassured to see that the probability of storms in this region at this time of year was extremely low.

At last, after three days of our lying semi-comatose in the cabin, the southwest winds gave way to calm conditions, and we could resume rowing. We had drifted backwards 60 kilometres, and it would take a full day of hard work to regain this lost distance.

Since leaving Portugal, our goal was to travel west as quickly as possible, to distance ourselves from the onshore hazards of Europe and Africa. We hoped to pass the westernmost tip of the Canary Islands, at which point the winds would begin to stabilize and blow fairly consistently from the northeast.

Contrary winds had blown us farther east than we'd like, so it was disappointing when these southwest winds returned, after only a day of rowing. At least it was only a breeze, at about 10 knots, so we were able to make progress, however slow.

October 8 dawned with altocumulus and cirrus clouds streaking across the sky. It seemed an unusual display and I didn't know what it meant. The sun, a quivering peach on the horizon, painted the seas with shimmering red. It was Julie's birthday, and I was determined to make it a special day.

While Julie laboured into the headwinds, I made pancakes. We had no syrup, but I solved this problem by caramelizing sugar in the pan and adding water. The resulting breakfast of pancakes, butter, syrup, strawberry jam, and whipped cream (which we carried in small TetraPaks) was scrumptious.

Julie made a birthday wish. She kept it secret, but I suspected it might be for better weather. The winds were rising, and once again we had to abandon our rowing and drop the drogue over the side.

I had planned on making an equally decadent dinner, complete with a bottle of Mario's wine, but the ocean had other concrete plans. Despite Julie's secret wish, we found ourselves on an even more wretched sea, blown in the wrong direction. Compressed in the cabin once again, I began scrawling in my notebook while Julie called her father on the phone. Shortly after her dad answered, Julie's tone changed.

"Are you sure?" she asked. "Where did you hear that?"

Pause.

"No, there's probably some kind of mistake," she continued. "There have never in history been any hurricanes anywhere near this region. It would be like a hurricane forming over the Great Lakes."

Long pause.

"I'm sure they made some sort of mistake," she assured her father. "Perhaps they mistook the island of Madeira for Martinique in the Caribbean."

I wasn't worried. There was obviously some kind of mix-up. Hurricanes couldn't form where we were situated. The water was simply too cold.

Julie finally closed the phone and turned to me. "My dad says a hurricane has formed just near Madeira and is heading straight towards us. Do you know what I wished for this morning? Favourable winds! Can you believe that as I made the wish, a hurricane was spawning 600 nautical miles from us?"

Granted, the weather *was* acting strangely. We'd never seen clouds like these before, and the air seemed unusually muggy. Still, we couldn't believe a hurricane was coming our way. I called Dean just to be sure.

"Would you mind checking the National Hurricane Center website?" I asked. I waited while Dean tapped on his keyboard. The boat was rising and falling on an unusually large swell from the south.

"Holy shit, guys," Dean said in a strained voice. "There actually is a hurricane, very, very close to you. And it's heading . . ." There was a long pause while Dean scanned the page for the information. "It's heading straight for you. It's moving east-northeast. Good god, I'm just looking at the satellite picture. This is definitely a real hurricane, with an eye in the middle with clouds streaking around it. It's pure evil!"

It sure was. I felt like this storm was hand-delivered straight from Satan himself, created for no other purpose than to destroy a quarter-inch-plywood rowboat.

The hurricane had formed in waters cooler than 24 Celsius, contrary to scientific consensus that a tropical storm needs sea temperatures of at least 26.5 degrees to intensify.

Because of this theory, meteorologists had debated about whether to categorize this one as a tropical cyclone. Finally, it became clear to them that it had to be a hurricane—a hurricane born in an area where it couldn't and shouldn't exist.

And one that was bearing down on Julie and me.

"So what did Dean say?" Julie asked after I turned off the phone.

"It doesn't sound good," I told her. "The hurricane is off the northwest coast of Madeira, directly west-southwest of us and about 500 nautical miles away. Unfortunately, it is slowly moving east-northeast, and is expected to continue doing so. At its current speed, it shouldn't hit us until tomorrow night. The good news is that all predictions for this hurricane are likely to be wrong. Since this storm is unprecedented, there is no history of patterns to go on. So perhaps the predicted direction of travel might be wrong."

"That's just fantastic news," said Julie glumly. "So the most likely scenario is that we are going to be in the middle of a hurricane in 36 hours."

I nodded.

It seemed like a bad dream. We were facing a high chance that we would not make it out of this predicament alive. Hurricanes are the most powerful weather phenomenon on the planet. They have the power to level entire cities, never mind tiny rowboats.

As a young man I spent five years offshore sailing, much of it solo. In total I travelled more than 20,000 kilometres in my tough little vessel, beginning on Vancouver Island and finishing in Papua New Guinea after exploring remote outposts of the South Pacific Ocean. My years of sailing had taught me just how powerful the seas can become when combined with a storm. Tempests half the strength of a hurricane had humbled me, and I prayed I would never have to face the wrath of a true demon of the sea. And now, in a tiny rowboat, with the person I loved the most on the planet, it looked as though I might be on my final voyage.

There was no denying the facts. If the hurricane struck us square on, our boat would likely founder and we would die. It was surreal knowing that we likely had only 36 hours left before our lives would be extinguished in a terrifying maelstrom of wind and water. Now I knew what it must feel like to be a prisoner on death row, 36 hours from the execution hour, praying for a last-minute pardon.

FASTER-MOVING BOATS, SUCH AS FREIGHTERS AND YACHTS, can scuttle out from a hurricane's path. Such manoeuvring was impossible for us. Rowing is slow at the best of times, but when a hurricane nears, the winds and rough seas render this form of propulsion useless. Even worse, the winds and currents move in a spiralling fashion and would draw us inexorably towards the storm's centre.

The low pressure in the centre of the depression is so great that it actually bulges the ocean's surface. This bulge draws water from thousands of kilometres around it and generates powerful currents of up to two knots. If the bulge reaches shore, higher water levels will overwhelm coastlines in what's known as a storm surge. One only has to look at the havoc that Hurricane Katrina wreaked on the U.S. Gulf Coast to appreciate the dangers.

These forces were already on the move. With the boat free drifting, we were travelling at about 1.5 knots towards the cyclone, pulled towards a giant black hole like the Starship *Enterprise*—and with no Scotty to fix our engines.

It was now late afternoon. The cloud ceiling was changing rapidly, alternating between thick grey clouds and blue skies that outlined corrugated cirrus clouds, like the bleached ribs of a long dead animal. The winds blew from the southeast at about 20 knots, and the air was extremely muggy, perhaps 28 degrees. Our bodies were greasy with perspiration. We could clearly see two sets of waves: a short, steep set from the southeast created by the local winds, and the slowly moving 20-foot swell rolling in from the direction of the hurricane—the den of Satan. These latter swells looked more like a rapidly rising and falling tide than distinct ocean waves.

Julie and I began to ready our boat as best we could for the storm. We secured loose items, such as cooking utensils and the stove, in lockers. We inspected all the hatches for leaks, made sure all our safety gear, including the life raft, EPIRB, flares, and radios, were easy to access, and checked the drogue.

Finally, there was nothing to do but wait.

We nibbled crackers, cheese, and cured meat in silence as the boat bucked on a darkening ocean.

"This is a birthday you'll remember for the rest of your life," I finally said, trying to pull a thin veil of humour over our grim state of affairs.

"Yeah, I'll treasure these memories for the next 30 hours," Julie replied.

I wondered what would be the weak point in our boat's defences. Would the *Ondine* simply disintegrate under the sheer force of 60-foot waves? Or would the hatches spring leaks and the boat start to swamp with each roll? Once the boat filled with water, the force of the sea would have more destructive impact, as the increased ballast would resist inertia—the boat itself would absorb more of the impact from exploding waves instead of transferring the energy into kinetic force by sliding away from the blow.

For the first time since we had left Portugal, we could see no lights from other boats in the distance. All shipping traffic had been routed away from the path of the storm. This diversion at least meant we didn't need to worry about getting run down in the darkness. Still, I suddenly missed the company of the bigger ships in our proximity. As we bounced around in inky blackness, it would have been reassuring to see a light and to know we weren't entirely alone. But we were.

JULIE AND I BARELY SLEPT at all that night. Instead we lay listlessly, every so often breaking into conversation—almost always focused on the approaching storm. We read the sections in our pilot charts about hurricanes and tried to find comfort in the fact that this storm shouldn't be happening. Perhaps the cooler water might suddenly extinguish this freak. Or perhaps it would start to curve in its path of travel, like so many of the Caribbean hurricanes.

The wind had increased to about 30 knots. The seas outside were confused as waves collided against each other. Despite the tumult, our boat seemed to be doing well.

The light of dawn illuminated a desolate seascape. The cloud cover, thick and black, had been reworked in the devil's palette. Breaking waves scarred the black ocean surface with wounds of white. And the shrieking wind eroded wave tops into foaming spray.

Julie phoned the National Hurricane Center in Miami to get an update. Nothing had changed, except that the hurricane was much closer. The storm was still classified as full-fledged hurricane and it was still heading straight for us. The official at the hurricane centre relayed the coordinates for the storm, and we were able to plot the new location. It was 300 nautical miles away, moving at 20 knots. We could expect to meet the brunt of the storm by evening.

We had packed plenty of safety gear, but like a man falling from a 50-storey building with an ample first aid kit, it didn't offer much consolation. If our rowboat foundered, we could launch our self-inflating four-man life raft and activate our EPIRB.

Throughout the day, the winds continued to increase along with the size of the waves. In the early afternoon, we made another call to the hurricane centre and received slightly better news. Although the hurricane was still moving in our general direction, it looked like it was now angling slightly towards the north. If it continued in this direction, the eye would pass from 80 to 100 nautical miles to our north, which might spare us the death blow. It was impossible to estimate just how severe the seas would be at this distance, but at least we might now stand a chance.

"This is great news," I said to Julie.

Julie was just completing the latest plot of our position relative to the hurricane. The two fresh Xs on the chart looked frighteningly close to one another.

"If it misses us by a hundred miles, the winds probably won't be in excess of 50 knots," I said with forced cheer. "We'll experience a bit of rocking and rolling, and soon we'll be back to our old routine of rowing through flat seas."

At this point, the winds were already blowing at close to 50 knots, and enormous waves slammed into our boat as they broke. An especially large wave slammed the hull, and the boat rolled until she was 90 degrees to the water. In the cabin, Julie and I piled against each other and the port wall. The boat held this awkward position for five seconds, as though it couldn't decide which way to go next, before finally rolling upright. As it did so, another wave hit the boat, and we heard a loud cracking sound.

"What was that?" Julie asked, eyes wide.

I pressed my face against the Plexiglas and strained to see, but my vision was limited in the fading light. In 15 minutes, we would be plunged into total blackness once again. I considered opening the hatch to investigate the noise and inspect the boat, but such a move would have been too dangerous with waves continually breaking over the deck. We could roll again at any time, too, so we couldn't risk opening the hatch for more than a few seconds.

Instead, I wrapped my arms around Julie and squeezed her against me. Tonight, we would learn once and for all just how strong our boat was.

WE CALCULATED THAT THE STORM WOULD PASS closest to us by about 11 p.m. As this dreaded hour approached, the movement of the boat increased in its violence, slamming Julie and me from side to side in the cabin like a pair of dice in a shaker. The wind emitted a shrieking whine, which was periodically drowned out by an even louder noise: the thunder of a breaking waves as they slammed into the boat. When the waves weren't breaking, the boat would simply rise up and up until it reached the wave's crest and then suddenly plummet with sickening speed like an elevator with its wires cut.

I was amazed at how well our boat handled the abuse. Perhaps the weight of our overloaded craft, and our food and gear packed low in the boat, made it impossible to capsize. Wave after wave slammed into *Ondine* with what felt like enough force to roll her over. Instead, she would just tilt 90 degrees, shed the tonnes of water that sluiced over the decks and then flip back to normal. She seemed to fare even better in the monstrous waves. The boat would submerge like a surfer duck diving through the break, and the force of the water would wash right over her.

Eleven o'clock arrived and our boat was still afloat. Julie and I weren't faring as well, though. We were covered in bruises as we endured what felt like a barrel ride down a never-ending staircase. Somehow, at least, we hadn't broken any bones.

The outside temperature must have been pushing 30 degrees. Inside the cabin, it was much, much hotter, like a floating sauna, and we were dripping in sweat. We had emptied our water bottles, and there was no way to get more until conditions calmed. After being hit by an especially large breaking wave, we would take advantage of the 15 or 20 seconds of calm to open the hatch a crack and allow hurricane-fresh air into the cabin.

"You know, I think we're going to make it," Julie said.

It was now past midnight, and for the first time we were beginning to feel we had a chance. The intensity of the hurricane seemed to have levelled off, or perhaps even decreased slightly. In a few hours, if the hurricane's direction remained constant, it would be past us.

Minutes ticked by like hours, and we cringed each time a churning wave thrashed our boat. It seemed, however, that fewer and fewer breaking waves were beating against the boat. By 3 a.m., we were certain—the worst was over and we had been spared.

By seven, the wind had dropped significantly, although we were still in confused seas, with waves rushing from every direction, frequently colliding and sending water exploding skywards. Julie and I clambered onto the deck and found everything intact, apart from the drogue. The force of the ocean had ripped the ropes from the fabric, and the rope hung limp in the water. I noted how our boat was handling the ocean without the drogue, and realized that losing it was the best thing that could have happened. Our boat sat at a much better angle to the waves, with the stern pointing windward at a

45-degree angle, which seemed the ideal angle to deflect the waves' force while making the boat less inclined to surf. With the drogue, the boat would frequently turn broadside into the waves—the worst angle to take them on. Even though we had a spare drogue, we decided that it would only be used to slow our drift and not as a heavy-weather tool.

We waited another 24 hours. Finally, the ocean had calmed enough that we could resume rowing. The seas had settled down, and the air had stilled. Julie beamed as she pulled long, steady strokes through the sea. Once again *Ondine* was moving forward.

"The good news," Julie announced merrily, "is that we don't need to worry about being hit by any more hurricanes. The chance of being hit by two hurricanes outside of the hurricane season and hurricane belt must be less than being hit by lightning twice."

I had to agree. The chance of our even being hit by one hurricane had been about nil, but somehow it had happened. We had made it through alive, and the pilot charts indicated relatively smooth waters ahead.

17

WATER, WATER EVERYWHERE

T HE NEXT FEW DAYS PASSED SMOOTHLY, and we were finally becoming adapted to life at sea. With the seasickness and accompanying lethargy completely gone, we were now able to focus more on the beauty of the ocean around us.

Hawksbill turtles, dolphins, and occasional sharks would pass alongside, seemingly oblivious to our lumbering vessel. Julie and I would leap into the ocean to cool off in the clear blue waters. Although the danger of a shark attack was extremely low, we could never quite shake the uneasy feeling that large sea creatures were observing our dangling legs from the watery depths. We each took turns swimming while the other person stayed in the boat on shark watch.

As we continued southwest at a steady pace, Dean relayed updates about Erden and Tim's progress, all of which Erden outlined in great detail on his expedition website. They had ended up pushing their departure date from October 4 to October 12, as both Tim and the boat had arrived in Lisbon later than anticipated.

On October 11, the night before their departure, heavy rains revealed that their hatches were leaky. They hadn't tested the watertightness of the boat with a hose, it seemed, so it was a stroke of good luck that the rains had exposed the problem—Erden had failed to lubricate the O-rings with silicone—before their sea journey. Repairs would be made and a new departure date was set in three days, for October 17.

Their send-off entourage included Lisbon media and the ambassadors of both Canada and Turkey. As the bright yellow rowboat reached the cleaner waters of the open ocean, though, Erden decided to test the water maker, a task he hadn't yet gotten around to. Bad news. The machine didn't work, so the duo had to turn back to shore and row into the marina of Cascais, about 15 kilometres from Lisbon. It was an inauspicious first day.

Tim and Erden managed to find a local technician to diagnose and fix the water maker's trouble: the intake and outtake hoses had been reversed during installation. They planned to set off again the next morning. However, marina authorities demanded to see registration papers for the boat. Erden had none. That snafu took two days to resolve. A new departure date was announced. But this day came and went, and the men remained on shore.

Then the unfortunate duo encountered their biggest problem yet. The Portuguese trade winds had faltered, so it was too late in the year to leave safely from the Portuguese coast. Erden had earlier admitted that he had gotten much of his advice from Kenneth Crutchlow of the Ocean Rowing Society. It seemed likely that Kenneth had given Erden the same advice that he had offered us: to depart from Lisbon any time between October and April. In an earlier update, Erden had stated that the beginning of October was on the early side to depart safely from Lisbon (in fact, it's on the late side), so he was likely unaware of the degrading weather off the coast.

Now, stuck in the expensive tourist town of Cascais, Erden and Tim had to wait and pray for a window of opportunity as storm after storm rolled in from the Atlantic.

Julie and I couldn't help but feel a little relieved. Although we were concerned for their safety, it felt good to have a little more distance on our round-the-world rivals.

THE POST-HURRICANE WEATHER PROVED PLEASANT, and we continued to make good progress towards the Canary Islands. We would remain near a busy shipping lane for the next 2,000 kilometres, so large freighters remained a common sight. Sometimes we would spot five or six in a day. A Spanish fishing boat, 400 kilometres off the coast of Africa, sighted us and changed course to investigate. As the 80-foot red wooden vessel pulled close, all hands emerged onto the deck to hoot and holler. They circled a few times before resuming their northeast course.

We also discovered some other visitors, who took up residence beneath the boat. Three small striped fish, perhaps 10 to 15 centimetres long, began to follow our boat across the ocean. When we rinsed our plates over the side, they would swim to the surface to eat the scraps. They soon became our pets. Julie named them Fred, Ted, and Ned, and we could tell them apart by slight differences in their markings. The fish were so tame that we could dive under the boat with a mask and snorkel and swim alongside our new friends. Our little fish would swim frantically, keeping pace with our vessel, as we moved relentlessly across the ocean. Their determination was rewarded every time we washed our dishes.

Finally, after more than a month without seeing land, we made out the faint outline of the Canary Islands in the distance. The Canaries are a chain of volcanic islands, beginning about 60 kilometres off the coast of Africa and extending 500 kilometres. The weather in this region is extremely dry, with the winds coming off Africa, and the rocky outcrops we saw were devoid of greenery. The islands' subtropical latitude of about 28 degrees creates a pleasant climate for much of the year, ideal for European beach lovers. Resorts abound on the various islands, and the sky was constantly streaked with the contrails of jetliners shuttling sun-seeking Europeans back and forth.

We had no intention of stopping in the Canary Islands, though, as any landfall in a rowboat is fraught with danger. Instead we wanted to get through the island chain as quickly as possible to avoid the dangers of being blown into a lee shore. Fortunately, as we approached the island chain, the winds calmed even more.

"What's that?" Julie asked one day as she peered over the side of the boat.

I looked into the water and made out the unmistakable iridescent colours. "That's a dorado," I said. "I ate them all the time when I was on my old sailboat." So far, despite several attempts, we had not caught any fish.

Julie grabbed the fishing rod and lowered the green rubber squid, which we had packed for bait, into the water. Immediately, the dorado surfaced from the depths to investigate. Once near the squid, though, the fish lost interest.

"Try moving it back and forth," I ventured.

I remembered on my sailboat that I would catch dorado only when the line was being trolled at four knots or more. They are used to catching fast fish. Our boat was stationary in the water.

Julie swept the end of the rod above the water, and the rubber squid dashed back and forth. With incredible speed, the dorado lunged after the lure and was immediately hooked. A few minutes later, Julie hauled her three-kilo catch on board.

I gutted the fish, and Julie breaded the pieces in flour, salt, and spices and fried her catch in oil. Along with a can of vegetables and some instant mashed potatoes, our dinner that evening was by far the best that we had eaten since Portugal.

IT WAS NOW LATE OCTOBER, and we received the latest update on the competition. Tim and Erden were still stuck in Cascais. Storm after storm had buffeted the Portuguese coast, and the winds kept coming from the south and southwest. Erden contacted a variety of experts for their advice. Carlos Ribeiro Ferreira, a European sailing champion, reiterated the information from the pilot charts and told Erden that, at this time of year, once the southern winds establish themselves, they can stay for months. "If you don't go now," he warned the men, "you may never be able to leave."

It was clear that Erden now understood the implications of approaching winter, and that the months of October to March were not the ideal months to depart. "At this point the delays are not in our favor," he wrote on his website. "The later we wait, the more entrenched the winter wind patterns will become."

Erden and Tim were so desperate to leave before the full brunt of winter was upon them that they even pondered "harbour hopping," or taking advantage of short-lived calms to row from marina to marina, where they could weather the rougher conditions. In theory it sounded feasible; however, any such attempt would almost certainly result in disaster. Inevitably, the men would be caught out on the water where an onshore wind might propel them into the cliffs. Fortunately, more experienced seamen advised Erden against such a rash decision.

Finally, after weeks of waiting, Erden and Tim concluded that they would not be able to depart from Lisbon. In an October 29 update, they announced radically changed plans: "We have decided with Tim that moving the launch point of the boat is essential to make progress this season. We financially cannot afford to remain in Portugal until spring . . . We are now preparing to ship our boat to Morocco in a container just like it arrived at Lisbon. The port of entry for the boat will be Casablanca. Depending on the wind patterns, we may launch as far south as Agadir."

Erden explained that, for millennia, early explorers had avoided departing from Portugal during the fall and winter months. I thanked providence that Erden had made the mistake of following the advice of Kenneth Crutchlow rather than making decisions based on historical records. Erden had publicly chastised Julie and me for our haste in leaving from Lisbon, completely oblivious to the fact that our primary reason for our rapid departure was safety.

In Erden's new update he explained that Tim would ride his bicycle to the Strait of Gibraltar and from there kayak or row across the Mediterranean to Africa. Here, he would continue pedalling down the coast of Morocco towards their new departure point. Erden, meanwhile, would handle the logistics of shipping, receiving, and readying the boat for the next leg of the expedition.

It never ceased to amaze me the lengths that Erden was willing to go to help Tim across the Atlantic Ocean and finish his human-powered odyssey. In total the project had cost tens of thousands of dollars and hundreds of hours of labour. Now he planned to embark on a challenging and dangerous endeavour—rowing across the Atlantic—for someone else's glory. As costs continued to mount and the logistics became more complicated, Erden continued to make sure that Tim had all the support he needed.

"As much as I would like to ride with Tim, I must remain in a logistical support role," he reported in another website update. "This particular journey remains Tim Harvey's trip to Vancouver. I will attempt to film and to document Tim's progress, and make sure that the boat is delivered safely and intact to our launch point."

Erden's intervention must have seemed a winning lottery ticket to Tim. I often wondered why Erden had become so inspired to go, quite literally, to the ends of the world to help a man whom he barely knew. Erden had his own expedition, so it couldn't be that he was looking for a little adventure. Tim and Erden had exchanged a couple of emails and perhaps a phone call prior to Erden's making his life-altering offer. Had this limited interaction been enough to trigger a bond of brotherly affection? It was hard for me to comprehend. Of course, as with most people, I would go to great lengths to assist another human in danger. However, only for someone I loved dearly would I go to the extraordinary efforts that Erden was now devoting to Tim's personal pursuit.

WHILE TIM AND ERDEN WERE ATTEMPTING TO SHIP their boat, Julie and I were slipping slowly through the Canary Islands. The withered island of Lanzarote passed by our port side. Volcanic and extremely dry, the island seemed a crumpled canvas painted using only two colours: brown and black. Sheer cliffs dropped into the sea, but we didn't dare venture too close for a better look. Ironically, one of the greatest hazards on this Atlantic voyage came whenever we got too near terra firma.

It would take us about three days to pass through the string of islands. Despite the dangers, a festive atmosphere prevailed on our boat. We expected to reach the long-awaited trade winds and currents shortly after the islands. In the meantime, we were enjoying the calm conditions as much as possible by fishing, swimming, and experimenting with gourmet fish dishes.

Our Iridium satellite telephone had allowed me to keep in touch with my mother almost daily, and I was relieved that her health was fairly good. She complained about her new drugs and said she felt some energy loss. But these complaints seemed trivial considering that she was still able to go on her regular 10-kilometre runs. Not bad for any 74-year-old. Now that Julie and I had weathered our first month at sea and survived a hurricane, I think my mother felt less stressed about our well-being. Now she was able to enjoy our stories about the rowing and the wildlife.

As we neared the islands of Fuerteventura and Gran Canaria, *Ondine* felt increasingly sluggish. The culprit, we discovered, was a thick carpet of gooseneck barnacles and algae that had blossomed on the bottom of the boat. Every time we went swimming we could see the filter-feeding crustaceans firmly attached to the vessel, their small oarlike appendages sweeping the water—in the reverse direction of our own oars—in search of plankton. Their long muscular stalks hung five to eight centimetres from the bottom of the boat, and this mass of tendrils generated a lot of speed-sucking drag.

Julie stood on shark watch while I swam in the water and cleaned the hull of our boat with a paint scraper. Thousands of little barnacle bodies dropped like snowflakes into the depths. Soon dozens of fish arrived to feast on the shellfish. Julie and I would have loved to have eaten the large barnacles, which are considered a delicacy in both Spain and Portugal. However, we were worried they might have absorbed toxins from the anti-fouling paint.

Shortly after I was back on deck, a large pilot whale surfaced nearly 50 metres from our vessel. I noticed the sleek black shape with a disproportionately small dorsal fin only when I was startled by the whale's loud exhalation, like an old man gasping his final breath. The creature dove and resurfaced twice quickly before disappearing into the depths. Moments later, a pod of four bottlenosed dolphins cavorted near the surface. Soon they, too, disappeared.

I stood watching across the water and hoping that the whale would reappear when a fin started rising out of the water. At first I thought it must be the dolphins or the whale.

But as the fin extended farther out of the water, cutting along without the typical rise and fall of a marine mammal, I realized I was looking at a shark.

The fin lifted to about a metre in height and circled the boat with great velocity. In all my years on the ocean, I've seen hundreds of sharks, but I had never witnessed a fin anywhere close to the size of this creature's.

"Julie, get the video camera, quick," I yelled. "There's a *huge* shark out here!"

Julie clambered out of the cabin with the big video camera. "Where is it?"

I pointed towards the Jaws-like fin. Julie's eyes widened.

"Holy shit!" she exclaimed. "That's huge!"

After two more circles of our boat, the fin slid back into the water and disappeared. We stood quietly for a few minutes and waited to see if any of our recent visitors would return. To be honest, I was surprised to have seen the shark. I had often been told that sharks will leave if dolphins are in the area, as dolphins often ram their gills. I now reshuffled this notion into the category of ocean myth.

Suddenly, a large grey shape materialized in the water about 40 metres from the boat. This one was headed straight towards us. The undulating mass had such enormous proportions that I assumed it must be the whale again, so I was pleased that it was approaching the boat. Whales are gentle creatures, and good navigators, too, so I didn't worry that a near-sighted cetacean was about to run us down.

As the creature closed on the *Ondine,* though, I noticed its body's movement seemed more like that of a fish. Marine mammals pulsate their tails up and down rather than side to side.

I was momentarily confused. The shape seemed too big to be a shark, yet it wasn't moving like a whale. Julie aimed the video camera at the mysterious creature.

The animal closed on the boat, and its features became clear. It was nothing other than an enormous great white shark, the infamous king of the ocean. The grey and white creature moved with alarming speed near the surface, and just before reaching the boat, it descended just enough to avoid a collision. The shark was close enough to the surface that we could have reached into the water and grabbed its dorsal fin as it slid past. It was probably about six metres long, but more astounding was its girth. The creature was nearly as wide as our boat, with a whale-like belly. That this huge beast was actually a lightning-quick, razor-toothed killing machine made me shiver.

The shark seemed interested in our boat, and I wondered what was attracting him. Was it the aroma of freshly scraped barnacles? I thanked providence that the shark hadn't decided to visit two hours earlier, while I was in the water. Even though we had only a thin layer of plywood between us, I doubted he would try to attack our vessel.

The shark emerged on the other side of the boat and then disappeared from view for good. We felt lucky to have seen the ocean's most spectacular carnivore and acquired a renewed respect for the waters around us.

Unfortunately, movies such as *Jaws* have given great whites a bad reputation, and their numbers have been reduced drastically through hunting by humans, their only predator. Today, great whites are protected in many parts of the world, and conservationists hope their populations will bounce back.

The ruthless nature of the shark begins in the earliest stages of its development. They are born within their mother through a process called aplacental viviparity. Unlike other types of fish, the mother carries the fertilized eggs inside her until they hatch. The baby sharks remain inside their mother until they develop further. Without a placenta to provide nourishment, the baby sharks feed on unhatched eggs and weaker siblings. Finally, the mother gives birth to the surviving members of her family. The newborns have developed enough by then to fend for themselves—and to swim quickly away from their mother before she gobbles them up.

The life expectancy of a great white is unknown, but biologists reckon they may live up to a hundred years. Our recent visitor, if size is any indication, was one of these ocean-going geriatrics. A five-metre great white is considered large, although there have been reports of sharks as large as seven metres.

AFTER OUR SHARK ENCOUNTER, we began to row again and moved half a knot faster with the boat's cleaned bottom. We were 15 nautical miles from the island of Gran Canaria. As night fell, the bright lights of this major tourist destination filled the sky with a yellow glow. Julie and I had been out at sea for almost a month now, with only each other for company, and it was strange to see the lights of civilization again in the distance. Just a few short miles away, there were freeways, resorts, fancy restaurants, nightclubs, and all the decadence that comes with such an island getaway. Despite the proximity of land, though, nothing had changed in our world. The ocean was as inky black as ever, the noises were the same, and the company was the same, and so was the food. Tomorrow we would pass between the islands of Gran Canaria and Fuerteventura, and soon afterwards the Canary Islands would fade into the distance.

Navigation was becoming more of a hazard, as shipping grew increasingly concentrated in the funnel-like passage between the islands. Local fishing boats also contributed to the offshore traffic.

At about 11 p.m., midway through her rowing shift, Julie awakened me as I dozed in the cabin. "Hey, Colin, do you mind coming out," she said. "We've got a Christmas treat coming towards us."

At night, ships run a system of red, green, and white navigational lights. The lights are shielded so they can be seen only from certain angles, which allows observers to figure out which side of the ship they are looking at and roughly calculate which direction the boat is heading. A green light indicates the starboard, or right, side of the boat, while the port side emits a red light, and the stern a white light. If you can see both the red and the green light simultaneously, it means you are looking at the front of the boat—in other words, it's coming straight towards you. Julie and I jokingly called this very serious display of red and green a "Christmas treat."

We couldn't gauge how far away the ship was, so we began to take defensive precautions. Julie climbed into the cabin to fetch the handheld VHF radio and the flares. I began rowing at three knots and a 90-degree angle to the ship's line of approach.

"This is rowing vessel *Ondine*," Julie said into the radio. "We are trying to contact the ship bearing towards us. Do you copy?"

Silence. The green and red lights continued to get brighter.

"This is rowing vessel *Ondine*. We are displaying a white flashing strobe light. We are asking the vessel heading towards a bright white strobe to alter course."

Nothing.

I was surprised that my own efforts on the oars weren't moving our boat out of the ship's line of travel. I realized, to my alarm, that this large night traveller must be steering towards us, homing in on our small craft like a heat-seeking missile. I let go of the oars and pulled hard on the rudder cords, turning our boat 180 degrees. I then resumed rowing in the opposite direction at almost 3.5 knots. It was no use. The other vessel changed course, too, and continued steaming rapidly towards us.

Julie's efforts on the radio continued to be fruitless. Suddenly, the black form of the ship's hull materialized a few hundred metres from our boat and charged full speed straight towards us. We had maybe 30 seconds until impact.

"STOOOOOOOOOOP!" Julie screamed into the radio, and then dropped the handset and grabbed the flare she had placed on the deck. As she fumbled with the flare's trigger mechanism, I made one last desperate attempt to dodge a devastating impact by reversing our direction yet again.

The vessel was upwind of us, and we could smell in the warm air a pungent stench of fish, tar, and wood. I could make out the dim glow inside the pilot house and two men, one behind a large steering wheel, staring out into the distance.

Julie fired a flare but it failed to detonate. My agonizingly slow evasive turn was only half completed. The ship was moving at close to 10 knots. A collision was seconds away.

Suddenly, the man standing beside the steersman grabbed the wheel from his companion and began to crank it with all his might. He must have seen us. The large wooden fish boat heeled over as it reacted to the hard rudder movement. Fortunately, he turned the vessel in the opposite direction that I was turning, and our boats missed each other by two metres. I had to tuck in my starboard oar to prevent it from being sheared in two by the ship.

The rumbling diesel engine continued at full bore, and the fish boat disappeared back into the veil of darkness.

"Holy shit!" I panted, dripping with sweat. "That was too close."

Julie could barely speak, she was so terrified. This was the second ship that had almost mowed us down. This time it was more of a mystery what had happened.

Our strobe light should be visible for miles. Since the ocean was calm, it would have been impossible for the fishermen to miss it. The only explanation was that the two men were heading towards the light on purpose. Perhaps they had mistaken it for a distant lighthouse or a strobe that marked their nets. It's next to impossible to gauge distance with light coming from a single source, so perhaps they assumed they were still miles away. It wasn't until they saw the shape of our boat materialize in the inky blackness that they reacted.

Our first near miss with the freighter had been because we were not visible enough. Our next close call was because we were too visible. The most obvious solution would be for us to display the usual red, green, and white navigation lights as well as the strobe to reduce confusion. I hadn't installed such lights in Lisbon because most ocean rowers think that, at such a low vantage, they can't be seen by other vessels. Combined with a rowboat's slow speed and erratic movement, these lights aren't of much use. On this occasion, though, I was sure they would have helped. Now, I felt frustrated that there was no way to remedy the situation.

THE CANARY ISLANDS SLIPPED BEHIND US like a fading dream. Once again, we were alone on the ocean. Our path of travel now diverged from the main shipping lanes. Within a few days, we stopped seeing other boats. Steady 35-knot winds blew from the northeast and helped propel us, but they also stirred up very large seas. Our boat held out flawlessly. Besides, after passing through a hurricane, all other rough weather felt like a kids' ride at the amusement park.

By satellite phone, my mother informed us that two men had departed the Canary Islands in a rowboat just a few days behind us. Jerry Rogers, 57, and Keith Oliver, 53, both grandfathers, were aiming to be the oldest to row across the Atlantic from the Canary Islands to the Caribbean. As 20-foot waves toppled around our boat and the wind blew ceaselessly, I hoped the men were all right. It certainly wouldn't be a pleasant introduction to the sea for them.

Dean passed along some news from an article on ExplorersWeb entitled, "Erden: All systems go, NOT!"

Erden had been unsuccessful in getting the boat placed in a freighter, and he and Tim were becoming increasingly disheartened. Finally their luck changed, and the winds switched to the north and provided reasonable conditions to depart from Portugal by oars. The long-term forecast was good, so the duo wasted no time getting their ocean rower ready once and for all.

They departed from Cascais, waving goodbye to a smaller crowd, and headed towards the open ocean. Unfortunately, several miles out, the duo learned that once again their water maker wasn't working. They called for a tow, and a motorboat pulled them back to the marina. The problem was solved, and the duo headed back out into the rough ocean.

The winds were strong and the seas rough, but the wind blew them in the right direction, and the determined rowers worked hard to get south as quickly as possible, before another storm or extended southerly blow hit them. The boat, however, didn't possess the same stamina as her rowers. Soon, systems started going down one by one. First the water maker stopped working again, and the men had to hand-pump water with the emergency unit when they weren't rowing.

Even worse, the hatches started leaking again, and the boys could barely keep up bailing out the inflow of water. Another problem was equally as dangerous. Their electrical system was faltering, and Erden worried that the navigational light and GPS would soon fail—a serious predicament, as they were in a major shipping lane.

Tim and Erden had no choice but to make landfall in Africa to repair their unseaworthy vessel. As they neared the coastline, the winds switched to the south and they struggled for three days into heavy winds.

"The guys are still at sea," ExplorersWeb reported, "and the boat is falling apart—piece by piece."

The GPS plotter shut down because of the ailing electrical system, and the men had to resort to using their handheld emergency GPS. Part of the electrical system had been completely submerged in salt water along with the now-defunct water maker. Things just kept getting worse.

Finally the boat limped into the fishing town of El Jadida, Morocco, waterlogged and exhausted. Erden vowed that, once and for all, he would straighten matters out with his boat. "Once on land, remaining round hatches on deck and the rectangular hatches will have to be redone," Erden stated on his website. "I will personally supervise the work and no longer trust that when money is paid we will get a seaworthy vessel."

CONDITIONS FOR JULIE AND ME REMAINED DISMAL, as strong winds continued to blow from the northeast. A thick haze spread across the ocean and limited visibility to about one kilometre. The haze also blocked a significant amount of sunlight. It felt like we were perpetually in late dusk. I'd read that dust blowing out from Africa can create such conditions, but I had never before experienced such a strange, otherworldly atmosphere. Ten days after leaving the Canaries, we'd seen only one ship, a ghostly freighter that appeared through the hazy fog and briefly shared our world.

In mid-November, we received word that the two grandfathers, 200 nautical miles behind us, had set off their emergency beacon and were rescued by a freighter on its way to Rotterdam. As the grey haze thickened and breaking waves pounded our small vessel, we felt more alone than ever.

18

FROM DELTA TO EPSILON

NO MATTER HOW LONG WE SPENT ON THE OCEAN, we never became completely accustomed to rough seas. Our tasks, from cooking and rowing to just climbing out of bed, became infinitely more difficult. Just trying to hold a plate often meant spilled food everywhere. Pots would topple from the stove and render entire meals a sloppy mess in the bilge, testing the limits of our patience. It required often dangerous feats of gymnastics to crawl around the boat in a world of constantly changing gravity.

Our optimism would diminish during the rougher weather, only to return with vigour when the seas finally calmed. Twelve days after passing the Canary Islands, the winds finally sighed their last. The seas became calm and lifted our spirits significantly.

Numerous dorado followed our boat, so we took advantage of the calmer conditions to drop a line and stretch our food supplies. The fish were getting bigger now, and Julie and I took turns and caught four fighting specimens. We ate one of the fish immediately in a dish of macaroni and cheese. The rest were cut into strips and hung out in the sun to dry.

The school swimming around our boat had grown in size and variety. Our finned entourage now included dorado, trigger-fish, a type of spotted smaller fish, and little crabs that would crawl along the outside of the hull. Our pet fish, Fred, Ted and

Ned, had either left or were eaten, much to Julie's dismay, but the 20-centimetre polka-dot fish seemed equally tame and did a good job of filling their shoes.

We speculated about why so many fish followed our boat for such great distances. Dorado are often found near floating debris, so fishermen run their gear near logs or other large flotsam coming from the deep ocean. I have heard theories that dorado like the shade, though this didn't seem to be the case with our companions. Although the smaller fish spent time directly under the boat, the dorado ranged far from it most of the day as they searched for their favourite prey, flying fish. We saw impressive displays of up to a hundred flying fish launching skywards. The dorado would rip through the water in pursuit and often chase the airborne fish for up to 100 metres to catch them when they landed. The dorado would then return to the boat briefly before continuing with their hunting sorties.

Dorado can change colours between bright yellow, blue, and grey, and they seem to use their colours for both hunting and communication. When we trailed our lure through the water, the fish giving chase would transform to a nearly invisible grey, while members of the school watching the chase from a distance would remain brightly coloured. It seemed almost as though they worked together, with some fish using bright hues to intimidate prey towards their camouflaged companions.

Dorado mate for life. It becomes immediately apparent after catching a fish whether it has a partner or not. Upon being hooked, the fish would immediately change to a bright yellow—perhaps a danger signal—and all the other dorado adopt camouflage colouring. The partner of the hooked dorado would usually come to its side and swim around it, helplessly trying to assist its mate. Often the mates of lost fish would stick within metres of our boat for days, and even forfeit hunting as they waited for their partner to return.

Once, bringing dinner aboard brought Julie to tears. We had hooked a male dorado, distinguished by its bulbous head and larger size, and he was flanked by his mate the entire time we played him in. Finally, when we were about to haul him into the boat, their two mouths met, as though his mate was giving him a farewell kiss.

It is a sad exercise eating such social creatures, but it was an important dietary supplement for us, and we consoled ourselves that we were existing in a fish-eat-fish world, and that the dorado were eaten all the time by dolphins and sharks. Dolphins, in fact, were the most voracious dorado killers, and we began to resent their presence because they would decimate our floating larder. The dolphins didn't show up often, but when they did, it would be in the early mornings or late evenings, after daylight had all but disappeared from the sky.

On our second day of calmer conditions, while manning the oars, Julie heard heavy breathing and splashing just after sunset. A slightly fishy smell permeated the air, a giveaway of marine mammals with their notoriously bad breath.

"The dolphins are back," Julie said.

I groaned. We were pleased with how quickly our school of dorado had grown. This would soon change.

I could barely make out the dolphins rising and falling in the water, a frenzy of activity below the surface. At night, dolphins have the advantage. Although dorado can out-swim a dolphin with speeds of up to 50 knots, they are blind at night, while a dolphin navigates precisely using sonar.

Like the sightless dorado, Julie and I couldn't see what was going on. We only heard the splashing, occasional squeaks, and heavy breathing. Our imaginations filled in the rest. The following morning, we saw that our dorado stock had been plundered: only two of about 30 fish remained.

Interestingly, the dolphins ate only the dorado, and our school of about 40 triggerfish and polka-dot fish remained intact, swimming lazily beneath the boat.

Each type of fish around our boat had a crucial role in our mobile ecosystem. The polka-dot fish became our pets and companions. When Julie and I swam in the water, they would stay by our sides. The dorado provided both food and a constant source of entertainment, as we marvelled at their complex hunting techniques. The relative newcomers, the triggerfish, also had a positive impact on our lives—they ate the barnacles off the bottom of our boat and kept it clean.

THE PLEASANT WEATHER DIDN'T LAST LONG. As we rowed westwards, we sighted an evil-looking squall. We were still bathed in sunshine as we watched the black line of clouds running from south to north. The dark mass seemed stationary, and only our own slow speed brought us closer to the storm.

Eventually, after 24 hours of rowing towards the system, we reached the periphery of the squall. The spectacle left us awestruck. Although it was 3 p.m., the base of the storm had gone as black as pitch. Heavy clouds rose out of this darkness, roiling and twisting into the heavens. Lightning flashed everywhere—a new burst every five seconds or so. A continuous, low rumble issued from the system, like the growl of a rabid beast. I couldn't help but feel terrified by this display of pure, dark energy. It felt alien and primeval, as though the sea were giving birth to a mythical monster.

In less than a minute, the winds amped up from calm to 60 knots out of the east and blew us towards the heart of the storm. The waves picked up, and salt spray spritzed across the water and almost blinded me. Nearby, two sets of short, steep wave systems collided and exploded. Just a few hundred metres from the boat, two waves impacted in such a way that water shot skywards almost 30 metres, as though a mine had exploded in the sea. What would have happened if our boat had travelled over such turbulence?

As we neared the storm, sheets of rain poured down with a force neither of us has ever seen. The torrents, fortunately, seemed to subdue the wind, and by the time we reached the heart of the squall, the winds had stopped entirely. In this mega-deluge, I rowed like a madman and tried to stay warm in my naked state. The clouds drowned out the light, and our world became a sound-and-light show as lightning flashed non-stop in the clouds above. The continuous roar of rain and thunder was deafening, and I couldn't help but fear that this monster wanted to kill us. There was just too much energy, and we felt so vulnerable in our little rowboat.

I had changed course slightly to cut through the system at a 90-degree angle. After two hours of rowing hard through the front, we emerged from the torrential rain and lightning and entered a world of varied clouds, small squalls, and patches of blue. The sun was just setting, and it created myriad hues as its light shimmered through alto-cirrus and cumulonimbus clouds.

"Maybe we should phone Dean again," Julie suggested. "I haven't seen such distinct-looking stratus clouds since Hurricane Vince."

I had to agree. Conditions were looking ominous. I picked up the phone and called Dean.

"Hey guys, are you catching lots of fish?" he asked cheerily.

"Yeah, we're definitely getting our vitamin D," I said, trying to equal his cheer, as though a shot of optimism would chase the bad weather away. "We've got a few weird clouds around us. It's probably nothing, but if you could check the hurricane centre website, that would be great."

"Sure thing. I'm sure it's nothing—you can't get hit twice by a hurricane outside of the hurricane belt," Dean assured me. "I'm not a gambling man, but I'd bet you guys are going to be just fine . . ."

Suddenly, his voice trailed off.

"Holy shit!" he announced. "There's another one heading towards you. It's called Tropical Storm Delta and it's on the border of becoming a hurricane."

I groaned. Julie clasped her head in dismay. She had guessed the nature of the news.

"So where is it?" I asked.

"Roughly a thousand miles west of you, and it's heading east."

"Another cyclone heading towards us," I moaned. "I'm getting sick of this."

"You know, I had an idea," Dean said brightly. "I thought of it after you guys made it through the last hurricane, when you told me about how much you got thrashed around the cabin."

"Uh huh," I said, only half listening.

"Well, it seems that one of the greatest dangers is having your heads slammed against the wall or into each other's. Maybe you guys could make some kind of hurricane helmet, or turban out of clothing, to protect yourselves from head injuries."

It seemed like a good idea. Maybe if we survived this next storm we could patent and sell Hurricane Helmets to other unlucky sailors. Right now, though, we had bigger worries.

I turned the satellite phone off, and Julie and I considered our strategy. The heart of the storm was still a day and a half away, but the weather was already getting too rough to row in. The winds were coming from the southwest, so we dropped the drogue over the side to slow our rate of back-wards drift. We secured all of our loose gear, gathered water and food inside the cabin to last a few days, and then sat back and waited. Again.

"I've thought of a good way to make our hurricane hel-mets," Julie said, as we lay staring at each other across our tiny bed. She wrapped some Helly Hansen fleece around her head and pulled a set of pantyhose (given to us by a German sailor as a plankton sieve) over the fleece to hold it together. Julie then tied the legs of the pantyhose under her chin to create a secure noggin protector.

Julie looked so ridiculous in her pantyhose helmet that I couldn't help but burst out laughing. Then I fashioned my own goofy-looking helmet from another pair of stockings. We began banging our heads together, like rams in rut, to test the cushioning. Two thumbs up! We laughed uproariously, before reality once again set in: We were going to die. But at least not from a head wound.

We lay in the cabin as the seas grew in size. Every four to six hours, we would call the hurricane centre to get an update on the storm. It seemed impossible that yet another cyclone was heading towards us. It was November 24, the extreme end of hurricane season, and we were still outside of the hurricane belt. According to the pilot charts, the general trend for the few hurricanes that form at this time of year is to begin much further west than our present position and then head west towards the Caribbean Sea. This Cyclone Delta, however, had decided to go in the opposite direction—straight towards us.

The sky continued to look like a devil's cauldron. Slanting yellow sunbeams cut between black squalls, and corrugated cirrus clouds interlaced the remaining areas of blue. Huge anvil heads roiled and billowed, like slow-moving atomic explosions. Flashes of lightning illuminated the horizon. Such energy and volatility would have been breathtakingly beautiful if we had been watching from anywhere else, if it weren't simply the prelude to a killer storm.

THE FOLLOWING MORNING, we received some good news. The storm was veering slightly more northwards, now bearing towards the Canary Islands. If it remained on this course, the eye would miss us by 200 miles. That was still too close for comfort, though.

It seemed as though the Canary Islands had caught Delta's fancy and taken her attention off our little red rowboat. True to prediction, the eye of the storm overshot us by a little over 300 kilometres. The winds reached 40 knots, accompanied by 25-foot waves—both well within the storm-weathering capabilities of our well-made rowboat.

On November 28, the storm seemed safely past us. Once again, we escaped unscathed. Others weren't so lucky. Delta passed 170 kilometres north of the Canary Islands and 19 people died from its fury.

November 29 was my birthday, and the weather was reasonable. Julie made a tantalizing breakfast of pancakes, whipped cream, strawberries, and caramel syrup.

"Don't make any birthday wishes," she joked. "You know what will happen."

Even as Julie voiced these words, though of course we couldn't know it, another entity was marking its arrival into this world: Hurricane Epsilon, born November 29, 2005.

Having dodged Delta's brunt, and now two days from the official end of hurricane season, we felt ecstatic. Finally, it seemed, we had made it through the worst of the hurricane season. I phoned Dean to relay our coordinates. I was greeted by a chorus of "Happy Birthday" sung by Dean and his girlfriend Sarah.

"Guess what?" Dean said. "Erden and Tim have headed back out to sea, and almost nothing has been fixed on their boat. The water maker is still broken, the electrical system hasn't been tended to, and nothing has been done to the sieves they call hatches."

"Why?" I asked, incredulous. "They don't need to worry about missing their weather window any more now that they've made it to Africa. What the hell are they doing risking their lives going out to sea in their unseaworthy banana boat?"

"I've got not the slightest idea," Dean said. "They've at least got a good weather forecast ahead of them, and I think that's what they're banking on. They've loaded extra water into the boat to compensate for the lack of a water maker and are headed for the Canary Islands. I think they're planning on doing all the work there since it has more advanced facilities."

Their risky plan seemed like a game of Russian roulette with two bullets in the gun. The first and most obvious danger would be encountering rough conditions in an ailing vessel. Even more disconcerting was the prospect of failing to make landfall in the Canary Islands. Due to the low power of a rowboat, you can never count on landing where you planned to. Contrary winds and currents can quickly overpower the rower and force an entirely new route.

If Tim and Erden encountered steady easterlies, they could be blown too far west to reach the Canaries. The prevailing winds would prevent them from turning around, and the two men would have few options except to instigate a deep-sea rescue or to continue on a journey of many months across the Atlantic Ocean with a broken water maker and a dodgy boat. Neither were scenarios I would care to risk.

19

A BIRTHDAY AND A CHRISTMAS AT SEA

"**S**ARAH AND I have a birthday present for you," Dean announced, from 14,000 kilometres away, over our satellite-phone connection, "which we are able to send to you in the middle of the Atlantic."

"What's that?"

"The end of the hurricane season!" said Dean. "Tomorrow's the last day. From here on, it's a piece of cake for you guys."

I celebrated my thirty-fourth year on the planet by swimming, fishing, and eating a treasured can of lychee fruit. Julie hauled in our catch of the day with the speargun. She waited patiently by the gunwale, spear in hand, looking like a Bond girl, until an unsuspecting dorado sidled alongside. She then made the fish into a chili using beans, spices, canned tomatoes, onions, garlic, well-aged cheese, and rice.

We devoured the dorado chili like it was haute cuisine. It was hard to believe we had been at sea for more than two months and could still eat like royalty. Just when I thought it couldn't get better, Julie pulled out a birthday cake, complete with burning matches instead of candles.

"Happy birthday to you!" Julie sang as I blew out the matches.

She had created the cake from a base of ladyfingers soaked in coffee and rum. She'd then covered this tasty foundation with a layer of home made, vanilla-flavoured tapioca pudding, another layer of raspberry jam, and then topped it with whipped cream. I had no doubt in my mind that this was the best meal ever eaten in a rowboat, and I marvelled at Julie's mid-Atlantic culinary magic.

When Julie and I left Moscow five months earlier, countless people had warned us that the expedition would be the ultimate test of our relationship. If we made it through the inevitable stresses, we could make it through anything. The rowboat crossing seemed like the greatest trial. On land, you can always find a little personal space and privacy. Such physical and psychological luxury didn't exist in our tiny boat. Our shared world had shrunk to a doghouse-sized cabin and a rowing seat. That was it. The rowing seat faced the cabin, so the rower would stare, for hours on end, at the person inside. Even going to the bathroom over the side of the boat was something of a shared experience, as the cabin hatch offered a panoramic view of the decks and everything that occurred on them.

Despite the lack of privacy and personal space, and the constant stresses and dangers, Julie and I were able to work together extremely well. We are both strong-willed, independent thinkers, and our mutual respect for one another helped forge our harmonious personal and expedition relationship.

Even after months together, our conversations never ran dry. We would talk about a wide range of subjects, such as our plans when we reached home, our experiences in Europe, our wildlife observations, or just our strategies to ensure the success of our ocean row. The romance never left our relationship. On special evenings such as my birthday, we would take a break with a bottle of wine and—just like young lovers around the world—watch the setting sun with our arms wrapped around one another.

THE DAY AFTER MY BIRTHDAY, we were awakened by a loud crash at 6 a.m. It sounded like a battering ram coming up from the depths and striking our vessel. Julie rushed outside to investigate.

"Oh my god!" she exclaimed. "It's a huge turtle attacking our boat!"

I poked my head through the hatch to see an enormous loggerhead turtle coming up for air. It then submerged, its one-metre-diameter shell disappearing under the boat, and the crashing noises resumed.

Perhaps he was trying to eat the few stray barnacles the triggerfish had missed. Or maybe he had mistaken our boat for the mother of all turtles and fallen in love with it. Still, every time *Ondine* lifted in the swell and crashed against the turtle's shell, it felt a little worrisome. After all, the turtle probably weighed 110 to 140 kilograms, and our boat was not designed to take this kind of beating.

We took a few pictures and videotaped the turtle. Unlike the smaller loggerheads we had seen, this big guy showed no fear of us. We had learned from earlier encounters with turtles that their eyesight is quite good. They will observe the boat from up to 100 metres away. When they discern a human on the decks, they invariably flee. If we hide in the cabin and peek through the hatches, though, the turtles will swim about and inspect the boat.

This fellow swam right up to us, poked his wizened head through the water two feet from our own, and stared into our eyes. His face looked like an old man's, and his unblinking stare made me a little uncomfortable.

Finally, we felt it was time to say goodbye to our guest, as there was a real danger he might damage the boat. I leaned over the side to touch the turtle and scare him away. Surprisingly, my touch caused him no fear, so I ran my hands over his leathery flippers and shell and even inverted the giant creature to examine his underside.

The turtle seemed to enjoy our playful interaction. At last, Julie hopped on the oars and rowed as fast as she could. The turtle swam a few half-hearted strokes after our boat before giving up and disappearing into the distance.

The loggerhead turtle is endangered, and most of its troubles come from man. It has been heavily hunted for its meat, eggs, and shell. Fishing gear that targets other fish inadvertently kills large numbers of these creatures. Unfortunately, its thick carapace, which protects it from sharks and other sea creatures, does nothing to save it from man. In Mexico and parts of Central America, turtle eggs are considered a tasty bar treat and, falsely, thought to boost a man's virility. After looking into the wizened eyes of our prehistoric friend that morning, I was saddened to think that the population of loggerheads was being destroyed thanks to the gullible beliefs of limp-dicked drinkers.

I called my mother on the Iridium phone to tell her about the turtle.

"Have you heard about the hurricane yet?" she offered in greeting.

"Good god, no. There's another hurricane?"

"Yes, this one is called Epsilon," she explained. "It's near Bermuda and is expected to head towards Europe."

I sighed with relief. Bermuda was thousands of miles northwest of our position. If the hurricane travelled towards Europe, it would pass nowhere near our boat.

"Don't worry, Mom. We're way south of that one: It shouldn't even affect our weather."

My assurances didn't assuage my mom's maternal instincts. She wasn't entirely convinced that we didn't need to worry about Hurricane Epsilon. Still, she did her best to listen to my tales of birthday cakes and curious turtles.

SOMETIMES, MOTHERS REALLY DO KNOW BEST. As my mom listened politely to my travel stories, hurricane forecasters at the U.S. National Hurricane Center were puzzling over the latest anomaly on the Atlantic. Epsilon had formed in waters averaging between 21 and 24 degrees, well below the minimum of 26.5 thought necessary to generate a hurricane, and in a region with much atmospheric shear (adjacent air movement of different speed or direction)—conditions not conducive to tropical storms.

With conditions so contrary for maintaining cyclonic activity, the forecasters predicted that Epsilon would soon dissipate. It defied those forecasts and continued to struggle for its life. On December 2, the tropical storm intensified into a full-fledged hurricane. Meteorologists continued to predict it would weaken, but Epsilon had other plans, which included veering away from its predicted route to Europe. Instead, it seemed to have eyes for a little red rowboat.

"There are no clear reasons—and I am not going to make one up—to explain the recent strengthening of Epsilon," noted Dr. Lixion Avila, forecaster at the National Ocean and Atmospheric Administration, in a public statement.

Julie and I thought we knew the reason. Both Vince and Delta had been unsuccessful in sinking the *Ondine*. Epsilon was the hurricane that might finally complete the job.

Hurricane Epsilon was spawned almost 6,500 kilometres away from us, so it took almost a week for it to travel into our region. It was a week of anxiety, and our spirits once again sagged as we prepared for yet another cyclone. Periodic phone calls to the hurricane centre informed us of Epsilon's progress. We couldn't help but think of it as the world's largest homing missile.

·🌏·

"IT'S CURVED AND IS NOW HEADING DUE SOUTH, straight towards you," Dean informed us on the morning of December 5. Epsilon was now 1,600 kilometres away and closing fast.

"I don't get it," I said. "How the hell do we get all these tropical storms and hurricanes coming at us one after another? This defies all logic. Epsilon isn't supposed to exist, and it was supposed to go to Europe. Now it's about to mow us down."

"Well, there is some good news," Dean said. "They're forecasting that it will curve into a southwest direction from the south it's presently at. It should miss you then."

This news didn't offer much solace. The prediction came from the same forecasters that had said the storm was heading towards Europe and would dissipate a week ago. At that point, I would have trusted a Tarot card reader more than a meteorologist.

The weather had changed drastically. Again the sky was shrouded in cirrus and cumuli altus clouds. An enormous swell rose and fell from the north. This steady roller coaster was benign in its effect on the boat, but still a terrifying indicator of what was charging towards us. There was no wind, and the sea's surface remained smooth, apart from the oily 30-foot swells. The boat rose up and down these monsters so gently that with our eyes closed it felt like we were on a mill pond. We could still row now, but we faced a dilemma.

If we continued to row, and the hurricane did travel southwest as predicted, our progress would take us closer to the hurricane's path. On the other hand, if the hurricane continued to travel south, any forward movement could move us slightly away from its line of travel.

We decided to give the forecasters another chance to get it right. We stopped rowing. We lashed the oars into the boat, and our vessel became a lifeless piece of flotsam on an unforgiving sea. Our well-rehearsed hurricane preparations completed, Julie and I sat outside and watched the still-calm sea and ever-stranger skies.

"Do you think this is going to be it?" Julie wondered.

"Be what?"

"You know," Julie said with a rueful laugh, "the hurricane that finally sinks us?"

A dorado chased a school of about a dozen flying fish. The glittering animals glided through the air, passed close to our boat, and splashed into the water 50 metres distant. I envied them. All they had to do was dive deeper to avoid the effects of the hurricane.

"Of course not," I said. "We're tough, and our boat couldn't be more seaworthy. You'll make it, won't you, *Ondine?*" I slapped the plywood deck affectionately.

"It must be reassuring for people like my mother and father to have faith in an afterworld," Julie said. "It would make things like hurricanes so much less significant."

"Yeah, but they're going to different heavens," I said. Julie's mother is Christian while her father is a Muslim. "That must have been quite difficult when they were together— knowing that they would live for eternity away from their loved one."

Julie sighed. "I guess we don't need to worry about that. If this hurricane does destroy us, we'll both be together—at the bottom of the ocean."

I put my arms around her. "We'll make it. We set out to row across the ocean, and whatever the demons of the sea are conspiring, our strength and determination will get us to the far side."

I really felt my sentiment was true. In all my expeditions, I had encountered the most formidable obstacles, but they were always overcome. This was the pattern, and I felt the pattern would continue.

Julie called Dean for the latest update.

"Good news," she said upon hanging up. "The hurricane is changing course as predicted and is now heading southwest. If it continues on that course, we'll be spared."

Although it was a good start, we couldn't yet relax. The storm had been behaving erratically and there was no guarantee that it wouldn't change course again. The bad news was that Hurricane Epsilon was still as intense as ever after almost a week of predictions stating otherwise. Even if the hurricane stayed on its current course, we would still receive a pounding. If it deviated, we could be killed.

The lead-up to the storm might have seemed monotonous if it weren't for the anxiety of not knowing what huge natural force might hit us, or when. Julie and I once again lay cramped and sweating in the cabin as the seas churned outside and buffeted the boat. The worst hit after nightfall, and we lay in complete darkness hoping that *Ondine* would make it through yet another storm.

While lying in the cabin, we were able to track the hurricane's progress via the Iridium telephone. This time, forecasters were correct: Epsilon continued moving southwest. The brunt of the storm would miss us by 480 kilometres. The winds peaked at about 45 knots at 3 a.m., and then began to die down. Once again we had survived a hurricane.

By late afternoon the following day, we were able to unlash the oars and continue rowing. We had been blown backwards during the hurricane and had plenty of ground to recover.

Overall, we were disappointed with our rate of travel from Lisbon. The effect of one cyclone after another had slowed our progress drastically. It wasn't just the volatile weather. These massive meteorological systems disrupted the usual balance of pressures that creates steady trade winds from the east. So far, the "trades" had been mostly AWOL, along with their accompanying currents—an almost unheard of phenomenon at these latitudes.

It was now two and a half months since we had departed Lisbon, and we had made it just over a third of the way across the ocean. If we continued at this pace, it would take almost seven months to complete our crossing instead of the initially anticipated five months.

We struggled onwards against persistent light headwinds, slowly losing our humour. We didn't have enough food to last seven months on the sea, at least not without severe rationing. We ate dorado for lunch and dinner to stretch our supplies.

On the morning of December 16, Julie laboured to move our boat through a sea of glass. The headwinds had finally died, but the trades still hadn't kicked in. We had been rowing for days on a sea of mercury that cooked beneath a cloudless sky.

Even though it was only 7 a.m., I was already dripping with sweat as I made pancakes. Normally, we had simpler breakfasts, but today we were celebrating reaching the halfway point after 84 days at sea.

"Is that a sailboat?" said Julie, squinting into the distance.

I leaned out the hatch and made out the outline of a sailboat about one nautical mile away.

"Let's call it on the radio," Julie said. "Maybe they'll come on over to say hello. Maybe . . . maybe they'll give us big bags of goodies for Christmas."

I handed Julie the VHF radio, and she made the call.

"This is rowing vessel *Ondine* calling a blue sailboat under power. Do you copy?"

Almost immediately we received a reply: "This is sailing vessel *Ripple* calling rowboat *Ondine*. Where are you?"

"We're ninety degrees off your starboard side, about one mile away," Julie said.

"We can't see you yet, but we will change course to come and say hello."

We watched as the blue boat changed course and began motoring in our direction. As it grew closer, I realized it was a lot bigger than I had first guessed—almost a hundred feet in length. Six crew members stood on deck hooting and waving as the luxury yacht neared our far smaller vessel.

"Good god, you two need to get yourselves a set of sails," said the man at the helm.

The crew members were all young and attractive, in their 20s and 30s, and they gaped at the spectacle before them.

It was incredible to see other people at such close quarters after almost three months on the ocean. The only other people we'd seen had been the Spanish fishermen in the distance. The skipper's name was Alex, and he and his crew were delivering the boat to Antigua, where the owner would meet them. Alex was from England; the rest of the crew came from elsewhere in Europe, including Switzerland and France.

We shouted back and forth across the water for an hour, exchanging tales of the sea. *Ripple* had left from the Canary Islands seven days previously, and the crew expected to reach Antigua in another six or seven—a stark contrast to our anticipated half-year at sea. The winds had been dead all the way from the Canaries, so they had been motoring non-stop.

Alex eyed our drying dorado on deck and said, "I guess your food must be getting pretty monotonous by now. Do you guys fancy a few treats?"

Julie and I nodded in excitement. Fran, the chef, disappeared below decks to see what she could muster. Minutes later, the sailors lowered several sturdy grocery bags down to our boat at the end of a docking pole. Julie opened the bags and cried out. Our generous visitors had given us several dozen chilled cans of pop and beer, large bags of assorted potato chips, a big box of chocolates, Tetra Paks of milk, Kellogg's Corn Flakes, and a variety of more nourishing dishes. They had also included nine pulp-fiction paperbacks and several magazines, including *Men's Journal* and *Cosmopolitan*.

Our new friends wished us luck, put their boat into gear, and began to move steadily westwards once again. Silence closed in, and again we were alone.

"Wow, I can't believe that just happened," Julie said, sipping a chilled can of iced tea. "It seems like a dream."

I had to agree. After drinking only 30-degree water for almost three months, a chilled beverage had become one of our most vivid and frequent fantasies. We thought we wouldn't enjoy such a treat until we reached shore. Now that the *Ripple* was gone, our cold beverages seemed almost unreal.

We wrapped our drinks in a blanket to prolong the chill, and took a two-hour break from the oars to feast on chocolate, chips, pop, and beer while flipping through the glossy magazines.

"Santa didn't forget about us here in the middle of the Atlantic," Julie said dreamily while studying the deranged photo of a serial killer in *Maxim*.

It was perfect timing. With Christmas coming in 10 days, and all our new goodies, we were able to make holiday plans. Unfortunately, our Christmas season would also involve 18 hours of rowing a day, seven days a week.

WE CONTINUED OUR STEADY ROWING. As Christmas neared, the trade winds finally started up again and gave our progress a welcome boost. Although our speed westwards increased, we still faced a serious navigational challenge. The distorted weather patterns and currents surrounding the tropical storms had pushed us much farther south than was ideal. Even the current trade winds were blowing from the northeast, which was making it difficult to regain our lost latitude. In order to make landfall in Miami as intended, we would need to gain 10 degrees latitude north, something that was looking more and more impossible. The winds continued coming from the northeast, and we would gain significant latitude only if the winds came from the east or lower.

Finally, Julie and I decided we had to change our destination. We scrutinized our charts, read the pilot books, and decided that Limon, Costa Rica, would be the ideal port to aim for. The wind and currents would push us in this direction and, most importantly, once we reached the congested Caribbean Sea, the stretch of ocean in this direction was relatively clear of reefs and islands. We would have to row an additional 1,000 kilometres, but it still seemed like the most prudent route. It would also add more than 2,000 kilometres to our bike ride home, but at least a road connected Limon to Vancouver.

After we altered our course towards our new landfall, we learned that Erden and Tim were also hoping to land at Limon. The weather had started out in their favour and allowed the team to make excellent progress on their voyage from Africa to Gran Canaria. The men looked forward to getting to the Canary Islands as quickly as possible. Along with leaky hatches, a failing electrical system, a defunct water maker, and some structural damage (incurred while in the African port), they had a new problem: "On top of everything else," they wrote in a December 6 update, "five of our food-storage hatches are seized tightly shut, locking our own food away from us!"

With the prospect of starvation and thirst staring them in the face, the men must have been dismayed when the wind began to deteriorate into gale-force southeasterlies as they neared their destination. Eventually Tim and Erden struggled to just 22 kilometres from land, but then could no longer make headway and started losing distance, drawn back towards the open Atlantic. The situation was beginning to look desperate, and the men were all too aware of the likely outcome.

"If we did not make landfall on the next island, we would be doomed to pumping water by hand for five months, with our survival water maker, our back up, our only safety margin," Erden later noted on his website.

Suddenly, faced with the prospect of being blown out to sea in their decrepit boat with limited access to food and water, Tim and Erden realized they had no choice but to call for a deep-sea rescue.

"Erden again exemplified the boy scout motto of 'be prepared,' when he produced the telephone number of the director of the Real Club Nautico de Gran Canaria (the Royal Sailing Club of Grand Canary)," Tim recounted on their website.

They called the director of the yacht club, who immediately notified the authorities. The Gendarmerie Maritime dispatched the rescue vessel *Salvamento Maritimo* to save the rowers. After being towed through the storm to shore, Erden was determined to make the boat seaworthy for the 7,000 kilometres of open ocean that lay before the duo. "While I stayed focused on the boat," he wrote, "Tim was able to get away for a day of excursion to explore farther inside the island."

Meanwhile, Julie and I were enjoying our lead-up to Christmas with fair winds and holiday cheer. Earlier, Julie had hidden away some decorations, so we decorated our boat with silver garlands and glittery stars. We described our holiday plans to Dean, and he posted our account of the festive scene on our expedition website:

"With *Ripple*'s input, we have now planned Christmas Day. Our festivities will involve warm beer, sweet treats, and the bellowing of Christmas carols into a chasm of blue. Dinner will be homemade dorado and cheese macaroni, made with a hopefully-caught fish and our last block of Portuguese cheese, aged to perfection for over 100 days. In some respects, we are pleased to have such a minimalist Christmas. The holiday season is about being with loved ones, and we have that."

We made fantastic speed on all 12 days of Christmas, never ceasing our shifts at the oars. In between rowing sessions, Julie or I would rush through our chores and then partake in more relaxing activities, such as swigging warm beer and entertaining whoever was manning the oars with a few off-key carols. It was, we had to agree, our most memorable Christmas ever.

20

INTO THE TROPICS

A WEEK OR SO AFTER NEW YEAR'S, I hung the fishing rod over the side to troll for dinner. We had left Portugal with only two lures and three hooks. One of the hooks had broken, and the rubber squid had had all but two of its legs bitten off. We'd retired the squid and now used a plastic plug shaped like a flying fish to catch the dorado.

An enormous dorado of about 35 kilograms had joined the school beneath the boat, and we had done our best not to snag it. The fish was so extraordinarily large next to his peers that it seemed a shame to kill such a magnificent creature. It was also too big to carve up and dry, so we focused our efforts instead on catching the smaller fish. We had named the giant fish Legend, and took care not to drop the lure when it was around.

Today, however, I didn't see Legend under the boat and assumed he was off hunting. A smaller seven-kilogram dorado sidled near the starboard side and I dropped the lure towards it. I began swishing it back and forth to get the fish's attention. A flash of fish shot out from under the boat and, before I could react, Legend bit the lure and was hooked. Immediately, the giant fish ran and the reel screamed until Legend was fifty metres from the boat. There he leaped 4 metres into the air, shook his head, and broke the line.

I was shocked. The monofilament line had never before broken. What we had just lost was worth its weight in gold on the ocean—the lure, the hook, the connecting wire leader, and a small lead weight. Normally, such an occurrence would be a mild disappointment, just the loss of a favourite lure. But out there in the middle of the Atlantic Ocean, our health and safety were jeopardized by the unexpected loss. We needed fish to stay strong, and all we had left was a two-legged squid and a single hook.

Legend still had the hook in his mouth, and his new body piercing was driving him mad. The two-metre-long fish swam away from the boat and then pirouetted to impossible heights to try to shake the lure free. Even from a kilometre away, I could still see his body shoot from the water and sparkle in the sunlight.

"We have to catch him again," Julie said.

"What?" I said, incredulous at such an idea.

"If we can somehow catch him with the other hook," Julie reasoned, "we can get our fishing lure and hook back."

"What if he breaks the line again?" I cautioned. "Then we've got absolutely nothing left to fish with."

"I think it's worth a try. We can play him in really gently—have the tension as loose as possible."

We pulled the two-legged squid out of retirement and affixed it to our final hook. We then waited for Legend to return to the boat.

"There he is!" Julie exclaimed as she peered into the depths.

Sure enough, among the smaller dorado loomed Legend's immense form. I could even see the plug hanging out of his mouth. Julie skipped the pathetic green squid over the surface, but Legend was unmoved. Several other fish chased the lure, so Julie had to pull it momentarily from the water to avoid catching them. We tried for over an hour, but couldn't interest Legend in the gimpy squid. Instead, he went back to leaping into the air, snapping his enormous body back and forth, trying to shake loose the metallic annoyance in his lip.

"It's not working," I said. "We need something that looks tastier than a two-legged squid."

"Let's catch another dorado and cut it into bait strips," Julie suggested.

We had used strips of dorado as bait in the past, and the technique had worked well. Dorado will dine cannibal-style as long as there is no tail attached to the spoils. Perhaps the tail is a visual clue that the fish is one of their own.

Julie hooked a smaller dorado. As I processed the fish, a lead weight tumbled from its stomach and onto our deck. I was dumbstruck. Where had this fishing weight come from, out here in the mid-Atlantic? Then the only possible explanation dawned on me: When my line had snapped, the weight would have been freed. This fish must have snatched it up as it sank towards the bottom of the ocean. It was simply the greatest of coincidences (or maybe because this was the hungriest fish) that out of the 30 or 40 dorado milling around our boat, we had caught this one and retrieved our piece of tackle.

I cut a 20-centimetre strip of dorado flesh into the rough shape of a flying fish. Julie affixed this strip onto the hook and began skipping it across the surface. A dozen dorado gave chase, but Legend didn't stir. After an hour, we finally admitted defeat. The sun was setting and we had to get back to rowing.

Just then, Legend began another round of his leaping, dashing away from the boat and then slowly returning. When he was about 50 metres distant, the golden fish took another giant launch into the sky. As we admired Legend's acrobatics, something parted from his body and arced through the air and into the water. It was the lure! Legend had finally shaken it from his lip.

I dove off the side of the boat and swam for the tiny floating object. Moments later, I was back in the boat triumphantly holding the hook and lure in the air. We had done the impossible and retrieved the lure, hook, and weight. We would be telling our grandchildren about this Legend.

OUR ROUTE TO COSTA RICA would take us through the Windward Islands, a chain that fronts the eastern end of the Caribbean Sea. These would be the only islands we would encounter before reaching our intended landfall. If all went according to plan, we would slide between the islands of St. Lucia and Martinique and continue the remaining 2,500 kilometres to Limon.

As these lush tropical islands grew closer, we analyzed our pilot books to get a better idea of the currents, weather conditions, and dangers. Our pilot books also featured exotic colour photos of black sand beaches, coconut trees, and turquoise waters. The islands looked like the most beautiful idyll on the planet.

Our main reason for not wanting to make landfall came down to minimizing danger. Any time a rowboat approaches shore, the risks increase greatly. Faulty navigation, unmarked offshore hazards, and onshore winds can lead to disaster. At the same time, the temptation to touch down was very strong. We had been on our rowboat for a third of a year. The allure of eating fresh fruit, spicy Caribbean cuisine, and ice-cold beverages proved impossible to resist. The winds had stabilized, and we were now more confident in our seamanship. As long as the winds didn't change unexpectedly, we figured we'd be all right to make a pit stop at St. Lucia.

Dean passed on a message that Sarah Petrescu, a *Globe*

and Mail reporter, was trying to get in touch with us. I gave her a call between rowing shifts.

"Hi Colin, I was just wondering if you know what's happening with Tim Harvey?" Sarah asked.

"Yeah, he's in the Canary Islands with his new partner Erden Eruç. They plan on heading out to sea as soon as the boat is fixed . . ."

"Actually, no," she corrected me. "I guess you haven't heard. Tim has just dropped out of the race. He and Erden are parting ways."

"So what happened?" I asked.

"I don't know yet," Sarah said. "It was posted this morning on the expedition website and gave no details. I'm trying to get a hold of Tim myself to gather information."

Sarah asked a few questions about life on the sea and then bid us goodbye.

I was stunned. It was hard to believe that Tim was finally out of the picture. I had travelled halfway around the planet with him on my tail. It wasn't until Dean read the article in the next morning's *Globe and Mail* that I believed it was for real.

"On Jan. 1, Mr. Harvey dropped out of what would have been an around-the-world journey," the article read.

The article didn't explain what had caused the break-up. I imagined that Tim and Erden had been extremely guarded in light of the media circus that Tim's and my split had created. The article indicated that the crack in the relationship began as the men neared the Canaries. "But their journey ended," Petrescu wrote, "when the boat began to fall apart and the two men couldn't agree on what to do next."

Tim admitted that his lack of involvement in making decisions was a contributing factor. "Not being able to make decisions made things go very bad for me," he had told the reporter. Tim added that his funds were depleted and he was sleeping on benches and on the beach. He planned to return to North America by hitching a ride on a sailing yacht. The article hinted that Tim's long-distance relationship with his fiancée Yulya was also faltering. "Things have cooled off a bit," Tim admitted about their relationship.

So that was it. Erden had made what was probably the biggest sacrifice of his life and Tim was now leaving him behind. I couldn't help but wonder if Erden still saw Tim as a modern-day Shackleton, as he had earlier told ExplorersWeb.

Erden would continue solo. "There is only one reason why I am on this side of the Atlantic, and that was to help Tim Harvey's journey," he explained on his website. "My solo row to Puerto Limon in Costa Rica is a salvage operation. My boat is committed on the wrong side of the Atlantic, our funds were depleted to support Tim's journey, and the only affordable way remaining for me is to row it across."

It seemed like one hell of an inconvenience. Erden was being forced to row across an ocean because it was the only affordable option. He had exhausted his wife's finances, had spent a year of his life labouring for Tim, only to have the foundation for the expedition crumble beneath his feet.

So that was it. There were only two remaining teams attempting to be first around the world: Expedition 360 (Jason Lewis) and Expedition Canada. Jason Lewis and team were still in Southeast Asia with 15,000 kilometres to go. Julie and I now had just 12,000 kilometres between us and Vancouver. The prospect of completing the planet's first human-powered circumnavigation was starting to look very real.

ON JANUARY 18, after we'd spent 120 days on the ocean, a faint blue smudge on the horizon revealed the presence of St. Lucia.

"LAND HO!!!!!" I screamed.

Julie scrambled out of the cabin and we wrapped our arms around each other while gazing at the tiny dot on the horizon. It looked like a cloud, except that its shape was unchanging— a little smudge that represented so much. Behind us lay 7,500 kilometres of ocean. I couldn't believe we had traversed such a vast watery expanse in our little plywood rowboat.

For four months, Julie and I had subsisted within the confines of our 24-foot rowboat on what we had been able to carry with us. The primitive simplicity of our world was almost beyond comprehension, and the prospect of stepping ashore and into civilization again seemed surreal, like arriving on a distant, inhabited planet after years in a spaceship.

The winds now were stiff and we also had a one-knot current in our favour. Although these elements helped our speed, it was vital that we position the boat correctly on this aquatic conveyor belt. If we drifted too far south, we could be smashed against the volcanic cliffs on the windward side of the island. If we veered too far north, we would be swept helplessly past the tip of the island.

Once we reached the northern cape, we had a margin of error of only a few hundred metres to row quickly into the shelter on the lee side of the island, out of the winds and current.

The wind increased to 35 knots. Our anxiety over the imminent dangers of land superseded the excitement of our arrival. The island's profile became more distinct, and we could make out clouds shrouding volcanic peaks. In the darkness, we could see the glow of electric life filling the sky, hinting of not-too-distant treats and luxuries. But we were still in our tiny, isolated world, rowing anxiously.

In the early morning of January 19, the mountainous island of St. Lucia loomed 15 nautical miles away. We had been up all night trying to keep the boat on course in the increasingly turbulent ocean. The waves reared up to 18 feet while winds gusted at 40 knots. We needed calm conditions for a safe approach, and these were anything but. Waves swamped the boat throughout the night and bashed whoever was toiling at the oars. Normally we would have abandoned the rowing station at this point for the safety of the cabin and allowed the boat to weather the storm on its own. But with land nearby, we couldn't. Mountainous waves slammed into sheer cliffs not too far off in the distance, so we were forced to remain at the oars to stay on course.

At one point, before the light of dawn, I had to turn the boat sideways into the waves to struggle northwards and correct our direction. In this vulnerable position, a rogue wave picked up *Ondine* and threw her onto her side. The port oar caught against the vessel and snapped, while *Ondine* teetered on the brink of capsize. I fell from the rowing seat and onto the port lifeline, immersed in the water. Only by looping my arm around the line did I manage to keep from washing away as the boat righted itself.

It was the first oar we had broken since leaving Lisbon. I untied a spare and replaced the floppy remnants of the old one. When a red sun finally lifted above the horizon to illuminate St. Lucia, it was a chilling sight. We were still 25 kilometres from the island, but the power of the waves against the cliffs was unmistakable. Swells that had built up energy all the way across the Atlantic collided with sheer volcanic cliffs and shot white plumes 30 metres into the air. Above the cliffs, thick jungles stretched up the slopes of jagged mountains, an oasis above the chaos. Maybe an island stopover wasn't such a great idea. Our precarious entry into St. Lucia was beginning to feel like snatching a diamond out of a crocodile's mouth.

A HEAVILY-POWERED OPEN FISHING SKIFF motored through the waves towards us. Six men of African ancestry waved merrily. "Where'd you come from?" one of them yelled with a French accent.

"Portugal!" I shouted back.

"That's a long way to row!" the man laughed. "Do you have many fish under your boat?"

I knew what was coming next. We couldn't help but feel dismay as the men trolled their fishing gear, circled our boat, and hauled in dozens of our dorado. Fortunately, Legend wasn't among those taken. After catching most of the fish, the men waved goodbye and aimed towards Martinique, effortlessly gliding over waves that must have been close to eight metres high.

The winds relented slightly in late morning, and we made a flawless pass of Pointe Du Cap, the northernmost point of the island. Julie and I were now rowing together to double our power whenever we turned into the wind and waves. Cutting a few hundred metres from the cape was terrifying as the waves thundered against black cliffs.

The current funnelled past the headland at almost 2.5 knots, so we had to get out of the flow as quickly as possible to avoid being swept past the island. We were drenched in sweat, rowing with all our might in perfect synchronization. Slowly, we moved into the lee of Pointe Du Cap, and the enormous waves and current began to subside. Another 15 minutes of rowing took us into waters almost as calm as a lake as we hugged the sheltered coastline.

Numerous resorts dotted the shore. Hobie Cats and windsurfers skipped across the aqua-blue shallows. We eased our boat into crowded Rodney Bay. A flotilla began trailing our vessel: small fishing boats, yacht tenders, and locals sporting dreadlocks, tie-dyed shirts, and colourful open wooden boats with names like *Bob Marley* and *Rasta*.

People on the shore clapped and cheered as we rowed through the narrow entrance of the Rodney Bay Lagoon towards the marina. I felt dizzy and confused by the eruption of attention. And immensely happy. We had made it all the way from Lisbon to the Caribbean by oar.

A local Rasta man, helming a service boat named *Sparkle Laundry*, led us to an empty dock in the marina and helped us tie up. A crowd of about 20 people, mostly yachters from foreign sailboats, had gathered on the dock to watch us disembark.

"Well, this is it, honey," I said. "After four months in a row-boat, I'm going to take my first steps."

I clambered onto the concrete pier and almost toppled into the water, saved only by a sailor who grabbed my arm. I could barely stagger a few paces without tilting over. I felt like a toddler taking his first few steps in front of proud parents.

Julie was just as wobbly. Everybody roared with laughter as she took one tentative step after another. The astonishment in her eyes said it all. Atrophying of the muscles used for walking made two-legged transportation precarious and hilarious. Even my knees felt loose, as though the ligaments and tendons had stretched a few sizes. After two minutes of staggering around the boat, Julie and I plonked our bottoms on the dock, exhausted. A French man named Jean-Marc pressed an ice-cold bottle of local brew into each of our hands.

"Congratulations," Jean Marc said. "To a voyage well done."

ST. LUCIA IS A WORLD-RENOWNED TOURIST DESTINATION due to its idyllic beaches and tropical climate. It was first inhabited by the Arawak and then by Carib Native Americans. Columbus sighted St. Lucia in 1499, the first European to encounter the island, although he did not go ashore.

The first European to settle on the island was Francois Le Clerc, a pirate more commonly known as Wooden Leg. He based himself on Pigeon Island, the tiny outcrop of land that Julie and I passed on our way in, and attacked passing Spanish ships.

Starting in the mid-1600s, the French and English fought fierce battles for possession of this strategically placed island. Ownership juggled back and forth between the two nations for 150 years until St. Lucia was finally ceded to the English in 1814. Since then it has remained part of the Commonwealth Empire. In 1979, it became an independent country within the Commonwealth.

During the 1700s, slaves were brought from Africa to tend the sugar plantations, and their descendants make up the current predominantly black population. Although the official language is English, many of the islanders still speak French, a legacy of past French colonial control.

Rodney Bay Marina seemed to be a world and an economy on its own, fenced off from the rest of the island and catering to the yachting industry. Gleaming million-dollar boats from around the world dwarfed our tiny vessel.

St. Lucia had a laid-back feel to it, and this atmosphere extended to the customs and immigration officials, who strolled down the dock and told us to visit them after the weekend so that we could go through the clearance formalities. The marina waived the $30-per-day moorage fee for the duration of our stay.

Our time in St. Lucia flew by in a whirl of activity. The boat was still in immaculate shape and needed minimal work. However, we had much business to attend to.

One of the most exciting developments was an emerging partnership with Truestar Health, a Canadian company that provides nutritional supplements tailored to individual requirements. On the ocean, we had constantly bemoaned the fact that the only supplements we carried were a generic brand of multivitamins. Christine Leakey, a friend of Julie's who had been helping with various expedition tasks, happened to work for Truestar, and she had mentioned our journey to her boss, Tim Mulcahy, CEO of the Toronto-based company. Mulcahy immediately saw the opportunity for a partnership. For us, the chance to tweak our diet with high-quality supplements for the rest of the expedition would be priceless. Truestar planned to send a representative to St. Lucia to deliver the supplements and acquaint us with the company.

It was more than a week before Julie and I were able to shuffle more than a few hundred metres without feeling spent, so all our initial activities took place near the boat: cleaning and inspecting it, discarding food of questionable quality, and tending to business in the marina's Internet café.

We received some more good news from our sponsors Wallace and Carey. They were proud of our recent accomplishment, and offered additional financial support for us to make it to the end. Julie and I were overjoyed. Unforeseen expenses kept cropping up, and it had become apparent that our $50,000 wouldn't last until Vancouver. The support of Truestar and Wallace and Carey had come at a pivotal point in the expedition.

Once we had our land legs again, Julie and I explored the island. We walked through the nearby village, eating local treats such as jerk chicken and fresh fruit. Many of the locals looked like disciples of Bob Marley and peppered their conversations with the Caribbean phrase, "Yeah, mon." One colourfully clad fellow with dreadlocks introduced himself as Jamon (pronounced, of course, "Yeah mon").

"Your name is Jamon?" I asked, pronouncing the *J* hard.

"Yeah, mon," he said.

I wasn't sure if this was meant to be the affirmative or if he was correcting my pronunciation.

During our time in St. Lucia we devoured bananas, papayas, passion fruit, grapefruit, oranges, prickly pears, and mangoes. Soon we would be back out at sea and fresh fruits and vegetables would vanish again from our diet, so we were excited to meet up with Gary McIntosh from Truestar Health, who had just flown in from Toronto. A fit man in his 20s, Gary arrived at the marina with a duffle bag full of cold-pressed multivitamins, protein powder, energy supplements, reparative compounds, and clothing.

AFTER 14 DAYS ON ST. LUCIA, Julie and I felt recharged, had the boat shipshape, and were ready to head back out to sea. We expected it would take about a month to cover the 3,000 kilometres to Limon, Costa Rica, and we would encounter no more islands en route. We were both excited and apprehensive about doing this final leg of our Atlantic crossing. Many sailors had warned us of the Caribbean Sea's dangerous reputation. The winds get strong, and waves reflected from the shorelines of the surrounding island chains stir up confused and powerful seas.

A family of Norwegians in a sailboat berthed next to ours helped us out during our stay in St. Lucia. They let us use their motorized inflatable to fetch groceries from the waterside supermarket, loaned us a laptop computer, and gave us Kevlar cloth to fix our broken oar. As we made our final preparations, Erik, the father, handed us his laptop.

"You will need this out at sea for your communication," he said. "You can send it back to us when your journey is over."

We rowed out of the marina at 10 a.m. February 1. Air horns blasted, and a fleet of yacht tenders followed us into the bay to wish us good luck. Julie pulled hard on the oars and soon put St. Lucia in the distance.

The Caribbean Sea was a new experience for rowing. The currents increased in speed, often reaching two knots, and gave us a huge boost. In the first two weeks, we made good speed with consistent tailwinds and strong currents.

As we neared the shore of Colombia, the currents reached a powerful 4.5 knots. Here, at the northernmost stretch of South America, currents coming across the Atlantic collided with the continent and were funnelled across its top. Accelerated by these currents, we moved at speeds of 5.5 knots, even when rowing lightly.

Two weeks out of St. Lucia, it had been a flawless run. Then Dean passed along disheartening news. Winds were expected to exceed 50 knots for a few days. Although the approaching storm wasn't cyclonic in formation (not having the spiralling characteristics and generally not as intense), the wind speeds were as strong as those we had experienced in our glancing encounters with the hurricanes.

Over the next two days, the winds intensified and the waves grew to 35 feet. We tried to continue rowing, but after snapping three oars (including the one repaired in St. Lucia), we decided instead to take turns rudder-steering the boat and keeping its stern to the waves. This involved sitting stationary on the sliding seat while controlling the rudder using two cords connected to the tiller.

The ocean turned grey and spray whipped off the tops of the waves. Breaking waves turned the waters into a tempest. They broke over our boat with frightening force and often launched our small rowboat down their steep faces like a bulbous surfboard. *Ondine* would plane like a power boat and accelerate until huge rooster tails sprayed up both sides. As it surfed, the boat would reach speeds of 20 kilometres an hour and feel like a runaway train.

We had rowed almost 9,000 kilometres and were only 1,000 kilometres from our final ocean landing, and yet I felt that this storm might be the one to snuff out our journey at last. The waves were the most powerful we had encountered, and our vessel was continually being rolled on her side.

During shift change on the second day of the storm, Julie opened the hatch to switch places with me. As I released the rudder cords, a 35-foot monster broke over the vessel, and 10 buckets' worth of water washed into the cabin, drenching food, clothing, and some electronics. The laptop given to us by the Norwegians was doused and destroyed.

It wasn't a good day.

21

ON DRY LAND AGAIN

W E ENDURED A HELLISH THREE DAYS in a wet, smelly, perpetu-ally rocking boat. Once again, *Ondine* endured. Our excitement grew as we neared the end of our five-month ocean crossing. The prospect of not having to row 10 hours a day, every day, had been the subject of our fantasies for the past four and a half months.

Unfortunately, our final days before landing weren't the period of contemplative celebration that we had hoped. Currents of up to 2.5 knots pushed against our boat, and we had no choice but to row 18 hours each per day. The six hours of overlapping rowing, when we were powering in tandem, was the only period we would make any forward progress, moving at about one knot. The remaining 18 hours per day of single rowing would just hold our ground.

As we struggled forward with almost no sleep, and no time to even cook (eating nothing but cookies, crackers, milk, and Truestar supplements), we turned into exhausted zombies. A ceaseless tropical deluge soaked and chilled us to the bone as we entered a thick cloud belt that enshrouded the coast of Costa Rica, like the approach to King Kong Island. The thick clouds and rain prevented us from seeing land, even as we drew close.

Limon is the only port in eastern Costa Rica, but the city has no harbour. Instead, it simply has large piers jutting into the sea, which act as both unloading terminals and breakwaters. While the freighters wait to be processed, they anchor in the open sea, fully exposed to the rolling swell of the ocean.

At 2 a.m. on February 23, through driving rain, we finally made out the lights of the anchored freighters and the glow of the town. We had been rowing like mad for three days, and even with the excitement of the end of our Atlantic row being so close, our energy was waning.

At 4 a.m., we reached an anchored freighter. The outwards current was still 1.5 knots. I threw the anchor over the side, hoping that the depth would be less than 25 metres—the deepest we could safely anchor with our 100 metres of rope.

At 20 metres, I felt the anchor connect with the solid ground of North America. We could rest.

I put my arm around Julie as the rain continued to pour. The lights of the city formed a kaleidoscopic blur through my sleep-deprived senses. Too tired to feel the joy we'd earned, we climbed into the cabin and passed out. After 145 days at sea, we had crossed the Atlantic Ocean.

AT 10 A.M., JULIE AND I rowed to a concrete pier. On the wharf, a crowd had gathered for our arrival. It included the Costa Rican press, customs, immigration, and a crew from the Canadian Discovery Channel.

We stepped onto terra firma, our legs swaying, and hugged each other. The contrary currents, hurricanes, and near-misses with ships were all behind us now. Julie had just become the first woman to row across the Atlantic Ocean from mainland to mainland, and I had completed the last major hurdle on my round-the-world quest. From here, only 8,000 kilometres of road lay between us and Vancouver.

Customs, immigration, the media, and the port authorities all vied for our attention, giving orders about where to tie our boat, firing off questions, and asking us to pose for photographs. I felt dazed facing such a mob after so many days of solitude on the sea. The contrast could not have been more complete. I longed for a quiet room in a hotel, and wished I could fast-forward a few hours.

Among the crowd were two men from the Canadian consulate who had driven from San Jose with an emergency passport for me. When we left Lisbon five months earlier, I was concerned that my passport would expire in four months, but felt that it wouldn't pose any serious problems. We had planned on arriving in the U.S.A., where I wouldn't need a passport. Furthermore, we had expected to reach North America before my passport expired.

Prior to reaching Costa Rica, I contacted the Canadian consulate and they queried the Costa Rican immigration department on my behalf. I would be jailed and deported— no exceptions— the consulate was told. To prevent this from happening, the consulate went to great lengths to create an emergency passport that would be handed to me as I stepped ashore. Since the consulate lacked a photograph of me, the men came armed with a Polaroid camera, and snapped a travel-weary picture of me stepping off the boat, then pasted it into the passport.

The uniformed immigration officer looked approvingly at the new passport, and demanded to see the rest of our papers. Julie diverted her attention from the gaggle of press around the boat to leaf through our damp stack of documents. After filling out a myriad of forms against the side of a parked car for both customs and immigration, the officials were satisfied and we were free to stagger into Costa Rica.

Seven hours passed from the time we first touched land to when we were finally finished with the bureaucrats and media.

As the last of the reporters left, Julie and I tied our vessel securely to the coast guard ship, added plenty of bumpers to compensate for the large swell, and finally ventured away from the sea.

Although walking was difficult, it wasn't the impossibility it had been when we reached St. Lucia six weeks earlier. We staggered across the industrial expanse of asphalt, past shipping containers and large forklifts, towards the entrance of the port compound. It wasn't the most beautiful arrival point, but it was our only choice. The rest of the coast is guarded by pounding waves crashing onto rocks or sandy beaches.

The heart of the city lay just beyond the loading docks, and Julie and I emerged through a heavy gate like a couple of curious monkeys escaping from the zoo. We were tired, and our legs already hurt, but the excitement of finally being able to celebrate the end of our Atlantic row kept us going.

We knew absolutely nothing about Puerto Limon, not having had any time to do research, so we eagerly absorbed our surroundings. The town has a rough edge to it, with a large number of homeless people and beggars on the streets. Nonetheless, it exudes the seedy charm that is so typical of port cities around the world. Sailors and longshoremen frequented its many pubs, run-down hotels lined the streets, and vendors were everywhere, selling anything from freshly squeezed orange juice to floral knickers. A few old colonial buildings still survive, hinting at the town's longevity.

Puerto Limon is where Christopher Columbus first stepped onto North America in 1502. The town itself was established in 1870 and soon became a thriving port servicing the banana plantations in the region. A large percentage of the present population is composed of black workers brought over from Jamaica to work on the banana plantations, which gives the region a Caribbean flavour.

We quickly found an inexpensive but comfortable hotel to store our belongings, before searching for a restaurant in which to celebrate. We'd eaten nothing all day apart from some crackers from the boat. Not far from our hotel we found a vibrant restaurant and seated ourselves behind a heavy wooden table. Within minutes the waitress brought us frosted mugs of beer and large platters heaping with fries, salad, and broiled burgers.

"To a successful crossing of the Atlantic Ocean in a rowboat," Julie said with a huge smile. Our glasses met and clinked a note of finality.

An enormous weight had lifted off my shoulders. From the journey's inception years three years earlier, I had been haunted by doubts. A small part of me always felt that I was embarking on an impossible journey, that I was wasting my time and risking my life. Now that we had finally reached North America, suddenly those niggling fears were quashed. Of course there were still dangers ahead, but the journey no longer seemed impossible. The end was drawing near. All the same, we couldn't be lulled into complacency. Ahead were still more than 8,000 gruelling kilometres by bicycle. Central America and Mexico are notorious for aggressive drivers, and highway bandits are common.

We retired to our ten-dollar-a-night hotel and collapsed into a soft bed. This would be our first night's sleep outside of the rowboat in more than five and a half months. Even in St. Lucia we had bedded each night in our vessel. The room seemed to rock back and forth as I fell into the most satisfying sleep of my life.

LIMON WAS THE PERFECT PLACE to base ourselves for the two weeks we needed to ready ourselves for the next—and final—cycling leg. The city nestles into a crook of paradise where rainforests meet ocean. Nearby beaches offer world-class surfing and the backdrop of jungles harbours some of the world's greatest bio-diversity, including monkeys, parrots, sloths, and colourful butterflies. Plentiful rains at a latitude of 10 degrees north cre-ate ideal conditions for the flora and fauna.

Limon itself is a working town, its main industry being the port where bananas and pineapples are shipped to distant cor-ners of the planet. Apart from cruise-ship day trippers, most tourists give it a miss and head instead to nearby beach com-munities such as Puerto Viejo. For Julie and I, however, the cheaper costs and plentiful goods and services made Limon just what we needed. In Limon, unlike in many parts of Central America, English is common because of the large number of Jamaican immigrants. The fusion of Caribbean and Central American cuisines means regular feasts of meals that combine fresh fruit, fish, coconuts, and plenty of spice.

The boat was lifted from the water by a crane and placed in a port storage facility. Later it would be shipped to Canada. We had been unable to ship our bicycles from Portugal, so Norco sent us two new VFR4 performance bikes along with Axiom racks and waterproof panniers. These ultra-lightweight bikes would allow us to travel fast, and yet still had the strength to endure the rougher roads.

To maximize our speed, we would carry only two small panniers between us. These we'd pack with the barest of essentials. Apart from what we wore, our clothing would con-sist of one pair of socks and underwear each, two T-shirts, and Julie's fleece jacket. We would also tote two small down sleep-ing bags, an extremely lightweight tent that cost $12, a basic tool kit, a small video camera, and a digital camera. We would forfeit the luxury of sleeping mats, raingear, a camp stove, and heavy tools. Our cycling equipment might be considered spartan by even the most gram-shaving of long-distance cyclists, but it was all we needed to make it home.

IN MID-MARCH, we rode our bicycles into the port, glanced nostalgically to where the boat had been tied, and then began the long ride home. The main highway leading west to San Jose is extremely busy and has no shoulders. Most of the traffic was composed of large transport trucks carrying their goods to and away from the port. I felt petrified as we cycled on the shoulderless edge as they rumbled past.

We rode as close as we could to the edge of the asphalt, which posed an additional danger. The heavy rainfall in the region created a slick of algae, and when our wheels came too close to the edge, the increased gradient would cause them to lose traction. At one point, when traffic was particularly heavy, Julie rode too close to the edge and her bicycle slipped out from under her in the blink of an eye. She sprawled the opposite way into traffic and was stunned by the impact of her fall.

I was cycling a few metres behind her, and was shocked that she didn't take immediate evasive action. Instinctively, I screamed at the top of my lungs.

My crazed scream spurred her into action, and Julie scrambled off the road, just seconds before a truck roared over the spot where she had been. With non-stop traffic coming in the other direction, there was no way the driver could have swerved.

We were both shaking as we stood by the side of the road, Julie's hands bleeding from road rash. It had been too close for comfort. We walked our bikes in the ditch for half an hour, regaining our nerves. It was our first day and Julie had almost been killed in the first 40 kilometres.

I didn't know what to think. The expedition meant nothing compared to Julie's life. Between here and Canada there would be a lot of busy roads and bad drivers. Were we just being stupid? I wanted to keep walking our bikes in the ditch forever, to keep Julie away from the traffic. It seemed it was just a matter of time before something tragic would happen. I kept thinking that we could simply hop on an airplane, fly home, get a house in the country, forget about this ridiculous expedition, and live happily ever after. But we eventually left the ditch and returned to the road.

Fortunately, we would later find that the highway out of Limon was one of the worst we would encounter all the way home. About 100 kilometres from Limon, we turned north onto a much quieter road following the eastern side of the continental divide. This rural highway passed through lush jungles, farmland, and small villages. No longer fearing for our lives, we were able to enjoy the surrounding landscape.

Due to the moisture-laden trade winds blowing onshore, huge amounts of rain fall on the eastern side of the continental divide, which runs along the spine of the Andes–Sierra Madre chain. The jagged mountains, cloaked in lush jungles, were an oasis beckoning to be explored. Spirited streams dashed down the flanks of volcanic mountains and passed under our road. The downside to such splendour was the regular downpours that would soak us to the bone. We carried no raingear, hoping the tropical climate would keep us warm. When the deluges carried on for hours, however, we would start to feel chilled.

Due to their low cost, and the fact that we carried minimal camping equipment, we elected to stay in hotels while in Central America. Further north in Nicaragua, Honduras, and El Salvador, this would be even more important for safety. Most villages and towns had hotels, so we would plan our days to end at centres marked along our route.

Costa Rica is much more developed than its neighbours, and most of the villagers we encountered seemed to be reasonably well off, wearing stylish clothes and occasionally owning cars. They would wave cheerfully as we passed.

On our third day the road turned to dirt, and our lightweight bikes forged through 20 kilometres of rough, potholed roads without complaint. The asphalt soon returned and we crossed the lowest point on the continental divide, barely noticing the incline. Within a few hours of reaching the western watershed, we arrived at the Pan-American Highway and the Nicaraguan border.

From here, we would be travelling mainly on the Pan-American Highway, a network of roads that runs from Alaska to the bottom of South America—with a swampy and dangerous gap of 87 kilometres in Panama.

We waited at the border as cars and trucks and long queues of bus passengers waited to be processed. A Costa Rican money changer approached us while we waited for our entry stamps.

"Change money?" the stocky man inquired.

Several others had approached us earlier and we had declined. This time, however, we relented, since it would save us a trip to the bank on the other side.

"What rate will you give us?" Julie asked.

The man tapped a reasonable figure on his calculator.

"Okay, we'll exchange 10,000 colón (about $20)."

A few more taps and he showed us what we would get. The man flipped out the cash and handed it to Julie. By the time she counted it and realized she'd been shortchanged by $19, he had disappeared into the crowd.

After paying about $10 for our entry permit, we cycled into Nicaragua. Poverty there was much more widespread than in Costa Rica. The crisp uniforms of school children we had grown accustomed to seeing were replaced by grimy rags. Fewer vehicles navigated the roads, and the ones that did often belched black smoke from their exhausts. Even more striking than the lack of wealth was the abundance of firearms. Almost any type of business more sophisticated than a shoeshine operation was protected by security guards wielding menacing rifles.

The road we followed had very light traffic, and was in much better shape than the potholed highways of Costa Rica. It also included wide shoulders, a very welcome surprise. We were told later that much of the Pan-American Highway was financed by the American government, hence the excellent condition of the road through Nicaragua, Honduras, and El Salvador.

We were pleased to see that bicycles have been adopted as one of the major modes of transportation, and we shared the road with other human-powered commuters, their bicycles often loaded with sacks of corn, tools, or a passenger or two. In the towns and villages, pedicabs were ubiquitous, and the old or frail, unable to pedal their own bikes, would be transported by the physically capable.

Almost immediately after entering the arid lands of southwestern Nicaragua, Lago Nicaragua came into sight. Strong easterly winds ripped over its wave-tossed brown waters. Covering an area of more than 8,000 square kilometres, Lago Nicaragua is the twentieth largest lake in the world. It is connected to the Atlantic Ocean via a navigable river, and its western shore is only 19 kilometres from the Pacific Ocean.

Although this murky windswept lake is anything but beautiful, it has held the world's attention since 1825, when it was determined to be a prime spot to run a canal connecting the Atlantic and Pacific oceans. The colonial administration of Spain decided that the ideal locations to build a canal were either through Panama, due to its lowlands and narrow breadth, or through Nicaragua which, although wider, has the geographical advantage of a navigable river and lake spanning most of its width.

But the Spanish never built a canal, and the U.S. government negotiated rights for both the Panama and the Nicaraguan route. After much deliberation it finally chose Panama for the canal.

Nicaragua is still trying to get international support to build a canal, which would cost an estimated $25 billion. If the canal were built, it would cut 800 kilometres off the route from New York to San Francisco, and it would facilitate much larger ships than the Panama Canal can manage.

By late evening Julie and I reached the old colonial city of Granada at the head of Lago Nicaragua. Granada is considered an Atlantic port since it is navigable from the Caribbean Sea, and its inland location makes it a strategic base. It was founded in 1524, which makes it one of the oldest cities in the Americas. After Nicaragua became independent from Spain, Granada became the national capital for periods.

It was dark as Julie and I pedalled through the busy streets of Granada, but it was still easy to discern the magnificent colonial architecture as we reached the old city centre. So far we had witnessed only poverty, shanty homes, and disarray, and it was hard to imagine the world of wealth and order that had created these ornate stone buildings and cobbled streets. Granada is a tourist destination, and we were able to find a comfortable hostel in the city centre.

From Granada we made our way steadily northwards, across the centre of the country, passing through arid desert dotted with occasional villages. Three days after leaving Costa Rica, we reached a border crossing, a stark contrast to the bustling interchange at the Costa Rican border. The only sign of life was two immigration officers occupying adjacent shacks on each side of the border. The clearance and entry formalities were quick, and minutes later Julie and I coasted into Honduras.

Immediately after crossing the border, the road began a long descent that was the greatest we had encountered since Russia. For half an hour we relaxed while coasting at speeds of 30 to 45 kilometres per hour. As we descended from the highlands into the furnace-like lower valleys, I became almost sick with the heat even though we were free-wheeling. When we had to pedal again, our clothes were soon soaked in sweat and our faces flushed with the heat and humidity.

We passed through the narrow tongue of land separating Nicaragua and El Salvador in two long days. The roads were broad, smooth asphalt, with a reassuring white line dividing the shoulder from the traffic lane. We continued to stay in budget roadside hotels to minimize any encounters with road bandits.

We quickly cleared immigration and customs at the El Salvador border, and were surprised at the stark contrast to the last two countries we had passed through. El Salvador has been much more Westernized, and foreign investment is apparent in the presence of multinational service stations and fast-food establishments. The country appeared more politically stable than Nicaragua and Honduras, despite the fact that it has recently emerged from a civil war and is reputed to have extremely high crime rates.

Julie and I thoroughly enjoyed our brief three-day passage through El Salvador. We followed the number two highway, which skirted the Pacific coast. The southern portion of this route connects small surfing towns, located on lovely black sand beaches nestled between rocky headlands. As we travelled northwards, the region became increasingly remote, and the scenery even more pleasing. There were few villages, and Julie and I would frequently stop our bikes where the road cut along a precipice to admire the ocean crashing into the cliffs hundreds of feet below. Despite the roller-coaster route we followed, the road was in good shape with a wide shoulder remaining even in the frequent tunnels.

The people we encountered in El Salvador were friendly, prices were cheap, and the food was excellent. We took precaution concerning our personal safety, and continued our habit of staying in hotels whenever possible. In one small village that had no accommodation, we were invited to set up our tent in the middle of an open-air restaurant. In the morning we climbed out of our tent bleary eyed, took a seat, and ordered eggs and coffee.

We traversed Guatemala quickly, travelling through a flat part of the country punctuated by small villages and scraggly forests. The land was green once again with the more abundant precipitation, and the roads had degraded significantly, often having no shoulders at all.

Twelve days after leaving Limon, we finally reached the Mexican border at La Libertad. Upon entering the small town, we became lost in a maze of narrow alleys and streets.

"Donde esta frontiera?" I asked a soldier.

He pointed in a northerly direction, and we bumped over cobblestones towards a river. Upon reaching its banks we were greeted by a comical sight. Dozens of people were crisscrossing the 200-metre-wide flow on inner tubes. More enterprising souls used multiple inner tubes topped with sheets of plywood. These makeshift vessels were loaded with passengers, bulging sacks, bicycles, and even livestock.

"I have a feeling this isn't the official border crossing," Julie said, incredulous as she surveyed the scene below.

We followed the river westwards and found the proper border post located beside a large concrete bridge spanning the river. Twenty minutes later we entered the seventeenth country of our expedition, Mexico. We were now in the Chiapas region, famous for ancient Mayan architecture. I was a little nervous about passing through this stretch, as we had learned of some disturbing incidents of travellers being attacked by bandits.

Greg Bleakney, a long-distance cyclist travelling from Alaska to Tierra Del Fuego, had been in email communication with us, since we were travelling much of the same route in opposite directions. Just days before we entered Chiapas, Greg had cycled through the same region, and he had a grim story to relay to us. He and his cycling partner had been attacked by bandits, and Greg directed us to the website update that his partner had posted.

> At noon on Sunday March 5th, while cycling near the ruins of Palenque, Mexico, 4/5 men ran out of the jungle and attempted to attack us near the top of a long uphill climb. A car drove by and they all moved to the side of the road, giving us just enough time to accelerate past them to a downhill section where we distanced ourselves from the scene. We hailed the passing car and asked the driver to escort us to the next safe town or village. He agreed and one mile later, a police car passed and we stopped him to ask for help. He told us that he would drive ahead 3 miles to the major tourist attraction of Agua Azul Falls, secure the road, and then loop back and forth to make sure that we were safe. He guaranteed that the road ahead was secure.
>
> Two miles later, we were attacked again by two men wearing black masks and carrying machetes. They sprinted out of the jungle and were upon us in

only a few seconds making it impossible to escape. We put our hands over our heads as they struck us several times with the blunt sides of their machetes and attempted to tear our pannier bags off the bikes. They were only able to remove two of the bags from Greg's bike and over the next minute or so the conflict escalated as their frustration increased. They retreated to the side of the road to dump Greg's bags and hide from a passing car.

At that point, we turned around and cycled 300 meters to a family's roadside hut at the bottom of a hill. We asked them if it was OK if we waited there for help and they agreed. We then asked them if it was safe for us in that location and they said no. A few minutes later several shady characters with hostile looks on their faces appeared out of the jungle near the hut. We were both wary of a third attack and created a road block with our bikes and bodies to stop passing cars and draw attention to ourselves. Though several cars drove around us in the ditch and refused to stop, this tactic did buy us enough time for the police car to return on his loop back to assist us. He tossed our bikes in the back of his truck and escorted us out of the area.

Neither of us were physically harmed during this assault but have both been rattled mentally. We urge all tourists and cyclists to avoid the road from San Cristobol to Agua Azul Falls to the ruins of Palenque to the border of Bethel in Guatemala. After our discussions with local police we have learned that attacks on tourists in these areas are now occurring several times per week. Some of the attacks have even involved large tour buses and shuttle vans.

Greg told us that in the past five weeks, four other groups of foreign touring cyclists had been robbed by pistol- and machete-wielding bandits in this region. Since the number of touring cyclists in this part of the world was low, we reasoned the odds of being attacked were extremely high.

Much of the Chiapas region is controlled by the Zapatista Army of National Liberation, an armed revolutionary group in the poorest Mexican state. Their stated goals are to represent the rights of the indigenous Mayan population and to oppose capitalization. They have created their own governments in some communities and currently there are 32 "rebel autonomous Zapatista municipalities" in Chiapas. However, the Chiapas region continues to be unstable, and many unfortunate stories have been relayed.

Several kilometres past the border with Guatemala we reached a roadblock of burning tires and chanting villagers. As we skirted the obstacle and pedalled through the angry throngs, the crowd took notice, and a new chant was voiced, saying something about the gringos. We quickened our pace and cycled hard until Chiapas was in our wake, two days later.

Since leaving Costa Rica we had been navigating with extreme difficulty. In Limon we had purchased a road map of Costa Rica in a service station, and imagined it would be easy to find such maps in subsequent countries. Unfortunately, we soon learned that road maps are luxuries that are virtually impossible to find in Nicaragua, Honduras, El Salvador, Guatemala, and Chiapas. In desperation, we had taken a photograph of a map of Central America that we had found on the wall of a restaurant, and until now we had been referring to the grainy images in our digital camera to guide us through the region. Finally, in central Mexico, we were able to find a good road atlas in a bookstore.

With our detailed maps we planned a route that would

veer away from the Pacific shelf towards the continental divide and Mexico City. We had spent many days cycling through relatively flat land, and were dismayed to enter what would turn out to be the hilliest terrain of our entire journey around the planet. As we entered Sierra Madre del Sur, our windy, narrow road snaked up into the heavens. We finally summited the pass, relieved, thinking that after descending we would follow the bottom of a flat valley. Instead, the road ascended pass after pass, each higher than the previous one. The sun baked down and sweat dribbled off our bodies as our legs spun wildly in lowest gear. Large trucks passed within inches of our bikes as they flew around bends, and we constantly feared being hit.

The scenery, however, was beautiful, and rugged dry peaks stretched off into the distance. Tiny mountain villages were peppered along the road, their inhabitants tending to the agave plantations used for mescal production. Farmers raised their hats in greeting as we passed.

Finally, after traversing five enormous passes, and almost being hit by vehicles numerous times, we reached the state of Oaxaca, where the land flattened out. As we closed in on Mexico City, Julie and I found an alternative to cycling on the extremely treacherous narrow state roads. A network of toll highways criss-cross the nation and although they are decorated liberally with no-cycling signs, this rule doesn't seem to be enforced. The roads themselves are impeccably maintained and sport three-metre shoulders just begging to be cycled on.

On these improved roads we quickly drew closer to Mexico City. Cycling through the chaos of one of the world's largest cities was surprisingly enjoyable, an experience resembling a real-life video game. The roads seemed devoid of rules, as VW vans, buses, dogs, and pedestrians vied for position.

Despite the chaos, most drivers were remarkably adept at manoeuvring their vehicles, and remained in a state of good-natured calm. This was illustrated when the driver of a dilapidated bus pulled in front of Julie and slammed on his brakes, blocking our progress along with the rest of the traffic. He emerged grinning from ear to ear and holding out two frozen-fruit popsicles for us. The middle-aged man with a big moustache gestured towards our Canadian flags, explaining that he had worked in our homeland and had absolutely loved the experience. Meanwhile, the passengers in his bus and the cars behind waited patiently while the conversation continued.

Mexico continued to grow on us as we cycled northward. Prices were much higher than in Central America, but the locals were very friendly and helpful. Best of all was the improved quality of roadside diners, a stark contrast from the ones serving bland food throughout southern Mexico.

Despite the positive transformation in roads and food, hotels became infrequent in the north, forcing us to camp in the desert most nights. This we didn't mind, as it was a pleasure setting up the tent among the cactuses and beneath the perpetually clear skies.

Our travel-worn tires, however, continued to degrade, and as we neared the U.S. border our daily tally of flats increased, peaking at 14 in one day. About 60 kilometres from the border our tubes packed it in for good, and we worked fruitlessly to repair gaping holes and defective valves. We had no choice but to hitchhike to Nuevo Laredo to purchase new tubes.

The next day, we cycled back to the site of our breakdown so there would be no gaps in our human-powered journey. We continued northward, finally reaching the border at Laredo, Texas.

Amid throngs of Mexicans, we pushed our bikes across a bridge spanning the Rio Grande, which separates the U.S.A. and Mexico. An enormous American flag billowed in the Texan heat, marking one of the greatest milestones of the expedition so far. I had always felt that once I reached the U.S.A., I could finally relax. Although there was still a long slog ahead, the dangers were vastly reduced. For the first time in almost two years, I felt confident that we would make it to the end.

In Laredo, Julie and I would take our second day off cycling since leaving Limon 30 days earlier. It would be a busy day off, as I needed to write a 5,000-word article for *Reader's Digest* and Julie was writing for *Venus* magazine. However, we still found time to enjoy generous servings of Texan cuisine and to savour the fact that we had reached the final country before home. It felt good.

"MY WORD, I CAN'T BELIEVE Y'ALL ARE CROSSING THE U.S.A. on your bicycles," the gas-station attendant drawled. "I've heard of people doing things like that, but I've never actually seen it for real."

Julie and I had stopped at a Texas service station to buy snacks for the road. The attendant's wide-eyed wonder would be the standard reaction as we passed through America's largest coterminous state.

The Texans' curiosity and surprise seemed to stem from our novelty factor, as few long-distance cyclists pass through the state—despite the fact that Lance Armstrong, the seven-time Tour de France champ, calls the Lone Star state home.

Even though Julie and I spotted only four adults on bicycles during our passage through Texas, we found it to be the most bike-friendly region we encountered in pedalling through 17 countries around the world. All the roads we travelled sported three-metre-wide shoulders. Combined with courteous drivers who would pull out to give us even more room, these lanes offered a level of safety we hadn't previously experienced.

We travelled mostly north through the heart of rural Texas on Highway 83. This quiet road traverses ranch country in the south and then agricultural land in the north. Our route bypassed major cities, and most of the communities we encountered had a population of 300 to 1,500. The shorter distances between towns allowed Julie and me to chow down in diners. Hotels, too, were frequent and affordable, although most often we opted to camp in the fields and wilderness off the road.

Texas may not be renowned for its scenery, but the landscape comes alive in the red light and long shadows of the setting sun. Windmills are another charming (and common) sight, clattering and squeaking as they use dry winds to pump well water for thirsty cattle.

And—as a local explained to us—Texas doesn't have mountains but it does have holes, and the state is proof that holes can be beautiful, too. Deep canyons, carved by wind and water, evoke Wild West backdrops of hoodoos and cactus. The rich red clay changes hue throughout the day like a concave Ayers Rock.

The quiet roads allowed us to converse, helping to while away the kilometres, and our conversations generally revolved around our observations.

"Have you noticed that people here don't know what 'washrooms' are," Julie mused as we departed from a diner.

"Yeah, it's 'restrooms' here in the States," I said.

"I've got this theory that the word used for a lavatory is an indication of the collective psychology of a nation," Julie said. "For example, the British call it the toilet. Now that's to the point—typically British. Canadians call it the washroom, which is a realistic description of what you could be doing in there, without getting into details. That sounds Canadian to me—polite but still getting the point across. But 'restroom'? Who goes into a smelly porcelain room to rest? That's outright denial."

"Well, I'm going to start calling it the water room," I chuckled, "since we use it mainly for filling our water bottles."

After 10 pleasant days cycling through Texas, we crossed into New Mexico and through its drought-stricken northeast corner in a day before entering Colorado. The road conditions soon deteriorated compared to Texan thoroughfares, but were still excellent by international standards of asphalt.

Since starting our cycling journey in Central America, we had been averaging 130 kilometres a day (including our two days off), which made for long, arduous days in the saddle. In Mexico and Central America, the physical rigours combined with the stresses of navigation, finding food and water, and worries about bandits had taken their toll on our motivation. Our relationship remained strong, however, and Julie and I had had to work hard to keep each other in positive spirits.

In the U.S.A., however, with wide roads, cautious drivers, and no threat of road bandits, we could relax and enjoy the constantly changing panoramas. It was easy to keep our water bottles filled at roadside service stations or public washrooms, and food stores and roadside diners were everywhere.

After ascending Raton Pass at the boundary of New Mexico and Colorado, Julie and I were treated to a spectacular and yet familiar sight: the snow-capped peaks of the Rocky Mountains. Suddenly the scenery didn't look so foreign. Home felt achingly close.

The temperatures began to drop as we cycled along the base of the Rockies, and our shorts and T-shirts were no longer sufficient. We stopped in Colorado to purchase $60 of generic fleece clothing to get us through the colder temperatures ahead. Although it was early May, we were hit by a blizzard two days after entering the neighbouring state of Wyoming. The minus-3 temperatures contrasted sharply with the 37-degree afternoons we'd experienced in Texas only days earlier.

We were close to the continental divide as the snow deepened around us, and we found it increasingly difficult to keep our bikes moving through 10 centimetres of snow. We were now cycling through the most remote part of the U.S.A. we'd encountered so far, and I began to worry as melting snow worked its way into my clothing, chilling me to the bone. We hadn't expected the weather to be this severe.

A lone dilapidated service station appeared in the gloom, an oasis in a desert of white. Julie and I rolled our bikes off the highway and entered the small building.

"How're y'all doing?" a slender bespectacled man asked us with a Texan drawl. "What the heck are you doing on your bicycles on a day like this? I wouldn't want to drive my car in these conditions."

The interior was dimly lit and a fifteen-foot bar lined one wall of the 30 by 20 smoky room. A couple of older men sat nursing their beers.

The man behind the counter introduced himself as Kenneth, and told us to make ourselves at home. We gratefully poured ourselves a couple of coffees and joined the men at the bar to watch the Christmas scene through the window. Chickadees flittered around a bird feeder while the snow continued to dump. I couldn't believe that just eight days earlier we had been experiencing 38-degree temperatures in Texas.

"It's forecast to drop down to 14 degrees (minus 10 Celsius) tonight," Kenneth informed us.

I shivered at the thought of spending the night outside in our $12 tent with our summer sleeping bags and no sleeping mats.

Kenneth looked at us sympathetically. "If you want, you can spend the night in my trailer home out back. It's not a palace, but it's a hell of a lot better than being out there."

We gratefully accepted. As we waited for Kenneth to finish work, he described life at his remote highway outpost. Originally from Texas, Kenneth had come to Wyoming to help his good friend, who was the owner of the gas station. Kenneth had recently undergone quadruple-bypass heart surgery, and his present stress-free lifestyle was beneficial for his recovery.

While Kenneth chatted, he popped a frozen pizza in the oven.

"How'd you guys like Texas food?" he inquired.

"Very tasty," Julie said, "and big portions!"

"Texan cuisine is the reason my heart gave out," Kenneth grumbled. "Everything is deep fried and loaded with fat. I never knew until it was too late that Mama's cooking was killing me."

Kenneth noticed me glancing at his frame, lean as a rake, and answered the question I was about to ask. "It doesn't matter if you're skinny, it still plugs up your veins."

Changing the subject, Kenneth gestured towards five or six men coming through the door, "These are the local boys who work on an oil rig a few miles away. These guys are the reason why this place is able to exist. As you noticed, almost nobody stops here for gas any more."

The burly men stomped snow from their feet and ordered a round of beers. Through the evening Kenneth worked as bartender for the workers. Julie and I chatted with the friendly men, and learned about the strenuous life of an oil driller. A tattooed fellow in his late 20s, was proudly introduced by his co-workers as the nephew of Johnny Cash.

At 11 p.m. the last of the oil men left, and we followed our kind host to his cozy trailer. We quickly fell asleep as the snow continued to fall.

The skies were clear the following morning, and roads ploughed, so we were able to make an early start. We crossed the continental divide two times, because we were in a unique location where the divide splits and rejoins farther along the spine of the Rockies. The land between the two divides is a shallow basin with a desert climate. We were more than 7,000 feet above sea level, but the land was surprisingly mundane— treeless and flat.

Finally, we slipped off this highland plateau and down into Utah. Temperatures warmed as we cycled through the most eye-catching landscapes we would encounter in the U.S.A. Brilliant red sand hoodoos and wind-sculpted cliffs bookended highway vistas that seemed stolen out of car commercials. We descended through canyons until we finally reached an open expanse and the great Salt Lake came into view. Then we turned northwards towards Idaho. Tailwinds blew us along the flat highways that led through Idaho, Oregon, and into Washington State.

With the wind at our backs, we passed over the coastal mountain range on May 16 and the scenery transformed from rolling dry farmland to the typical northwest landscape— rainforests of cedar and Douglas fir cloaking high snow-capped mountains.

As I inhaled the rich scent of damp conifers, I knew I was almost home. Some 43,000 kilometres had passed beneath my feet since leaving Vancouver. Now our final destination was only 250 kilometres away. As Julie and I closed the gap between us and the Canadian border, I began to feel nostalgic for a trip that hadn't yet finished.

O N MAY 19 WE FINALLY REACHED the Canadian border. The border guard asked us a few simple questions and waved us
through. We climbed back onto our bikes and glided
slowly away from the booth and into Canada. Our destination
lay 60 kilometres to the north, and as I looked at the familiar
scenery around me I was overcome with emotion.

For two years, the road had been my home. Each night, I
would bed down in a new location—in the tent, the rowboat, or
the canoe. At times, our trip didn't even feel like an expedition;
it had transformed into an all-encompassing style of living,
deeply ingrained in my DNA. My life was characterized by a
state of perpetual travel and danger. Oddly, the whole process
had taken on a sense of normalcy, as though staying in one place
was the weirdest behaviour imaginable. It seemed strange to me
that all this would soon come to an end.

As the late-spring sunshine baked down on us, and the
North Shore Mountains became visible in the distance, my
memories of the previous two years blurred. It seemed I had
all of a sudden transformed from someone on an incredibly
difficult and arduous expedition to once again being a West
Coaster out for a casual bike ride.

Was I really about to complete the first human-powered
circumnavigation of planet Earth? As Julie and I cycled in
unison along familiar roads towards home, I thought back to

everything that had gone into creating these final moments. I thought of the years of planning and dreaming before the expedition started. I thought of the storms on the Bering Sea and the toil of our Siberian hike. I thought back to my time in the Siberian hospital and being lost in the minus-100 temperatures of Russia's Far East. And the thousands and thousands of kilometres of monotonous toil. Day after day, month after month, year after year.

For the past two years I had struggled an average of 16 hours a day striving to reach my goal. The physical aspect, doing about the work of a marathon a day in some of the most gruelling places on earth, was only a part of the overall workload. With only a couple of part-time volunteers at home helping with logistics, a large part of our time in the field was spent trying to raise funds, doing research, and dealing with the endless bureaucracy. When we weren't physically propelling ourselves forward we would be on the satellite phone, or a pay phone at the side of the road, calling shipping companies, sponsors, and bureaucrats in distant corners of the planet.

On top of everything else we continually had to take time out from our travels in order to meticulously document our journey with video and still images. Never once, in two years, had I had one day off to just sit back and relax. Christmas Day, birthdays, and other celebrations were no exception. We had to work from dawn until bedtime. Keeping focused and motivated was the only way we would ever meet our enormously challenging goal.

And finally, after voyaging 14,000 kilometres on water and 29,000 kilometres across land, I was almost back to where I had begun. I had done almost two thirds of it with my wife-to-be, and the strength, determination, and intelligence she had displayed in this journey made me feel privileged to think I would be spending the rest of my life with her. Earlier we had worried that the expedition might jeopardize our relationship as husband and wife, but instead our bond had only been reinforced to the point of unbreakability.

We reached New Westminster, a suburb of Vancouver, and began pedalling along a bicycle path that parallels the Sky Train route. We were now out of the busy traffic and would not need to enter it again. Apart from an errant mugging, almost nothing could stop us from reaching the end.

It was a gorgeous sunny day, and we slowed down so we could enjoy the last moments of the expedition. We blended in with the hundreds of cyclists we shared the trail with, and we weaved through some of the parks en route. We stopped at a small Chinese grocer and bought some treats and juice to savour on a bench.

"How does it feel," Julie asked, "to know that tomorrow morning you'll be done? It's not the end of just another leg, but you've completed the expedition, your life dream."

I reeled at the thought. Metres away a couple of toddlers were feeding pigeons, while the hum of electric trains whirred in the distance.

"It's exciting," I said.

I searched for better words to articulate what I was feeling. Sure, I was excited, but it didn't adequately convey the layers of emotion I felt. I was 12 kilometres away from the end of a two-year odyssey. It had been two years of barely sustainable emotional intensity. Frequently I had felt at the breaking point, due to the level of motivation and discipline required to keep going at a steady pace. In two years I had not allowed myself to slump down exhausted and relax mentally and physically for more than a few hours.

At times I hated it. I would fantasize about one day having a permanent home and not living in a perpetual state of struggle and uncertainty. Other times I felt euphoric as I revelled in the new experiences and the sense of accomplishment. The intimacy we experienced with the wildlife in the mid-Atlantic as we bobbed in our tiny rowboat is a memory I will treasure for the rest of my life.

When we travelled through Siberia, to the sound of howling wolves and skittering snowflakes, home was too distant a concept to be a motivating force. Our drive had come instead from the rewards of experiencing one of the most remote regions on the planet. Here we saw thousands of walruses cavorting off the beaches, and grizzly bears feeding on spawning salmon. The indigenous people, living symbiotically in this rugged land, would invite us into their skin homes.

Rapidly changing conditions in the Arctic were making life difficult for the northern people, but they still generously shared the food they struggled to obtain. I felt guilty that my counterparts in the so-called industrialized world were contributing to the negative changes taking place in their land so far away.

The original motivation for my journey around the planet was to illustrate the power of self-propulsion to combat climate change. Ironically, this two-year odyssey had taken our team through some of the worst meteorological disasters in modern history. First we had encountered the droughts in northern Canada and Alaska, which created record forest fires. In Europe we travelled from the floods of Central Europe, which killed 42 people and caused billions of dollars of damage, to the droughts and forest fires of Portugal. We then rowed from Portugal's smoky shores into the worst hurricane season in recorded history.

Although it is impossible to say for sure that these weather anomalies can be attributed to global warming, global warming is an indisputable fact, and it will bring an increase in extreme weather conditions.

Many people in the industrialized world are too apathetic to make lifestyle changes that would reduce greenhouse emissions. They feel that humanity as a whole will never achieve the required targets, so why bother? Granted, it may be the greatest obstacle humanity has ever faced, but the individual costs per human are minimal. Potentially, costs would go up slightly for goods, transportation, and energy. But people—and our planet—would be healthier.

In the past (and present) people have endured atrocities, hardships, and famines that would make the inconvenience of reducing fossil-fuel consumption insignificant. Yet the reluctance of humankind to make these changes will possibly destroy the most precious thing we have: planet Earth. Our little sphere is an oasis, alone in a chasm of lifeless space. My journey around this planet, using the simplest form of propulsion, human muscles, has given me an interconnected view of the entire globe. Humans, animals, and plants share our biosphere, but we are the only ones who can make significant changes using our brains. Over the next few years, humans can demonstrate whether we are an intelligent, unstoppable virus, motivated only by greed, or a creature that can coexist with others.

Most people had felt a human-powered journey around the planet was impossible. It was a journey too dangerous, too lengthy, and too complicated to ever be completed successfully. I had believed otherwise, and after two years of dedicated teamwork, and unfailing faith that it could be done, Julie and I were finally closing in on the end.

Seven kilometres from the totem pole, Julie and I stopped at the house of Mary Hearnden and Dan, friends of ours, to spend our last night of the expedition.

On May 20, 2006, Julie and I pedalled to the Museum of Anthropology at the University of British Columbia, a rendezvous point where cyclists wishing to finish the journey with us would accompany us on the remaining five kilometres to the totem pole at the Maritime Museum. We cycled the scenic route along Jericho Beach, with its memorable views of both ocean and forest. Finally, only two kilometres remained, and I felt as though I were passing through a dream. I had envisioned this moment so many times, scripted its finest details in my mind, and at last it was really happening.

Spotting the totem pole in the distance unleashed a flood of memories of the efforts it had taken to get here. It seemed impossible that I had crossed two oceans and three continents using my own power. The night in the snow cave in Siberia came back as a vague dream, in the same delirious format that my chilled neurons had recorded the near-fatal event. I had learned that the way to achieve my gargantuan goal was to break it into smaller steps, one day at a time. Each morning I would wake up, muster as much enthusiasm as possible and focus on achieving the daily goal. The overall objective was often too overwhelming to try wrapping our heads around. And when I did, the magnitude of it all scared the hell out of me. Eventually, after 720 days of hard work, I was about to complete what I had set out to do.

As Mungo Martin's totem pole grew closer, I could see a crowd waiting to welcome us home. Julie and I cycled side by side, and I savoured the last few seconds of the journey. A figure in a black jacket jumped up and down trying to get my attention. It was my mother. She looked every bit as healthy as when I had last seen her.

Our friend Dean had set up a tent, sound system, and finish-line banner next to the totem pole. His voice boomed through the microphone, cheering us along for the final moments of the journey. Behind the crowd of people who had gathered to see us home was the panoramic view of English

Bay. Sailboats slipped across the waters of the bay fronting the cityscape and panoramic North Shore Mountains.

Julie and I pedalled the last few metres through the banner, wrapped our arms around each other and then hugged the totem pole. My old friend and adventuring buddy Dan Audet sprayed a bottle of champagne over us.

Two years earlier Julie and I had stood at this same spot, apprehensive and unsure of our future. Since that time we had travelled 43,000 kilometres around our planet, while our world had moved 38 billion kilometres through space. But everything seemed the same. The totem pole, the scenery, the museum were all just as I remembered it. It seemed incredible that all this continued to exist, while my own life was unfolding in a different world.

Nothing had changed physically, that was true. But within, everything was different. The nervousness was now relief, anxiety replaced with hope, and my love for Julie was stronger than ever.

My journey of exploration had taken me everywhere and nowhere, but most important, it brought me back to the beginning. It brought me back to the West Coast of Canada where I was born and raised. It brought me home to a land of rainforests, mountains, glaciers, and ocean that I pray will always be there for future generations.

FIVE MONTHS HAVE PASSED since Julie and I completed our journey. It still seems strange to wake up in the morning and not have to drape myself, aching and tired, onto the saddle of a bicycle or rowing seat for twelve hours of toil.

We have found ourselves a home away from the hustle of the city, a quiet acreage to rent on Vancouver Island. A stream flows beside our house, and I happily amuse myself sitting on the bridge and watching the fish below. During our free time Julie and I are exploring the rivers and forests that surround our home. We have set our wedding date for August 11, 2007.

Although we live in the country, we are continuing our low-emissions lifestyle by exclusively using bicycles for our daily transportation needs. Everything from groceries to computers to a lawn mower is lugged home using bike trailers and panniers. We even haul our garbage out with the bikes. On the few occasions when we need to rent an automobile, we work with Zerofootprint, a company dedicated to offsetting carbon emissions.

One of the things we learned after cycling 30,000 kilometres is that if you want to encourage people to ride their bikes, you need to provide safe routes to travel. We have partnered with an organization that shares this conviction, the Trans Canada Trail. This charity is committed to building the longest recreational trail in the world, stretching over 18,000 kilometres and joining all three oceans bordering Canada.

Through our speaking tour and community events we are rais-
ing funds and awareness to help build the Trail, and to encourage people to use it. For those interested in learning more
about it, please visit www.tctrail.ca.

While Julie and I weaned ourselves from the nomadic
lifestyle we had enjoyed for so long, Tim continued on his own
zero-emissions journey. After parting ways with Erden Eruç,
Tim joined a crew of young Swedes sailing to Venezuela in
South America. He then cycled back to Vancouver completing
his own circumnavigation in mid-November. Tim is currently
living with his mother on Galiano Island where he is planning
another expedition. Yulya is still in Irkutsk.

Erden resumed his row from the Canary Islands solo. Shortly
into the voyage his back began acting up, and Erden mused in his
regular updates about how he could solve this problem. He
pondered struggling back to shore against the currents, trying to
flag down a freighter, or just doing nothing. Finally, after days
passed with no solution, Erden picked up the oars and began
rowing westward again. He made it all the way to the Caribbean
Islands, and continued rowing towards Limon, his stated destination. A low-pressure system threatened from the distance and
Erden decided to cancel his attempt and called for a tow back
to the island of Martinique where his journey ended.

Erden is back with his wife in Seattle, planning to continue with his own human-powered expedition around the
world. He will attempt to row across the Pacific Ocean, com-
mencing in the spring of 2007.

My mother continues to be the poster girl for geriatrics,
and is in great health. She hikes in the mountains and continues with her ten-kilometre jogs. She stands a good chance of
beating Julie and me in the upcoming Vancouver Sun Run.

Julie and I are still working hard to pay off our massive expedition debts. Through the summer we edited 100 hours of video

footage into a fifty-minute film, also titled *Beyond The Horizon*, and organized a 20-city Canadian speaking tour. As I write this, we have almost completed our tour and have shared our journey with over five thousand people. We are thrilled that the documentary has won several awards, including "Best Adventure Film" at the Taos Mountain Film Festival. We plan on using some of the other 99 hours to develop a multi-part TV series.

At times I have found it difficult to condense my two-year journey into the pages of just one book. Fortunately, Julie is writing her own book, *Rowboat in a Hurricane*, chronicling her incredible journey, which will focus more on the portion of the expedition that took place on the Atlantic Ocean. Julie's background in science will enable her to decipher and convey the workings of the natural world we travelled through. Her book will be released in Canada and the U.S.A in the Fall of 2008.

Just four days ago, Julie and I were honoured to receive the 2006 "Adventurer of the Year" award from National Geographic Adventure magazine. We accepted the award at National Geographic's headquarters in Washington, D.C., on November 14th. It was a humbling experience to be in the presence of so many great explorers, many of whose journeys we had enjoyed through the pages of their books.

Much of my inspiration to explore had come from the pages of the well worn National Geographic magazines of my childhood. I would look at the pictures with awe, mesmerized by remote regions that seemed as inaccessible as outer space. Now, as Julie and I sat in the crowd as our short film played in the National Geographic Theatre, I felt I was in a dream. Images of foreign landscapes, remote cultures, and wild oceans flashed across the screen. It was as though I was looking at someone else's journey. But it was ours. I looked down from an image of Julie rowing the boat and caught her eye.

"Time for another adventure," she said with a smile.

ACKNOWLEDGEMENTS

THE PHYSICAL EFFORT OF TRAVELING 43,000 KILOMETRES was overwhelming. Just as daunting were the logistical, financial, and bureaucratic challenges we continually faced. It was only with the generous help of numerous individuals and organizations that we were able to clear these hurdles, and ultimately to achieve our gargantuan goal.

My good friend Dean Fenwick deserves a huge thanks for the countless hours he spent labouring on our behalf. My brother, George Spentzos, came to the rescue when our expedition was at the brink of collapse, and offered moral support throughout the journey. Thank you George. The kind folks at Wallace and Carey, who became our second family while we were on the road, also deserve a heartfelt thanks.

Writing this book was an adventure of its own, and I'd like to thank all the wonderful folks at Doubleday Canada who offered guidance and helped bring this project to completion. Thanks Nicholas Garrison for all your help and encouragement. Another huge thanks goes to David Leach who spent long, hard days editing my jumble of words into something manageable.

I would also like to express my sincere gratitude to my mother, Valerie Spentzos, who was a pillar of support throughout this expedition. My sisters Jane and Patty have also been continual sources of encouragement.

Thank you to my father-in-law to be, Husam Wafaei, for welcoming me into the family, even though I was an accomplice to his daughter's daring escapades. I can't resist including Husam's most encouraging words, which came to us in the middle of the Atlantic Ocean as Julie and I bobbed helplessly, thousands of kilometres from terra fima, "Guys, you've got to get to land quick. There's a hurricane coming towards you!"

Big thanks also go to Helga Wafaei, Randi, Raine and Alexandria Spentzos, Frank and Anita Carey, Jackie Bellerose, David Morgan, Dan Audet, James and Shelley Campbell, Kris Byarnson, Valeriy Oralov, Carole Paquette, Mary Hearnden, Dan Carey, Mario DeAlmeida, Christine Leakey, Betty Angus, KJ and Murray Klontz, Brad Hill, Bob Pope, Jason Brannon, Liz Cameron, Lloyd Pritchard, Karen Best, Shelley Russell, Bob Stubbs, Terry McIsaac, Ben Kozel, and Corrine Hockley.

And thanks to the following organizations for believing in us: Truestar Health, Wallace and Carey, School District 51, Bema Gold, Mountain Equipment Co-op, Iridium Satellite Solutions, Denturistsoftware.com, Kelowna Flightcraft, Helly Hansen, Norco Performance Bikes, Axiom, Caorda, Liferaftrental.com, Mountain House, Freeze Dry Foods, Siteaction.com, the City of Provideniya, Rodney Bay Marina, Valandre, Hilleberg, B.O.B. Trailers, Croker Oars, Gerber Knives, Karhu Skis and Bindings, Serratus, Nokian Tires, Mack Printers, Vancouver Maritime Museum, Baffin Boots, West Marine, the Westin Bayshore, and Johnny Walker.

Thank you to the media outlets that helped to convey our message. This includes *National Geographic*, *The Globe and Mail*, CBC radio, CKNW radio, and Global Television.

And finally, thank you Tim Harvey. Although we had our differences, we both shared the desire to explore. It was our combined efforts that allowed us to experience some of the most beautiful places on the planet.

PHOTO CREDITS

"Yulya in the mountains shortly before reaching the village of Konergino." (credit: Colin Angus)

"A bitterly cold campsite in Siberia." (credit: Colin Angus)

"Colin in Siberia in the Fall, when the weather is still relatively warm. Eventually it got too cold for beards." (credit: Colin Angus)

"Kindergarten kids in Siberia." (credit: Colin Angus)

"The three Siberian policemen who invited Colin into their car for borscht, pilmenny, and, of course, vodka." (credit: Colin Angus)

"Colin decked out for Siberian winter travel." (credit: Tim Harvey)

"A Chukchi man and his son." (credit: Colin Angus)

"Julie on her bike at the Guatemalan border." (credit: Colin Angus)

"Dorado fish drying in the sun in the mid-Atlantic." (credit: Julie Wafei)

"Before and after photos. The one on the left was taken for Colin's Russian visa before the expedition started. The one on the right was taken minutes after Colin stepped from the rowboat onto land by someone from the Canadian Consulate in Costa Rica for an emergency passport." (credit: the Canadian Consulate, Costa Rica)

"Julie and Colin finishing the expedition in Vancouver after almost two years on the road." (credit: Bob Berkinoff)

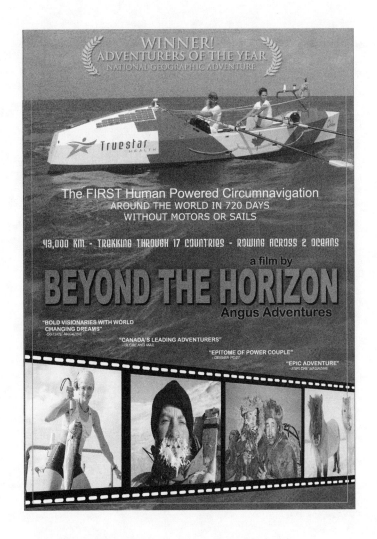

DVD available from www.angusadventures.com